D1029252

STRATEGY, CHANGE

AND

DEFENSIVE ROUTINES

CHRIS ARGYRIS

HARVARD UNIVERSITY

Pitman

Boston · London · Melbourne · Toronto

Pitman Publishing Inc.
1020 Plain Street
Marshfield, Massachusetts 02050
Pitman Publishing Limited
128 Long Acre
London WC2E 9AN

Associated Companies
Pitman Publishing Pty. Ltd., Melbourne
Pitman Publishing New Zealand Ltd., Wellington
Copp Clark Pitman, Toronto

Library of Congress Cataloging in Publication Data
Argyris, Chris, 1923–
    Strategy, change and defensive routines.

    Bibliography: p. 357
    Includes index.
    1. Organizational change. 2. Organizational behavior. I. Title.
HD58.8.A755   1985   658.4′012   85-584
ISBN 0-273-02329-2

Manufactured in the United States of America
10 9 8 7 6 5 4 3 2 1

To Charley Ellis

Contents

PREFACE

This book has its roots in two puzzles. The first perplexes individual managing organizations, be they big or small, private or public, wealthy or poor, growing or stable. For example, the top line and staff executives agree that a new strategy is required, that important organizational changes must be made, that new people must be introduced, and that a new set of values about excellent performance must be ingrained in the organization. The strategy is defined; new people are brought in; organizational changes are made. However, the strategy never achieves its potential, and the old values about performance still blunt the new ones.

A new economic and social program is designed by a young, bright group of government officials. The legislature approves and funds it. Everyone agrees that the money should not be turned over to the existing agencies because their rigid bureaucracy would eat up most of the resources and make effective implementation unlikely.

A new agency is created with the new young and spirited teachers in charge. Within five years this agency is taking on the same negative bureaucratic features as the old ones.

A new strategy is developed that has the backing of most of the executives just below the top. The betting by them is that the top will never accept it because the new strategy raises questions about the present leadership. Those delegated to sell the new plan to the top "massage," "round out," "sanitize," "mold," "shape" (to use the metaphors often spoken while planning the presentation) the data so they can introduce it in such a way that it will not be shot down.

The result is that the team of presenters, shackled by self-imposed censorship, make a presentation that does not have the unconflicted zip required to win over a conflicted top group. The latter are disappointed with the weak presentation. In the interest of progress and not disappointing them, the top keep their disappointments to themselves. The result is that they do not respond enthusiastically. The presenters sense it, but they interpret the lukewarm response as evidence that even their watered-down presentation was threatening. Thus, both groups leave disappointed with the other, acting as if this is not the case, sensing that it is the case, and colluding not to discuss it.

The puzzle illustrated by these examples is that:

- Key individuals agree on the important causes and solutions to critical problems, but with good intentions they deal with each other in ways that assure, if not failure, certainly mediocrity.
- Key individuals are able to define the characteristics of a rigid organization. They agree that they must create a new organization relatively free from those characteristics. They are given the resources to do it, and they succeed in creating what they condemn.

Why is it that when a difficult and threatening problem is correctly diagnosed, when a valid implementation plan is designed, when the resources are available, the implementation may fall short of everyone's expectations? It is almost as if there were a massive army of organizational pac-men ready to gobble up actions that could overcome these defenses and help organizations achieve the potential of which they are capable.

The second puzzle stems from trying to solve the first one. The organizational pac-men are activated by human beings who are acting defensively. Sometimes we are aware that we are activating the pac-men, but we maintain that we have no choice. "Someone had to take the bull by the horns." More frequently, however, we tend to be unaware when we are producing defensive actions that activate the organizational defensive loops.

What makes it difficult for superiors or subordinates to be aware of the fact that they are creating defensive reactions? What makes it easy for them to spot the defensive reactions others produce but not their own? If they do spot their own, why is it usually in hindsight? That's human nature. The trouble with that answer is that it tells us what we already know — namely, that human beings produce the defensive reactions. Worse yet, it implies that they are unlikely to be changed because — yes, you guessed it — that's human nature. So we have an answer that makes common sense but that gives few clues as to how to solve the problem.

I hope to shed some light on understanding these puzzles and on solving them. In so doing, I am going to be faced with a third puzzle, one that is puzzling even to describe. I will begin here and hope that by the time you have finished the book I have described it in a way that, at least, it makes sense whether you agree or not.

I will try to show that one critical cause of the first two puzzles is the reasoning we have learned to use early in life to deal with threatening issues. We may be socialized to deal with threat that is counterproductive to genuine solutions. But why would we be programmed with reasoning processes and skills that are counterproductive?

My research leads me to suggest two reasons. We are taught to act counterproductively in the name of being humane, thoughtful, and civilized. Moreover, the processes that the human mind uses to help us make sense of the world may be the same ones that help us to get in trouble.

If all this sounds a bit bewildering, I should say that was the reaction of my colleagues and myself. However, the data keep supporting this conclusion, as I hope to show in Chapters 2 and 3.

The result is that human beings come into organizations programmed to create intricate networks and layers of organizational defenses that become self-reinforcing and self-proliferating. Whenever I describe this position more fully, I usually get three reactions:

- Your diagnosis may be correct, but the idea of changing modes of reasoning and skills learned early in life is unrealistic. Implicit in this reaction is that the causes are irreversible or uncorrectable. Our experiences show that this is not the case. People can change these factors and then go on to change organizational defensive loops. It is not easy, but it is not impossible. It requires about as much time as it takes to learn to play a moderate game of tennis or a decent tune on a musical instrument.
- Your diagnosis is correct, but are you suggesting that people be stripped of their defenses? Of course not. Some defenses are necessary. We help individuals to choose which defenses and under what conditions they will alter them. There is one other point. Very often the people who take this position are those whose defenses make life miserable for others. The defenses that help one person to make life manageable may make another's life unmanageable.
- Your diagnosis may be correct, and it may have gaps and flaws. Let's work together to see how far we can go to reduce these defensive actions. These individuals are neither true believers nor automatic condemners. They are willing to explore the ideas and put them to a tough test. I do not ask for more.

I hope that when you finish this book you will have learned some hands-on strategies that you can use to overcome defenses as well as a theory about organizational defensive routines. It is true that reading this book will not lead to mastery of the ideas, but that is also true for playing tennis or the violin. Some instruction and plenty of practice are needed.

I emphasize, especially to those who are familiar with my work, that the basic theoretical ideas are not new. What is, I hope, a major contribution of this book is the application of these ideas to strategy implementation. A second contribution is being able to derive from the theory actual hands-on strategies and tactics, rules for producing effective language, as well as examples of effective conversations to deal with defensive routines. When concrete advice can be connected to abstract theory, then we have the best of both worlds. The analogy that comes to mind is the aerial camera. The higher up the airplane can fly, the more comprehensive the picture can be. The good camera produces comprehensiveness without losing specificity. A good photograph shows details with clarity.

I wish that I could thank the many strategy consultants who permitted me to observe and study them in action and who invited me to consult with them. Unfortunately, to identify them would break the promise of anonymity that I gave all the organizations in which I have worked.

As always, I have gained much from my discussions with Don Schön, Robert Putnam, Diana Smith, and Dianne Argyris. Professor Edward Bowman has been of more help than I have told him. Marina Mihalakis has been a wonderful co-worker in transcribing tapes, typing manuscripts, and making editorial suggestions. I am deeply grateful to Dr. Spiro Latsis and the Latsis Foundation for financial support to take a half-year leave of absence.

The book is dedicated to Charley Ellis. He is one of those rare human beings, who as chief executive officers, is continually seeking to reduce defensive routines and to increase excellence in organizations.

INTRODUCTION TO PART I

This book is about implementing change, especially the type of change that is difficult and threatening to the organization and to the individuals in it. The vehicle for thinking about change is strategy. I chose to focus on strategy because it is at the heart of managing any organization. Strategy formulation and implementation include identifying opportunities and threats in the organization's environment, evaluating the strengths and weaknesses of the organization, designing structures, defining roles, hiring appropriate people, and developing appropriate rewards to keep those people motivated to make contributions.

Although the book contains examples about implementing strategy, the thesis of this book applies to all types of consulting as well as the managing organization. In selecting strategy as the vehicle, I am not implying that somehow this function is more fraught with problems than other managerial functions. Indeed, I have found those professionals who understand strategy tend to be among the best, the brightest, and the most concerned with helping organizations be more effective.

The most important single audience, however, is anyone who wants to design and implement strategies that are difficult and innovative and that challenge the status quo. The advice given and the skills that are recommended apply, I believe, equally to line executives as to management consultants.

A second contribution that I hope this book makes is showing how to design and manage organizations that are populated with professionals, how to keep those organizations alive and innovative, and simultaneously how to reduce the rate of professional burnout that seems to exist in so many organizations. The ideas should be relevant not only to consulting firms but also to law firms, governmental bureaus (local and national), accounting firms, and health, education, and urban planning organizations.

There are many current ideas about how to formulate strategy. Simplifying quite a bit, yet not unfairly distorting I hope, these ideas can be grouped around two themes. The first is strategy formulation based on rigorous empirical (usually quantitative) analysis that is informed by the best theories available. These theories usually come from fields such as economics of the firm, finance, and marketing.

Using these theories and empirical methods effectively requires a good deal of professional competence in analysis and in conceptualization. These requirements often lead the strategists to seek to be left alone until they have formulated a sound strategy. This, in turn, usually leads to an autonomous relationship with the client organization. Certainly the client organization may contribute by collecting data, collating it, and so on, but the hard creative analytical work is done by the expert who has skills of empirical analysis and in relevant theories.

The second basic theme for formulating strategy is the collecting, discussing, and massaging of the data by the top management group that administers the organization. This perspective typically relies less on rigorous empirical analyses and model building than on the collective wisdom of the members of the organization and the power they possess to implement what they formulate. The process may appear less formal and more discursive, but it has a logic of its own.

The strength of each perspective is ironically their Achilles heel. Formulating rigorous strategies can lead to producing models that are distanced, if not disconnected, from reality. This danger, in my experience, is especially high when it is used by less competent analysts. The first-rate rigorous strategists are constantly concerned about connecting their models to reality. Without that connection, the models are not testable. Without testability, the rigor is empty. Probably the most fundamental problem with this approach is that strategists' knowledge about economics of the firm, finance, and marketing is primitive. However, this knowledge matures, and as it is coupled with advances in information science, the gap between models and reality will, I believe, be significantly reduced.

The Achilles heel in implementation of the first, empirical, approach is that the required stance of being autonomous from the organization could lead, as we shall see, to unwittingly collecting or receiving invalid data and being resisted by the organization when it comes time to implement the strategy. Thus, the Achilles heel is in the human side of strategy formulation and implementation, especially when the strategy may be threatening.

The Achilles heel of the second, discursive, approach is also in the human side and, again, especially when the strategy is threatening. However, the discursive approach was developed precisely to involve the human dimension, to overcome the problems created by the first approach.

This human dimension leads to the role of defensive routines. Defensive routines are probably the most important cause of failure in the implementation of sound strategy regardless of the approach used. Defensive routines are actions that are designed to reduce the individual's or the organization's pain, and when used effectively, they prevent correcting the causes of the pain. Defensive routines reduce pain and simultaneously inhibit learning.

As we shall see, when dealing with threat, we are programmed to create defensive routines and to cover them up with further defensive routines intended to bypass those that exist. I see no reason to believe that the discursive approach would not be especially affected by defensive routines.

This programming, by the way, occurs early in life. Organizations do not cause us to use our defensive routines. We are the carriers of defensive routines, and organizations are the hosts. Once organizations have been infected, they too become carriers. In Chapter 1, for example, we see how we use mixed messages to deal with the difficult problem of autonomy versus control in decentralized organizations. Mixed messages lead to reactions that, if such messages are to work, must be hidden. It is difficult for us to use covert protective responses overtly.

Change in dealing with threat, therefore, is the name of the underlying game. Such change requires that we learn new competences for dealing with threat. Change also requires new organizational policies and structures that, as they reinforce the new competences, will combine to create features of new organizational cultures.

The book is organized into two parts. In Part I, I describe defensive routines that exist at all levels of organizations (Chapter 1). In Chapters 2 and 3, I describe individual and organizational causes and reinforcers of defensive routines. In Chapter 4, I conclude that if you turn to the literature on competitive strategy, you will receive advice on strategy implementation that bypasses and therefore reinforces defensive routines. Thus, there exist society-wide defensive loops to deal with threat that reinforce the use of defensive routines. In Part II, I suggest what might be done to interrupt these societal loops.

one

INDIVIDUAL-ORGANIZATIONAL DEFENSIVE ROUTINES[1]

Defensive routines are thoughts and actions used to protect individuals', groups', and organizations' usual ways of dealing with reality. Defensive routines come between the individual or organization and any threats in the environment and can be both productive and counterproductive. They are counterproductive when, in order to protect, they inhibit learning — especially that learning about how we reduce the basic threat in the first place. Defensive routines are productive when they protect the present level of competence without inhibiting learning. Learning occurs when we detect and correct errors (a mismatch between our intentions and what actually happened). Learning also occurs when we produce a match between our intent and what was actually produced.

Counterproductive defensive routines are easily identifiable. For example, organizations may require individuals to think in a particular way about sales or marketing and refuse to reexamine these views. Sometimes groups may develop a conformity, or group-think, pattern that prevents them from seeing important features of reality.

An example of defensive routines that are easily identifiable is responses to intolerable superiors. Lombardo and McCall

(1984) interviewed 105 executives from the Fortune 100 industrial organizations. Seventy-three executives reported that they had bosses during some time in their careers who were intolerable. The types (characteristics) of intolerable bosses included Snakes in the Grass ("He was a living snake and a pathological liar"); Attilas ("Being wrong never slowed him down"); Heel-Grinders ("He treated people like dirt"); and Egotists ("He knew everything, wouldn't listen, and was pompous"). Clearly, these types of individuals are likely to generate defensive action.

The most frequent reaction is not to resist openly. Most executives continue to work for their boss. Life is made a bit bearable by believing it will not last long and by striving to learn how to deal with the superior. Thus, the vast majority tries to make the best of a bad situation.

Another set of skills is related to predicting the boss's actions. If he or she is a roller coaster, time your moves for the upswing; if you differ in opinion, first discuss something you can agree on; if the boss becomes personal, do your best to respond professionally. Needless to say, these responses are not discussable and their discussability is undiscussable.

Defensive actions not only protect but also simultaneously inhibit learning, especially about how to reduce the threat. In the case of the unbearable, dominating boss, subordinates may comply and salute while, at the same time, they may suppress their frustrations and anger during the encounter. They may do their best to act as if this is not the case, but the result is that the boss's actions and the subordinates' responses become undiscussable. It is not likely that the defensive actions (the boss's domination or the subordinates' compliance) can be corrected as long as they are undiscussable, and their undiscussability is also not discussable. The result is that the superior and the subordinates are protected by actions that simultaneously prevent learning. Consequently, the organization loses and often so do the individuals in it.

Few would argue that this is a healthy state of affairs for the individuals or the organizations, and many would lament the subordinates' defensive actions but probably would say they were necessary. Some might make the argument that if the superior was a genuine SOB, then it behooved the subordinates to protect themselves because, in doing so, they were probably helping to keep the ship afloat.

These defensive actions are in response to pathological or unjust acts. They protect all the players, inhibit learning, are difficult to alter, and become self-reinforcing. Once this is the case, the defensive actions become defensive routines. The defensive routines that are a response to pathological or unjust acts are *not* the most frequent defenses found in most organizations and are not the primary focus of this book. Another set of defensive routines is much more powerful, prevalent, and dangerous to the long-run health of the organization and the individuals in it.

I refer to those defensive routines that also are designed to protect individuals. They also inhibit learning and are undiscussable, but they are in response to thoughtfulness, caring, diplomacy, concern, and realism. They are not in response to some pathological or unjust actions. They are not limited to a particular organization or a unique situation. They are, as we shall see, part of the woof and fabric of most organizations. They are taken for granted because they are as inevitable as power, scarce resources, coalitions, and other features of everyday life in organizations.

Feldman (1984) suggests that executives in a large organization deal with tension between self-interest and organizational demands for conformity by becoming organization men or women but acting as if this is not the case. More important, the individuals develop secret intentions within and between other individuals to protect themselves: "If you don't tell people what you think, they don't know what you think. If you don't put your cards on the table, you cannot be attacked" (p. 13). Under these conditions great managers know how to blend deference behavior with secrecy. This leads to two types of conforming behavior: (1) acceptance of demands for conformity combined with (2) secret rejection of the demands.

These defenses are more dangerous to the long-run health of the organization because first they distort the truth in the name of helping others. Henderson is quoted as describing a particular senior consultant as one who "will tell you the truth, only that part he wants you to know, the partial truth" (*Boston Globe,* 1984,

p. 31). Second, in order to distort the truth, individuals must act as if they are not doing so. With every conscious distortion of truth goes a conscious cover-up as well as a cover-up of that cover-up.

The reason these defensive routines are not seen as counterproductive is that they are connected with caring, thoughtfulness, and effectiveness. We believe this because the routines are culturally taught to all of us early in life. We have been taught long before we joined organizations that these defensive routines are signs of mature behavior. If I am correct, the pathology involved in these defensive routines is created by our culture. It is very difficult to assert that culturally taught and sanctioned defensive routines are counterproductive because everyone uses them and they are supported by norms in doing so. By what reasoning do we arrive at this view, and with what evidence can it be supported? It will not be difficult to back up our case because we will invoke the criteria used by the very people who raise these questions. We will be able to show that these defensive routines will fail by their own criteria, not only by ours.

Defensive routines are protected by other defensive routines. I call them *bypass routines*. For example, the paradox that effectiveness is combined with failure is often rationalized away by saying that is life, or it can't be helped, or that's human nature, or that's what organizations are all about. The reason that these rationalizations can be used with impunity is that they are true, given the way the world exists. The challenge is to see if we can change the status quo because we live in a society that teaches us to use defensive routines that are contradictory to what we need to create and manage healthy organizations.

The reason we cannot ignore the challenge is that our organizations require that we use what I will call, temporarily, *tough reasoning*. Organizations are increasingly managed through the use of sophisticated information science systems that require tough reasoning. Recall, garbage in, garbage out. However, also involved in the defensive routines taught by our culture is what I will call, temporarily, *soft reasoning*. The difficulty arises when we must use tough reasoning on managerial problems that involve threat. The moment this occurs our instincts are to use soft reasoning to deal with the threat. The soft reasoning will undermine the tough reasoning, and the undermining will be rationalized away as a result of caring thoughtfulness.

The symptoms of defensive routines are actions that we can acknowledge as counterproductive and self-reinforcing but that we are unable to control or to eliminate. Some examples are the following:

- A leading firm on quality control has concluded that organizations have a hidden organization. These hidden organizations actively subvert quality and productivity up to 30 percent and in some cases higher (Feigenbaum, 1984).
- Researchers who have evaluated the effectiveness of quality circles and other forms of employee involvement report that even under ideal conditions, there is a decay in the well-designed programs after the initial phase, even though that phase was successful. One important cause of the decay is increasing mistrust on the part of all parties involved due to the way threatening issues are handled. Apparently few programs try to deal with threatening issues during the early phases. (See Chapter 12.)
- A large company that is world renowned for its personnel activities to assure employee justice recently discovered (as a result of a survey responded to by over 90 percent of its employees) that employees wished that management would take more initiative to deal with employees who are not productive.
- Many large organizations report what they describe as "middle-managementitis." They usually refer to the masses of individuals who are often layered on top of each other and getting in the way of productive effort.
- The task of many Washington, D.C., top-level bureaucrats is to protect the president from stress. This often results in distorted or censored information that has led individuals to believe that one of the services required by the presidents were people to help create "passports to reality."
- The auditor general of Canada asks why is it that the productivity of public service managers does not match their ability and

motivation? Why is it that there are auditor general's reports that say the same thing every year and yet not much seems to happen to overcome the basic problem everyone agrees exists (Brodtrick, 1984)?

• University faculties, especially those in research universities, often distance themselves from taking action on difficult issues. Eventually, deans are forced to take action that then is followed by faculty condemnation of the administrator for acting unilaterally and preceptively.

• Burnout of professionals is rarely caused by meaningful work, even with a heavy workload. Instead, it is caused by what they experience as defensive bureaucratic rules and meaningless nonchallenging work.

Let us turn to several examples to illustrate how these symptoms arise. Each case has been selected because it is an example of what we have observed frequently in organizations.

Case A describes the defensive routines that we have found in almost all our studies of attempts to decentralize large organizations. The case describes the defensive patterns that often occur between headquarters and divisions in private and nonprivate organizations — namely, how to provide the heads of the subunits with genuine autonomy yet, at the same time, weld them into a cohesive team where they are concerned about the organization as a whole.

In Case B, we examine the problem from the perspective of a thoughtful, concerned chief executive officer (CEO). He was responsible for allocating scarce financial and people resources to the divisions. He wanted to provide the division heads with a genuine opportunity to make their case for the scarce resources. He also wanted to involve the division heads in the final decision so they would begin to think of the organization as a whole, not simply focus on their own particular part.

In Case C, we examine the problem of resource allocation through the eyes of some players several layers below the CEO (in another firm). We watch how several senior executives try to educate a young up-and-coming line executive on how to act in front of the top corporate finance committee so that he wins rather than loses.

CASE A: DEFENSIVE ROUTINES IN CORPORATE-DIVISIONAL RELATIONSHIPS

In almost all decentralized structures, the perennial problem exists of corporate control versus divisional autonomy. The problem exists from the beginning. Decentralization is often sold to the organization as a way to push down decision making to the people who have the relevant information and can take action. CEOs are fond of saying to their divisional managers, "You are in charge; we will leave you alone but hold you accountable." They ask for performance and no surprises.

Divisional managers like this autonomous relationship. They want to be left alone to produce. Indeed, they often interpret the degree to which they are left alone to perform as indicative of the level of confidence and trust the corporate has in their competence. "If you trust me, you will leave me alone," is the attitude of the divisional heads.

There are two problems with this attitude. First, there may be times when the superiors can make important contributions to solving the problems. It is a misuse of human competence to exclude top management because including them means that they do not trust the subordinates. The challenge is to create a relationship where the superior can participate without endangering the autonomy of the subordinate.

This challenge is rarely met in practice. One reason is, as we shall see in Chapters 2 and 3, people are programmed to intervene with help in ways that do reduce the space of free movement of the subordinate. Note that I said people, not superiors. Our research shows that subordinates would do the same if they were the superiors and that they do the same to their subordinates. Thus, we are programmed to provide help in ways that create the problem the recipients feel.

The second problem with the if-you-trust-me-you-will-leave-me-alone approach is that it is unlikely that superiors with a deep sense of stewardship are going to remain uninvolved when they believe they can be of help. The superiors often realize the touchiness of the situation and try to intervene diplomatically. It is the very diplomacy they use to minimize the problems that triggers the defensive routines.

A typical reaction is for corporate to act cautiously and with concern. They may ease into the problem, usually by sending mixed messages. The first part of the mixed message takes the form of "You are the boss"; "We trust you"; "We are not trying to meddle." The second part is "Check with us ahead of time"; "Could you speed up the reduction of head count?", or "Why not clear with the financial people on this issue?" Corporate also may back off certain pressures only to reinstate them a few months later when, in their view, the heat is off. Heat is related to the feelings key executives have and not to a business problem that both sides believe can be solved if the feelings are resolved.

In most cases, however, the feelings are never discussed. Each side knows about the other's feelings; each side knows not to speak of them openly; and each side knows to act, as much as possible, as if nothing like this is going on. This problem places an important constraint on what is discussable and how to discuss what is not discussable without showing that is what is happening.

Mixed messages have a logic in them that tends to drive the actions of the executives. They are clearly designed to be vague. Mixed messages are vague and inconsistent because the senders are trying to communicate a message that may be threatening in a way that they believe will reduce the threat. The paradox of mixed messages is that the fact that they are mixed is clear.

When a message is designed to be clearly vague or inconsistent to reduce threat, it may succeed in the short run but rarely in the long run. Mixed messages succeed in the short run if the sender covers up the fact that the message is designed to be mixed and if the receiver colludes in the cover up by not discussing the mixed feature of the message. There is temporary relief at a cost of long-run difficulties.

The most prominent feature of a mixed message — namely, the fact that it is mixed — becomes undiscussable. Moreover, its undiscussability is also undiscussable. This is the beginning of ingrained defensive routines that will mushroom and deepen even though few participants may want this to be the case. The reason that they will mushroom beyond the control of their creators is that the rational and thoughtful actions we take to deal with mixed messages will lead to the escalating defensiveness. How so? Well, let us start with an obvious rational and necessary reaction on the part of the divisions. The divisions must find ways to explain the existence of mixed messages. Often these explanations take the following forms:

- Corporate never really meant decentralization.
- Corporate is willing to trust divisions when the going is smooth but not when it is rough.
- Corporate is concerned more about Wall Street than us.

These attributions of corporate motives are rarely tested with corporate. This is understandable because, first, if mixed messages are undiscussable, then publicly testing for the validity of these explanations is even more so. To make public such an explanation to test its validity is for the receivers to admit that they never understood the original message as anything but mixed. Second, since divisions are less powerful, their heads may find themselves being asked by their subordinates why corporate is acting inconsistently. Division heads are now in a double bind. On the one hand, if they go along without question, they may lose their autonomy. If this happens, their subordinates will see them as not having significant influence with corporate. Hence, the organization may be decentralized in name but centralized in fact. On the other hand, if division heads do not comply, they could be judged by corporate as recalcitrant and, if this continues long enough, disloyal.

Corporate is in a similar predicament. They sense the attributions as well as their cover-up. They also probably cover up their reactions in the cause of good relationships. For example, individuals who interact with corporate report the following:

- Corporate listens attentively.
- Corporate appears to empathize with our logic and agrees to let up.
- A while later corporate reintroduces the same requirements that we thought they agreed initially were unreasonable.

Soon, divisional people may eventually conclude they must learn to live with their binds by generating further explanations:

- Corporate encourages open discussions but ultimately cannot be influenced. Divisional representatives may eventually conclude that openness is actually a strategy to cover up the fact that corporate cannot be influenced.
- Since this conclusion assumes that corporate is covering up, the conclusion is not tested with corporate.
- Since neither the attributions nor the frustrations are discussed and resolved, both corporate and the divisions may eventually begin to distance themselves.
- A climate of mistrust arises that, once in place, makes it less likely that the issues become discussable and correctable.

Corporate then explains the distancing by divisions as:

- Understandable resistance by divisions when corporate is trying to manage more effectively,
- Evidence of their disrespect for progress.

These explanations, often made privately, are not tested because they could upset divisions who believe that the explanations are not accurate.

Notice what is happening:

- Divisions seek to find abstractions that protect their turf.
- Divisions assert that they are unique, which could be translated by corporate into "They are closed and not able to be influenced."
- Divisions appear to discuss issues openly with corporate and to develop a working agreement with them. However, if divisions send mixed messages, corporate may mistrust the agreement. Corporate may then conclude that divisions will discuss issues openly but basically that they are not able to be influenced.
- Hence, divisions begin to act in the same ways they perceived corporate to act and thus begin to create the same consequences.

So, now we have attitudes, assumptions, and actions that create self-fulfilling and self-sealing processes, emanating both from the top down and from the bottom up. Under these conditions, it is not surprising to find that all employees hold optimistic and pessimistic views about the others in their company and may say the following about each other:

They are bright people and well intentioned,	but	They are narrow and have a parochial point of view.
They are interested in the financial health of the company,	but	They do not understand how they are harming earnings in the long run.
They are interested in people,	but	They do not pay enough attention to the development of the company.

It is unlikely that there is a way to build on the positive features or to reduce the negative ones. The reason is that it is not possible to build on the features on the left-hand column without overcoming the features on the right-hand column. However, to begin to overcome the features on the right-hand column, they must be discussable, and this violates some key assumptions in the organization.

To summarize, we have a situation in which the individuals with more and those with less power, out of clean intentions, produced mixed messages. The logic of mixed messages drives behavior just as powerfully as the logic of economic competition. The only way that mixed messages can work is if the fact that they are mixed is not discussed. This creates undiscussable messages whose undiscussability is assured if individuals act as if they are not undiscussable. Mixed messages are cover-ups for threat, and they are protected by others who colluded in the cover-up. Hence, we have a cover-up of the cover-up.

If these issues become undiscussable, then individuals will try to deal with the consequences by finding issues that are discussable. Thus, divisions develop negotiation tactics. For example, they understate their goals or cushion their budgets, or they accept corporate goals but show compelling evidence that they need more people. If they get the additional slots, they may fill some of them with permanent employees but hire temporaries to use the newly obtained cash for other purposes. Information systems must then be designed to hide the specific finagling while at the same time to show the positive results.

We now have organizational factors that are built around the original defenses. Once these factors are built, they are no longer seen as connected to the defenses because they were sold to the top by compelling economic logic that then becomes part of the standards for the company. This is the process by which layering of people and units develops. For example, a small liberal arts college whose annual financial statement was barely balanced found itself in a situation where the faculty did not trust the president and vice versa. Instead of dealing with the issue forthrightly, the board attempted several defensive tactics. Each would work for a few months and then the problems recurred. Finally, the board voted to hire a provost who would be respected by the faculty and the president. The consequences were predictable. The faculty told the provost that they would trust him if he worked with them and communicated diplomatically to the president. The president soon complained of being poorly informed and unable to perform correctly. The president pushed for the provost position because he wanted to prove to the board and everyone else that it was the faculty who were ungovernable. He went into the arrangement, therefore, with the belief that if it succeeded, it would be to vindicate his views.

Summary

An important tension exists between corporate control and divisional autonomy. Both sides go into the situation with an attitude of cooperation and with some degree of concern about whether or not the other side really means what it says. All sides expect to test the validity of their concerns whenever an important difficulty arises, like failure to meet financial goals.

When financial troubles arise, corporate, in keeping with its stewardship, acts to reduce costs. Realizing that such actions might be seen by divisions as cutting into their autonomy, corporate eases in and sends mixed messages. The intent of the mixed messages is to keep divisional concerns at a minimum.

Divisions interpret the mixed messages as an unfair violation of divisional autonomy. However, they too ease in to keep corporate concerns at a minimum.

All the players know that what is clear about mixed messages is that they are mixed. They also know that mixed messages are used when threatening information must be sent since individuals do not wish to upset each other. In the name of getting along, cooperating, and being civilized, not only are mixed messages being used but also their very use is undiscussable. The latter is true because to discuss openly a mixed message is to violate the reason for mixing it.

It is difficult to learn more about undiscussable issues because they require not only that they not be discussed but also that their undiscussability not be discussed.

Each side must develop explanations for the mixed messages in order to design their responses. Explanations are causal explanations. Causal explanations are usually framed as motives. Why are they sending mixed messages? What do they have in mind? What are their motives? Each side psychoanalyzes the other, generating attributions: "Their motive is to reduce our autonomy little by little"; "They are Wall Street oriented."

Each of these attributions suggests different responses. Unfortunately, none of the attributions can be tested publicly because the motives are undiscussable, the two-bit psychoanalyzing is undiscussable, and diplomatic attempts to test are also undiscussable.

We now have a set of conditions where misunderstanding and error are increasingly likely while the correction of the error is less likely. The people know that this is the case, but they are almost powerless to do anything about it because they would have to surface the assumptions, the cover-ups, and the camouflage of the cover-ups. But how can they admit to all these features if they created them to protect the organization? To recognize all these features would be a cure that makes the illness worse.

Everyone is now in a double bind. If they continue to maintain these loops, the organization will be harmed. However, if they bring them up, the organization can also be harmed.

This model describes patterns of relationships among top and middle executives, staff and line, different divisions, and administrative processes like resource allocation. It is a model of organizational features. The content of the mixed messages, the way they are kept undiscussable, and the resulting misunderstanding between corporate and divisions may vary, but the pattern will not. There will be mixed messages, misunderstandings, and so on even though the specific players may leave and new players come in.

The next question is How do we actually behave to produce the mixed messages, misunderstandings, and counterproductive consequences? What do we say and do to each other? We must answer this question because we produce the causes and maintenance of the organizational patterns.

Many executives with whom our research has dealt would now agree that what was just said makes sense. "Of course, individuals interacting with individuals produce the pattern. So what?" The first "so what" is that if they truly believe that it is the individuals in the organization who create and become the agents of these patterns, then it follows, if they wish to change the patterns, that the focus will have to be on the individuals. This focus is often resisted by the same executives who accepted the analysis.

For example, I recently used the model to describe to the top 30 executives of a large corporation their particular pattern. They became highly involved and started to add illustrations as well as to raise doubts. In both cases the result was that they were talking about each other.

Bill: Yes, and our division has some painful history of how we got zapped by corporate when, in the early years, our budgets were honest.

Joe: What do you mean zapped? I don't think that is fair. Our intention has always been to be helpful.

Bill: Well that may be true of some in corporate and not of others. For example, ...

When we broke for coffee, quite a few executives told me that they were pleased: "Finally, we are getting at the real stuff." (Indeed, these evaluations were confirmed by the written evaluations sent to the CEOs after the session). However, quite a few also told me, "You don't waste any time, do you?" or "Aren't you cutting close to the bone?" or "I'm going to wait and see if this group really tackles these issues." The point is that the executives are willing to accept that it is individuals in the organization who create and maintain these patterns until they are faced with choosing whether they are to change the patterns or not. Then I am asking them to enter dangerous waters.

One of the most frequent requests I get about this time is, "Aren't there any organizational changes we can make?" The requests are to solve the problem by bypassing the players. In principle, the request makes sense. After all, if it is an organizational pattern, then why not create an organizational solution?

There are at least two reasons why a solution cannot exclude the individuals. Whatever the new pattern, the individual executives will have to implement it. They must have the necessary skills to create the new culture between corporate and divisions.

The second and more profound problem is that the pattern of mixed messages, undiscussability, and so on was not originally caused by organizations. There is nothing in organizational designs or in the rules of how to manage them that recommends or rewards such defensive routines. As we shall see, we (young or old, male or female, rich or poor, minority or not) are programmed by the larger societal culture to produce these defensive routines. We will produce them in any organization, large or small, young or old, private or public. All we need is to be faced with tasks that are threatening. Most alternative schools that have failed have done so because they could not deal with the threatening issues of curriculum, power, and involvement even though, in some cases, the teachers and students had volunteered to attend, the curriculum was under their control, the schedules were theirs to decide, and they had the buildings and money to accomplish their goals (Argyris, 1974).

If it is a societally caused problem, then we are dealing with how we are taught from a very early age to cope with threat. These defensive mechanisms are therefore highly skilled, are produced automatically, and are seen as the source of caring, maturity, and being civilized. Thus, to change these defensive routines is to ask us to re-examine the bases of our sense of competence as well as concern and even justice.

It is because these defensive routines are so automatic, so ingrained in us from an early age, so illustrative of what it means to be caring and concerned that the next two cases focus on examples of what individuals actually said and did to each other as they were trying to be of help to each other. I have selected two prototype relationships between superiors and subordinates and two between top line executives and strategy consultants (one internal and the other external).

CASE B: DEFENSIVE ORGANIZATIONAL ROUTINES CREATED BY A STRUCTURE DESIGNED TO PREVENT THEM

The case of the Corning Glass Works (Harvard, 1981) is often used to illustrate corporate-divisional relationships in an organization that is decentralized. One of their biggest problems was the internal resource allocation process, or who gets what and how they get it.

A management structure was designed to make it possible for division managers to watch over their own areas of responsibility yet not become so driven by strict organizational lines that they were unable to share with each other and the chairman the total responsibility for the corporation. A key structure was the Resource Allocation Committee (which one officer called an exclusive club for accountants) that was responsible for recommending priorities and funding levels for developmental projects. The review process was composed of some of the most senior officers of the company. The company's strategic planner described his role as "keeping the process on a strategic level so we don't get lost in the numbers" (Harvard, 1981, p. 24). Performance measurements and rewards were in place because as the president said, "People don't do extraordinary things for money, but it sure improves hearing" (p. 26).

At the end of the allocation process, a meeting was usually held where the divisions' financial plans were discussed with all the divisional heads. The idea was to gain everyone's commitment to the new goals. The president wanted the division managers to see the allocation process from the corporate point of view as well as their own. He thought this should lead the division managers to internalize the goals and eliminate the we/they view.

In the first such meeting ever held, all the projects were listed by priority and opened up for discussion. The president felt that the meeting took too much time. Moreover, having to reject so many projects after they were discussed in the meeting "caused a lot of pain" (Harvard, 1981, p. 26). The second such meeting, held one year later, was handled differently. One-on-one meetings were held with managers whose projects were cut or rejected. Therefore, when people went into the meeting, they knew what to expect. According to the president, "Things went much more smoothly than last year" (p. 27).

The president then described the case of Lee Wilson, who had asked for 12 engineers of a scarce and expensive variety. Wilson did a good deal of politicking before the meeting. Also, the president got together with Wilson before the meeting and prepared him for the fact that he would only get 6 engineers. He was therefore not only prepared to lose but also, when he appeared in the large meeting, to act as if that was not the case. The president felt that Lee understood and that he would play the role well. The case indicates that Lee acted as a good soldier and accepted the news with magnanimity. He acted as if he was not upset but that he understood.

Wilson reported privately, however, that the negative decision was earth shaking. He believed that it was important to get 12 full-time engineers to build continuity and involvement to his projects. Like his president, Lee realized the importance of commitment and involvement.

Moreover, Wilson found a way to get around the turndown. He decided to go outside to get 6 engineers on a temporary basis so that they would not be charged on his operating budget. According to the assistant controller, this strategy was understandable but unacceptable. The controller believed that Wilson's original request for 12 engineers was probably part of an opening bid in an administrative game. "They got 6, which is probably less than they wanted" (Harvard, 1981, p. 29), but they went outside and hired some temporary engineers. The controller then asked, "So how have we allocated resources? How have we limited the dollars spent for development? What has the process really accomplished" (p. 29)?

The solution the controller proposed was first a top-level determination of firm limits on capital resources and engineer head counts. The limits should not be subject to horse trading. Second, there should be more frequent allocation meetings for tighter monitoring.

The product and planning manager under Wilson was also disappointed and frustrated. He made several presentations into which he and his colleagues put a lot of time and energy. The response in all the premeetings was very positive, but when it came to giving out dollars, the response was significantly less positive. "I think they're saying yes to a lot of projects that add up to more time than they can spend. They cause wasted time and expense" (Harvard, 1981, p. 29).

There is a logic in this story about how to deal with potentially upsetting or threatening issues. When there is pain, design structures to bypass it and do not say that this is what you are doing. For example, the president sensed the pain the divisional managers experienced when their projects were rejected in the large meetings. He also attributed that one reason the meeting lasted too long was that it was difficult for divisional managers to face up to the scarce financial resources and bite the bullet. The president then designed a new process that he thought would greatly reduce the pain that would be experienced publicly. His intentions were clean and constructive.

If so, then why are these actions defensive and counterproductive? Why aren't they a sign of concern and caring for people? The answer is a paradox in that the actions are a sign not only of the president's caring but also of a counterproductive defensive routine.

We can tell if the action is counterproductive by using a few simple criteria. First, to what extent is there a match between the intention of the president and the result? The case material suggests to me more of a mismatch than a match. For example, from what the two principal subordinates said, the pain was still there, but now they had a new set of frustrations. First, the pain was no longer discussable and, hence, had to be suppressed. But that was not too upsetting because it was expected. Second was the time and energy spent at the divisional levels to get ready for the allocation meetings. Imagine the work done of the individuals at the divisional levels to collect data in order to win and not lose. Imagine also, if the controller was correct, the gamesmanship that was taught to all lower levels as they prepared a compelling argument for 12 engineers when they knew a lesser number was adequate. Powerful executive development related to budgetary games and how to cover them up!

The president wanted to reduce precisely these types of consequences. He wanted to create a spirit of corporate-divisional community in which we/they views were eliminated. However, Wilson and his planning manager used "they" when talking about corporate. Thus, we have a cure that made the illness worse.

The same consequences spread to the allocation process. The controller pointed out that if these games continued, the resource allocation process would be seriously undermined. His solutions are important because they represent a typical and automatic response: Tighten up. He wanted the top to develop firm levels of expenditures that were not negotiable. He also wanted more frequent meetings to monitor and control more effectively what divisions were doing.

If these recommendations were implemented, the divisional managers would feel that their space of movement and their autonomy was eroded. Decentralization as a concept and policy would become less credible, and the feelings of mistrust would increase. Again, we have a cure that is likely to make the illness worse.

We can now identify a second feature of a counterproductive defensive action. In addition to the mismatch or errors, processes are set in motion that continue or escalate the errors. For example, the president downplayed the controller's concern about budget game playing by saying, as we shall see, the controller was a financial type and, as such, a bit too rational. The president also said that it was natural for division heads to ask for more than they need because they want some slack to cover themselves. These reactions are then used by the division heads as tacit approval of the games they play and the games they teach others to play.

CASE C: EDUCATING A YOUNG EXECUTIVE TO WIN WITH TOP CORPORATE COMMITTEES

This case is an example of how a superior attempts to help a young subordinate to write a winning report as well as to develop his reasoning and skills of persuading superiors several levels above. The material comes from the Basic Industries case (Christensen et al., 1982, pp. 653–664).

Adams presents to his superiors (Courtney and Mason) a draft of a proposal to go to the top finance committee. During the conversations Mason gave the following kinds of advice to Adams.

> Look, Pete [Adams], this document has to be approved by Brewer and then the finance committee. If Chicago's our choice, we've got to *sell* [emphasis Mason's] Chicago. Let's put our best foot forward! The problem is to make it clear that on economics alone we would go to Akron, . . . but you have to bring out the flow in the economics. . . .
>
> All this should be in a table in the text. It ought to cover incremental costs, incremental investment, incremental expense. . . .
>
> Hey, why don't we put some sexy looking graphs in the thing? . . . See what you can do Pete. . . .
>
> Now, Pete, one other thing. You'll have to include discounted cash flow. . . .
>
> The biggest discussion will be, "Why the hell move to Chicago?" [pp. 660–661]

You will, I believe, easily recognize this conversation, as it has been replicated countless of times in organizations. The superior (Mason) wants to help a young subordinate (Adams) make a winning presentation with a high-level committee. He believes that the subordinate has not written a report that will win over the committee. With some degree of enthusiasm he advises Adams what to include. Mason believes that he is helping Adams by giving him sound advice and by not telling him that he was disappointed in Adams's draft. As the case writer reports, "Courtney and Mason had been disappointed with Adams's draft and were trying to help him improve it without really 'clobbering' him. Adams's draft was weak. His numbers were incomplete and his argument sloppy" (Christensen et al., 1982, p. 661).

The strategy of the conversation is for the superior to advise the subordinate on how to win and couple this with not discussing openly his disappointments, presumably in order not to upset Adams. The sentences quoted indicate that Mason was direct and forthright with the advice, but in telling Adams what to say and not to say, he was simultaneously telling Adams that the report was disappointing without saying it overtly. By keeping his sense of disappointment covert, Mason made it undiscussable. If Adams had doubts about the validity of Mason's disappointment, then he may take his cue from the one given by his boss and keep his disappointment to himself.

This is apparently close to what happened. Adams, we learn, was not convinced that Mason was correct. He was disappointed in Mason's help: "Mason is only interested in justifying the location of the new facility. . . . I think Mason doesn't really care what capacity we propose. He just wants 'sexy looking graphs.' That's okay for him, because I'm the one who's going to get it in the neck in 1968" (Christensen et al., 1982, p. 661).

Adams not only suppresses his feelings of disappointment with Mason but also justifies his sense of disappointment by making attributions about Mason's motives and evaluations of his help that Adams does not test publicly. Indeed, he covers them up and acts as if he is not doing so.

There is a story in this case that goes beyond the case. A superior tried to help a subordinate by being forthright about how to make a good presentation and by withholding his disappointment that the subordinate did not do that in the first place. The subordinate did not agree with his superior's advice and felt disappointed with the track the superior took. The subordinate used the same strategy regarding his disappointments: he kept his mouth shut and acted as if the advice was fine. Both left with disappointments, and both acted as if they were not disappointed.

It is not difficult to conjure up some further possible consequences. The superior may express his or her disappointment of the subordinate's performance when he or she asks someone to help the subordinate redesign the presentation. The superior may also keep the event in mind when making the annual review. In the former consequence, the superior is actually communicating a performance review to the one he or she is asking to help the subordinate without communicating the review and, of course, not testing for its validity. In the latter case, if the superior tells the subordinate during the annual review of the disappointment months ago, he or she would have confirmed the subordinate's fears that the superior had not levelled. This may lead the subordinate to feel unfairly judged. It may also lead him or her to continue communicating the untested evaluations and attributions being made in the subordinate's circle of friends within the firm. It is not unfair, I believe, to conjure examples where Adams, in the interest of helping some colleague, advises that Mason likes to focus on sexy graphs and so on. This is live on-line executive development, it is live culture building, and it is harmful to the development and the culture that most organizations espouse.

An additional consequence is related to the fact that neither person tried to explore the reasoning behind his actions. For example, it is unlikely that Adams knowingly would design a report that would disappoint Mason. It could have happened because Adams was inexperienced. It also could be produced by some sound reasoning that Adams never had a chance to express because he spent his time defending his views, not examining the reasoning behind them. Mason could have asked Adams, "What leads you not to include such and such figures?" or "Would you please step back from the content of the report and tell me what you see to be the shape of your argument?" In asking these kinds of questions, Mason could help Adams explore his reasoning processes that caused him to write the report as he did. This kind of learning is a different kind of on-line executive development. Imagine if Adams not only learns to reflect on his reasoning but also advises others to do the same (instead of advising them to have sexy graphs).

When I ask these questions of executives like Mason, most agree that the approach implicit in the questions makes sense. Some lament the fact that they cannot do it because of lack of time. I doubt that this is a valid excuse. First, when they try it they learn that it takes no more time to ask these questions than to try to sell Adams. Second, asking these questions may actually reduce the defensive responses by subordinates who, understandably, do not wish to lose. Third, it helps to produce a culture where undiscussability of key issues is not supported and where stories and legacies that inhibit initiative, creativity, and self-reflection in one's actions are reduced.

WHAT ARE WE LEARNING ABOUT DEFENSIVE ROUTINES?

The first lesson is that all the defensive routines in these cases produced consequences that were not intended by the actor. For example:

In Case A:

Corporate Strove	**The Consequences Were**
To generate a genuine sense of autonomy and responsibility on the part of the divisions.	Divisions felt the responsibility but not the autonomy.
To generate concern for earnings objectives.	Concern was generated as well as hostility and mistrust.
To generate a commitment on the part of divisions for the organization as a whole.	The commitment to the whole was increasingly weakened and covered up.

In Case B:

The President Acted	**The Consequences Were**
To protect the divisional managers from pain.	New and more important pains were created related to feelings of mistrust and lack of confidence.
To defend the integrity of the resource allocation process from unpleasant and long meetings.	The length of the meeting was reduced, but the number of private meetings increased significantly. The integrity of the process was harmed by the games the rejected divisional managers had to play.
To reduce the narrow parochial views often promulgated by organizational structure.	The expression of parochial views in the meeting was reduced, while the expression of the same views outside the meeting was increased.
To reduce we/they dynamics between corporate and divisions.	The expression of we/they dynamics between and in front of the corporate people may have been reduced but not when away from corporate.

In Case C:

The Corporate Executive Strove	**The Consequences Were**
To teach the young executive how to make presentations.	The young executive also concluded that he was being educated in organizational political games.

The Corporate Executive Strove	The Consequences Were
To hide his sense of disappointment as well as the reasoning behind his advice.	He made attributions about the executive's reasoning and hid his disappointment about his superiors.
To cover up this was the case.	He covered up this was the case.

The motives of the participants in all the cases were constructive. The president of Corning wanted to help the division heads. He also wanted to create a sense of commitment to the whole. The division manager was committed to the organization and wanted to cooperate with the president. Both cooperated but those very actions led to feelings of frustration, bewilderment, and we/they attitudes that reinforce the narrowmindedness the president wanted to reduce.

Why do individuals produce such errors so consistently? There are several causes for such errors. First is the reasoning behind them. For example, during a videotaped discussion with students (MacAvoy, 1982), the president of Corning said that he was not worried about the budget games as much as the controller because of the following:

1. Controllers are naturally suspicious. They want rational processes.
2. It is common for people to overestimate the resources that they need and underestimate the results. This is understandable because they want the slack in their budgets.

The first explanation holds the following logic. It is acceptable to discount the controller's fears because controllers are naturally suspicious. The inconsistency in that rule is that in order to hold it, the CEO must be naturally suspicious of individuals he considers to be naturally suspicious.

Along with the inconsistency involved in such reasoning

are injustice and overprotection. The injustice in such a rule stems from the fact that in order to accept the statement about controllers as true, we would need data that show they are more naturally suspicious than others. To my knowledge, such data do not exist. Second, it is unjust to accept the rule that we should discount controllers' views because they are naturally suspicious without also discounting others who exhibit natural suspicion — in this case, the CEO.

The overprotection lies in the fact that if this analysis is valid, the CEO is not being helped to see it. If the CEO is correct that at least his controller is naturally suspicious, then the controller is being overprotected from realizing that the CEO and others may be discounting his concerns. Or, if the controller is aware that his concerns are being discounted, the CEO is protected from examining why this is the case. Individuals do not design their actions to be successful if they are discounted unless defensiveness exists in the system. Finally, the organization suffers because the inconsistencies, injustice, and overprotection are not discussable.

Turning to the second explanation, the CEO asserts that it is common for individuals (in this case, divisional managers) to seek slack by overestimating the resources they need. Indeed, my own research would support his view (Argyris, 1962; 1964). If understandable means it is not a serious administrative crime, then why aren't such tactics easily discussed? Why cannot divisional managers state openly what insurance they have built into their budget? One explanation, if true, gets at the injustice feature in this rule. Some CEOs do not mind overestimation of resources and underestimation of results as long as the subordinates have good performance records. They are not so accepting of divisional managers with poor results. That, in turn, leads to a puzzle. Why play the games with the good performers and not with the poor performers? This question assumes, of course, that the poor performers are confronted.

The overprotection that occurred was that the CEO did not have to deal with the fact that the divisional manager was upset and did not agree that the CEO's actions were helpful. Imagine also the impact of these games on the subordinates. If it were true that the division needed only six engineers and if the division knew it, then playing this game was tantamount to teaching the individuals at the lower levels to lie administratively. I have witnessed many settings and describe several later in this book where subordinates sit around and design the appropriate administrative lies to be given in the report to the top. Again, the organization suffers.

Let us examine another example. In the Vick case (McGuire, 1981), the CEO had a misunderstanding with one of his subordinates. When a group of students asked the CEO about the misunderstanding, his response included the following comments: (1) Yes, there was a misunderstanding; (2) I was surprised (that it had occurred); (3) I do not know why (it occurred); and (4) I chose not to explore it because. . . .

The CEO Said	**The Operating Rule**
"I chose not to explore the misunderstanding because I didn't think anyone was going to win."	Discussion of personal misunderstandings are fraught with difficulties; therefore, I do not discuss them.
"The real question is do they understand the process now so that they will not repeat the same error?"	When you bypass misunderstandings, make certain that the organizational policies will not be violated.

The first explanation implies that an executive should not explore such an issue if it is likely that both parties may be at fault and/or both might become upset. The strategy overprotects both parties. In that sense both will win. The CEO remarked that he might have pressed the issue if the subordinate involved had a poor performance record. Again, we find two different sets of rules for the same error.

The example also illustrates a new way in which the organization may be the loser. The CEO stated that the correct criterion should be to ask if the parties involved now understand the process so that they will not repeat the same error. This is one of the most common responses that I encounter with such errors. The strategy is to put into place an administrative process and make sure it is understood. Once this is the case, then it is just to hold them responsible for not repeating the error. While I was writing this chapter, I attended a meeting with a CEO and his general managers. One general manager was describing the apparent insensitivity of a recent report. He said, "That guy has not worked on the issues that concern us and is insensitive to boot." The immediate reaction of his colleagues was "Have you and he discussed his job? Is he now clear what is his job so that this will not happen again?" "Of course," replied the general manager. Everyone relaxed because they knew if the subordinate repeated his errors, he could be justly punished.

Note that the immediate advice was not to ask the subordinate his reasoning behind his producing errors and not to deal with his insensitivity but to make sure the administrative processes were in place to punish him if he continued to err. This strategy deals with individual insensitivity and poor performance by making sure the administrative rules are clear. The difficulty is that where the rules are used as a device to control poor performance, the rules become not only clear but also rigid. They become rigid because they are often used with individuals who are defensive and who protect themselves with reasoning that exemplifies fancy footwork. Eventually, the superior gets frustrated and falls back on the rule. In effect, the superior is forced to communicate, "Look, I don't think we are getting anywhere. You know the rule and you know that you are not following it." Rigid and clear rules are not likely to deal with insensitivity. Indeed, the insensitive and poor performers are given a way not to face up to their responsibility. They can focus on the rigidity of the rules.

It is important to emphasize that the superiors' actions in all the cases were designed to be fair and firm. Moreover, in the Vick and Corning cases, there is no evidence to suggest that the subordinates felt badly or unjustly treated. The controller may have some doubts about his superior's views, but he may also believe that his superior intends to be just. All the problems I describe may be seen by the players to be as natural as the clothes they are wearing.

Herein lies the challenge. The reason, I believe, the players can feel this way is that it is consistent with the ideas in good currency about how to deal with such issues. Indeed, in this context the superiors are thoughtful, concerned human beings. They may be inconsistent at times, but who isn't? They may be unfair, but as President Kennedy told Mae Craig, "Life is unfair."

The reasoning involved, however, contains gaps and inconsistencies and depends on data that were never collected. In addition, reasoning about how each party should act was kept private. Any attributions or assumptions that were made were not tested publicly. This is defensive reasoning in that it protects us from learning about the validity of our reasoning. If the reasoning is private, if the testing of the inferences or conclusions is private, then the reasoning makes it unlikely that any errors will be detected and corrected.

Another feature of defensive reasoning is that it is usually protected by using culturally accepted assumptions that are valid but self-sealing. For example, whenever I ask the individuals in cases like those here what leads them to give such advice, they respond that this is the way to succeed in organizations. What leads them to keep their attributions about others private? They respond that if they made them public, it would be the equivalent of a cure that made the illness worse. What leads them to play political games in organizations? They respond that that's human nature and the nature of organizations.

All these responses have a good deal of truth in them. However, they also lead to the negative consequences that are polluting the problem solving and the quality of life in organizations. We are again faced with a paradox: What leads to success also leads to failure.

Before we accept this paradox as inevitable, we should try out new ways of organizing and dealing with each other to see if we can reduce the paradox. I believe it can be reduced. I also believe that it can only be accomplished if we go beyond the status quo. The trouble with the status quo is that it is self-sealing. To assert "that's human nature" or "that's organizations" is to assert that human nature and organizations have little potential for significant change. If those who make these assertions have power, then they are likely to be correct because it is a self-fulfilling prophecy. If the larger culture supports this kind of reasoning, then the self-fulfilling prophecy is reinforced by a self-sealing process.

Whenever the ideas in good currency are used in these ways, they act as bypass routines. A bypass routine is a culturally acceptable defensive routine that is used to bypass another defensive routine.

One final point is that I have been focusing on the way we reason when we deal with threat. I have been examining the human mind in action. In so doing, I have begun to explain behavior that is often explained by invoking the concept of motives or motivation. There are several reasons why I recommend examining the reasoning processes and not the motives of individuals. First, as we have seen in the cases so far (and in those to come), motives are not good explainers of what happened. In all the cases, the players were motivated to be of help, to be constructive, to be caring, to be consistent; yet the opposite occurred.

Second, some of the main problems with defensive routines are the reasoning behind them. For example, mixed messages will work if they are clearly designed to be mixed and if this is covered up and further if the cover-up is also covered up. No number of clean motives will erase the unintended consequences of such reasoning.

Third, the focus on the reasoning process gives us an effective lever for changing the status quo. If the ideas in good currency are to be questioned, if the skills learned early in life to produce these ideas are counterproductive, then change will threaten our sense of self-esteem and confidence. Under these conditions, it is very important to be able to build upon some competence, especially a basic one like reasoning. Then we will have a realistic sense of confidence that we have a competence — namely, the capacity to reason — to help us get from here to there.

PUZZLES ABOUT DEFENSIVE ROUTINES

I must explain several puzzles about defensive routines. First, although defensive routines are powerful and omnipresent, to my knowledge, we are not taught formally how to produce them. Also, to my knowledge there are no formal policies to encourage or protect them. We must understand how and why defensive routines arise. What is their source of power? What is their impact on strategy formulation and implementation? How can the counterproductive features of these routines be reduced? In answering these questions I focus on what I believe are the most powerful defensive routines that have a counterproductive impact on strategy, organizational change, and the everyday management of the organization.

This brings us to the second puzzle. The most powerful defensive routines are those where the intentions are honorable — namely, to increase the effectiveness of individuals or organizations. I do not mean to imply that there are not cases where the intentions are dishonorable and where individuals do threaten and hurt each other. In my experience, the number of these "dirty bombs" is small compared to the "clean bombs" that are dropped every day in organizations.

It is not easy to change these types of defensive routines. We will resist changing actions that are clean and have honorable intentions. Moreover, the facts that they are seen by so many as clean and honorable and that they exist everywhere are evidence that they are culturally supported. As we shall see, this support comes from the organizational culture as well as the culture at large.

The third puzzle related to defensive routines of the clean intentions–culturally supported variety is that they lose their effectiveness if they are discussed candidly. For example, it is difficult to help someone save face if we tell him or her that is what we intend to do. However, the only way such an action can work is if the recipients know what is being done and if they act as if that is not being done. It is as if the rules include, "I know I am face saving. You know I am doing that. Both of us know that we will not discuss it. Both of us will act as if this is not the case." In addition to being well intentioned and culturally supported, they are also undiscussable and their undiscussability is undiscussable.

In summary, defensive routines are used to protect us from pain. The paradox is that when they succeed in preventing immediate pain they also prevent us from learning how to reduce what causes the pain in the first place. Defensive routines can be self-protective in the short run and self-defeating in the long run. To anticipate a possible reaction from some to the effect that in the long run we are all dead is true, but the defensive routines live on as legacies to continue to overprotect individuals and organizations in the future.

two

REASONING AND DESIGNING TO DEAL WITH THREAT

One of the most important features of defensive routines like the mixed messages described in the previous chapter is how natural it is to create them or to deal with them. The reaction to producing them and to making them undiscussable is instantaneous and automatic. This chapter digs more deeply into these reactions. The vehicle is a case about an executive who must deal with a subordinate whose performance is poor. The case therefore deals with communicating potentially threatening information.

The way individuals reason in this case, we have found, is the way they almost always reason, regardless of the subject matter, as long as threat is a key component. This is true, whether the message being communicated is between individuals, groups, or intergroups (Argyris, 1982). The results are completely consistent with the data that have been collected, using several different modes and nearly 4,000 male and female respondents. Their ages range from 11 to 70, and they are minority and majority, wealthy and poor, and live in the United States, Europe, South America, India, and Africa (Argyris, 1982).

THE CASE OF JOHN AS SEEN BY BILL

Bill is a CEO and John is a vice-president and national marketing manager who reports to Bill. Bill likes John very much but believes that John will not succeed in his job or be a serious contender for more senior opportunities until he overcomes three difficulties:

1. Inability to distinguish important issues from all others.
2. Inability to delegate. When an assistant was hired to help John with his mountain of paperwork, John's performance did not change significantly.
3. Extremely poor relations with field people who consider him to be slow, negative, and pompous.

In writing about the case, Bill was asked to describe the strategy he used to talk with John and to recollect, as best he could, the conversation that occurred and any thoughts or feelings he did not communicate for whatever reason.

Thoughts and Feelings that Were Not Communicated	**Conversation**
Here I go again. I wonder how he feels? Well, it has to be done.	Bill: John, we have talked many times about the important role you play as our national marketing manager. I am still concerned about the issue that being a good technician is not enough.
	John: I work hard to keep good control over the area for which I am responsible.

Thoughts and Feelings that Were Not Communicated	**Conversation**
The truth is that he is working from the top of the pile.	**Bill:** What do you mean by "control"? Is control the *real* problem? Are you consciously establishing priorities or just working from the top of the pile? **John:** As we get more and more involved with field people, I have less and less time. You realize, I am sure, that the pressures of this job have increased and I am working very hard.
Part of the problem is that you are creating your own pressures.	**Bill:** What are you doing? How do you assess what comes first? **John:** Well, my door is always open. My people come to me when there is something I should be involved in.
How do I get him to broaden a "frozen" insight into an executive's job?	**Bill:** That still doesn't answer the basic issue of establishing priorities. That's the key to most of the problems we face in marketing. **John:** Bill, I'm sure you are aware that when I find out something is wrong, then I get involved immediately.

Thoughts and Feelings that Were Not Communicated	**Conversation**
The difficulty is that this means you have a passive stance to your job. I want you to take more initiative, to innovate. Can you do this? I wonder.	Bill: We have to do more than monitoring and waiting. We must find ways to organize, think ahead, plan, and *lead*.
I felt increasingly frustrated that I was not getting through to John. I thought I would go on to another difficulty that had been identified. I made a brief transition and said:	Bill: John, your peers like you. But the people out in the field describe your approach as "lecturesome," "pompous," "know-it-all."
	John: I try to "call 'em as I see 'em," that's my job. Surely you do not want me to sugarcoat everything.
I don't want to sugarcoat, just to create an atmosphere in which we can work *constructively*.	Bill: That is part of our job — as managers, we not only have to identify deficiencies, we have to identify and help resolve them in a fashion that generates growth, not hostility.
	John: They have a responsibility, too — you talk about hearts vs. minds — some of their hearts don't want to be changed!

Twenty senior executives (representing small and large organizations in the private and public sector; 40 percent were women) participated in a seminar and completed the test by writing a case using the same format. The instructions given them were as follows:

1. Please write (in a few paragraphs) your personal evaluation of how you feel Bill dealt with John. Describe your impression of Bill's effectiveness as you go through the case.
2. Next, assume that Bill turned to you and said, "What do you think of the way I dealt with John?" Using the same case format Bill used, write one or two pages of conversation between you and Bill. In the right-hand column write a scenario of what you would say, how you would expect Bill to reply, how you would answer him, and so forth. In the left-hand column write any uncommunicated thoughts and feelings you might have. Please do not write a scenario of how you would have dealt with John. Consider Bill to be your client.

Respondents' Evaluations of Bill's Effectiveness

The 20 respondents diagnosed Bill as largely ineffective. Examples of words that they used in the diagnosis were:

- Bill handled the situation poorly.
- Bill did not accomplish the objective of his conference with John.
- Bill missed the mark. The intended strategy was on track, but he failed to get the job done.
- Bill's handling of the situation is very traditional and, naturally, ineffective.
- The conversation was a failure.

Respondents' Explanations for Bill's Failure

Although all respondents agreed that Bill failed, they differed on their reasons why. The explanations fell into two basic categories:

1. Bill was authoritarian, unilateral, and directive.
   - Bill spent most of his time *telling* John that he was wrong and not listening to John.
   - Bill was not supportive and did not express confidence in John. He decided that John was wrong and that was it.
   - Bill is accusatory.
   - Rather than being supportive, Bill dropped back to being an autocrat and exemplified a dominant hostile attitude toward John.
2. Bill was vague, wishy-washy, too indirect.
   - Bill talked around the problem . . . without getting to the point. Vague phrases were used throughout the conversation, without any concrete, constructive criticisms or suggestions for improvement.
   - Bill never addressed what was really on his mind. Bill was oblique (and too indirect).
   - Bill never defines the problem clearly.

The first conclusion is obvious and not particularly new. The polarization of responses is interesting: slightly under half saw Bill as being authoritarian, and slightly over half saw him as wishy-washy and too indirect. These data serve to remind us of the wide variance in opinion even though everyone read the same case. Our research suggests that when confronted with diagnosing incompetence or error, individuals often polarize, and either extreme often ignores the complexity of what actually occurred. Thus, Bill could have acted both unilaterally and weak; he could have distanced himself from and have been too close to Bill.

It could be argued that we may have to ignore full complexity; otherwise, we would be immobilized. There is some truth to this argument. Under real time conditions, we cannot sit around and diagnose all day. However, our research suggests an additional explanation that we may have theories in our heads about dealing with threatening issues that cause us automatically to polarize.

Consequences Predicted by Respondents

The respondents reported that the result of Bill's ineffectiveness would be to make John feel defensive and, hence, not predisposed to learning how to change his actions. The respondents who felt that Bill was being authoritative predicted that John would feel prejudged, misunderstood, and put down. The respondents who felt that Bill acted too indirectly predicted that John would feel, at first, bewildered and that soon these feelings would be augmented by a sense of being misunderstood and judged unfairly.

Both of these types of diagnoses contain the same "micro-causal theory" that goes something like this:

If Bill (after judging John as ineffective) acts unilaterally, authoritatively, or indirectly and weak, *then* John willl feel defensive and, hence, is not likely to listen and learn.

In effect, this is a causal theory of human defensiveness that is consistent with the ideas in good currency about human nature. The respondents are using a valid theory of defense.

Puzzle 1:

The respondents judged and evaluated Bill unilaterally. For example, to say to Bill that he acted authoritatively and unilaterally is to act unilaterally and authoritatively. Thus, our respondents automatically thought and reasoned about Bill's effectiveness in dealing with John using the same causal theory of defensiveness that they were about to tell Bill he should not have used with John. When they were diagnosing Bill's effectiveness, our respondents used a type of reasoning that, if described forthrightly, would probably make Bill feel defensive and self-protective.

Why do people think in ways that are counterproductive by their own criteria of effective actions, and what makes them unaware of these inconsistencies? Why do we find repeatedly that it is only the actors who are unaware and not the observers? Recall, Bill could see John's problems, the respondents could see Bill's problems, and I could see the respondents'. As we shall see, we appear to use a different theory to think about action from the theory we use to act, and we hold a theory of human defensiveness that helps us to be unaware of the inconsistency.

Puzzle 2:

The scenarios the respondents used can be categorized into three strategies. The first I call easing in; next is forthright; and finally is a combination of the two — that is, first easing in and, when Bill didn't respond as hoped, becoming directive. Note again the bipolar feature of action that we must explain.

DEFENSIVE STRATEGIES

Easing-in Strategies

Bill: What do you think of the way I dealt with John?

Respondent: How do you feel about it?

Bill: Well, I thought that I did as well as could be expected with John resisting.

Respondent: Why did John resist you?

Bill: Well, I guess he was upset.

Respondent: Is there anything that you might have done to cause him to resist?

Respondent: I liked your sincerity and your concern for John. I wish you had been able to get him to open up a bit.

Bill: That's the problem. Every time I try to talk about his performance with him, he gets very defensive.

Respondent: What are the things you like about John's performance?

Bill: [answers]

Respondent: When was the last time you told him the things you liked about his performance? . . .

Do you think the interview would have gone differently if you had told him up front what things you liked?

When executives try out scenarios like these with each other, the recipients (in this case, whoever role plays Bill) feel that the person trying to help them has judged them as being ineffective and is trying to tell them so in indirect ways like asking questions. Indeed, the questions are experienced as subtle cues. For example:

When Helper Asks	Helpee Often Feels
Why do you think John resisted you?	Oh oh, I think he thinks I may have caused John's resistance.
Is there anything that you might have done to cause him to resist?	See, I am correct. Why doesn't he level with me?
When was the last time you told him the things you liked about his performance?	She believes that if I had told him positive things more often, I would not have this problem. I do not think so.
Do you think the interview would have gone any differently if you had told him up front what you liked?	What is she driving at? You can't be up front with John without upsetting him. She is beginning to upset me.

Four features about easing in are important. The first is that the helpee feels prejudged. The second is that the helper has decided that he or she could not be forthright. The third is that all this is covered up. The fourth is that the cover-up is also covered up. For example, the helpees rarely state what is on the right-side of the column partially because they are taking their cues of how to behave from the helpers. If the helpers withhold their judgments, then the helpees will do the same but act as if they are not doing so.

Indeed, the helpers are withholding information. For example, following are some thoughts and feelings that the helpers reported on the left-hand column of their cases that they decided not to communicate:

1. Open up the conversation with Bill in a nonthreatening way.
2. I'll say this carefully to see if Bill is able to hear without getting upset.
3. My strategy is to get Bill to recognize that he's part of the problem, that as long as he keeps putting John on the defensive, John won't face up to his problems.
4. All Bill can think of is what is wrong with John's performance. I want him to think what's right!

In all cases, the respondents were thinking or feeling in these ways but did not say so in order to keep Bill from becoming defensive. However, Bill (and almost all the executives who have role played Bill) has inferred that the respondents were having thoughts and feelings like these.

Forthright Strategies

Bill: How do you feel I handled the situation?

Respondent: Not very well; you blew it.

Bill: How so?

Respondent: [John] listened. Then he defended everything he did. You didn't reach him! If you think that conversation indicated he accepted your premise, you're wrong. He's so convinced he's right, he endured the conversation. There was no contact between you.

Bill: What do you think of the way I dealt with John?

Respondent: I always admire a manager who has the courage to confront a problem. I think it took courage to have that conversation with John, but I feel you could have gotten more mileage out of the situation.

Bill: What do you mean?

Respondent: Well, I think you could have thought out your objectives more specifically. I know it was clear to you, but it wasn't clear to John or me exactly what the problem was and, more important, what was needed to fix it.

Bill: It sure was clear to me. It's clear to him too.

In the forthright strategies, Bill knows that he has been judged as being ineffective. During role playing of scenarios like these, the executives who take the role of Bill become defensive and protective of their strategy. They tell the helpers, in effect, that they do not really understand John. The helpers, in turn, try to communicate that they do understand John and that Bill may be blind. What happens very soon is that the differences in views, as well as the feelings of defensiveness, escalate. If the helper is Bill's boss, then the Bills usually carefully begin to ease out. They thank their boss for the help and say they will give the advice a good deal of thought. When asked later what were they thinking and feeling, their reactions are consistent with the first forthright example. Paraphrasing, they usually feel that their helper blew it, that they (the helpees) were never reached, and that the helpers were so convinced they were right that they were closed to learning. Hence, the helpees must endure the conversation and act as if they are not enduring it. The helpers now are creating the same conditions that they were telling Bill he should not have created with John.

By the way, in all cases where the helpees decided to endure but act as if this was not the case, the helpers sensed the other was enduring the session and acting as if that was not so. The helpers also stated that they decided not to say so. We now have a reversal. In the forthright strategy, it is the helpers who sense Bill's resistance and cover up the mixed strategies.

Let us turn to two cases that contain a mixture of easing in and being forthright. All names have been changed in these cases.

Combination of Easing-in and Forthright Strategies

Uncommunicated Thoughts	Conversation
Let's review the objectives to be sure of mutual understanding.	Joe: Bill, your plan was to first identify the objectives. Am I correct?
	Bill: Yes, and I had them well defined.
I want to determine if he recognizes where he went off track and if he has an open mind.	Joe: I agree. You then developed a strategy to communicate them to John and get his involvement, right?
	Bill: Yes, and I felt that was handled well.
Get him to reflect on his actions, motives, and results.	Joe: Why do you feel it was handled well?
	Bill: Well, I covered the points, but from observing John's reaction, I could see it was a lost cause.
The truth — probably react defensive	Joe: Then the objectives were not achieved — you didn't change John, you left him confused.
	Bill: What do you mean?

Uncommunicated Thoughts	Conversation
This is possibly the underlying cause of Bill's frustration. Let's state it and measure the reaction.	Joe: Bill, you told me months ago that John was a holdover from the past regime and his tenure and contracts with the board of directors prevented you from removing him from the position. Bill: Yes, that's correct, but I am trying to make the best of a poor situation, and to date, it's been pointless.
Okay, now move from the emotional to a logical way to get these two people together.	Joe: Maybe in your eyes. But don't you feel that you may be leaving out several ingredients that could really help John to grow and contribute? Bill: I've tried everything: meetings, discussions, threats. Nothing works.
Easy, I don't want to discourage him, but there may be some shock value here.	Joe: Possibly, but how about being more direct, frank, honest, and open. Why beat around the bush? Bill: It will destroy him.
Bill really likes John. Now let's move in the direction of mutual problem solving. Both men are capable and both have needs that if solved, will benefit all involved.	Joe: No, I don't think so. John doesn't really know what you want from him. You told me about your discussions and now this latest meeting and your frustrations. Have you ever laid out specifics,

Uncommunicated Thoughts	Conversation
	point by point, for him?
	Bill: Not exactly, but we covered the necessary ground. What are you driving at?
Give my analysis of knowing both men and spending time with John.	Joe: Bill, the objectives are correct. The problem is that John doesn't see or perceive them in the same priority as you do.

Here we see a case where the respondent (Joe) felt that Bill dominated the session with John by telling him too much. Consistent with this diagnosis, the respondent began by asking about Bill's views. He also was covertly checking Bill's motive (Is he open?) and trying to get Bill to do what he wanted John to do without saying so openly (Get him to reflect on his actions, motives, and results). As the session continued, the respondent was beginning to act in ways that he was criticizing Bill for using. For example, he was beginning to manage, to tell, to control Bill. Note especially the comments on the left-hand side.

The following case provides an example of a senior executive (in the public sector) who appears to use psychodynamic concepts to explain what is going on:

Bill did not accomplish the objectives of his conference with John. It seems to me that they ended where they began — that is, Bill being frustrated with John and John feeling overwhelmed by his responsibilities. Since this seems to be a repetitive situation, an unhealthy psychological game of, let's say, "poor me" or "harried executive" seems to be going on here, with John playing the role of victim and Bill that of persecutor. Their psychological predispositions are playing into one another.

In other words, Bill is as responsible for the situation as is John. But as part of this repetitive play, he must project total responsibility to John.

This case is a good example of the great paradox of managerial behavior — that is, the conflict between the rational approach to getting things done in the most efficient way and our difficulties in overcoming the emotional barriers to making that happen. Bill and John both want the organization to succeed, but their unconscious needs get in the way. Managing this paradox is one of our greatest challenges, a challenge of which Bill does not seem to be aware.

Uncommunicated Thoughts	**Conversation**
I wonder if Bill is aware of the psychological game between him and John. I don't want to put him on the defensive. I must facilitate his process of self-evaluation and discovery.	Bill: How do you feel I handled the situation? Kurt: Before I answer that, I'd like to ask you a question. How do you feel about John right now?
You need to be in touch with what you're feeling, so I'm going to feed them back to you.	Bill: I'm still frustrated and angry with John. He doesn't seem to really hear me and be willing to change. Kurt: Sounds like you're still very upset with John.

Uncommunicated Thoughts	**Conversation**
He doesn't realize this is a repetitive pattern.	Bill: Yes, it's the same old thing, and I'm sick and tired of it. Kurt: So you feel about like you did before you met with John.
He's beginning to think about the repetition.	Bill: Yes, it's the same thing every time. Kurt: You've felt like this a long time.
Need to change gears here to problem solving.	Bill: Ever since John and I have been working together. Kurt: Have you thought of some ways in which you and John might get out of the rut you're in?
Need to switch back to reflecting.	Bill: I've considered letting John go, but he is a friend and a good man. Besides, what would a man his age [52] do if he were without a job? Kurt: You're really concerned for John's welfare.
You are ready to look at some ways to help John do a better job.	Bill: Yes, he's really a good guy, but he's not doing the job I need done. Kurt: What are some ways you can help John do a better job?
He is open for a suggestion now.	Bill: Continue to talk with him like I have, I guess?

Uncommunicated Thoughts	Conversation
	Kurt: Your discussions really haven't resulted in any improvements so far, have they?
He's beginning to realize the nature of the situation. He may be open to change.	Bill: No, not really, I just get angry and frustrated.
	Kurt: Would you be willing to identify some specific behaviors you'd like to see for John and ways he can be helped to initiate them? This will mean your taking a look at some new ways of relating to John. How about it?
He's reluctant, and his relationship with John is important to him for the wrong reasons. He needs to try some new behaviors with John.	Bill: I'm willing to explore some things with you, but I wouldn't want to destroy my relationship with John.
	Kurt: Let's start with something that is easy for both of you but gets you started working together in a new way.

The respondent believed that Bill and John were acting out unconscious needs and using psychological defenses that are playing into one another. Note how this kind of analysis requires high levels of inference that are difficult to check so they can be disconfirmed. Indeed, the scenario the respondent wrote indicates that he never checked out these inferences but assumed they were valid. The inferences he did attempt to check out were related to how John felt and the repetitive pattern. Note also that the two major recommendations that were made were not, as far as I could tell, carried out. I could find no evidence that the unconscious psychological barriers were overcome first.

I also found no evidence that the respondent showed Bill what good behavior is and how to do it. For example, the respondent suggested that Bill identify some specific behaviors that he would like John to produce and ways John "can be helped to initiate them." If I were Bill, I would agree, but I would still be left wondering what these behaviors are and how to communicate them without getting into the unconscious forces that the respondent believes are operating.

Finally, note that using a strategy based upon the psychodynamic view illustrated in this case led the respondent to do what all the other respondents did — namely, to withhold his thoughts and feelings that related to the way that he intended to control Bill unilaterally. Thus, Kurt begins by wondering if Bill is aware of the psychological game between him and John, while we are left wondering if Kurt is aware of the psychological game that he is creating between Bill and himself. Kurt is trying to get Bill in touch with his feelings but does not appear aware that he is doing so without telling Bill that is what he is doing. Kurt makes inferences that Bill does not realize this is a repetitive pattern that he never tests publicly. Finally, note how much Kurt believes he is controlling Bill's mind. For example, he decided when to change gears, when to switch back to reflecting, when Bill was ready to look at ways to help John, when he was open, or when he was reluctant.

Other Examples of Inconsistencies

All the cases contained inconsistencies that the writers did not appear to recognize but that could affect the effectiveness of their approach. For example, this respondent advises Bill to act in ways that he cannot produce:

Advice	Problem
Be more specific and firmer.	He is unable to be more specific with Bill. When Bill asked about being firm, the respondent advised Bill to tell John that if he doesn't change, he will be fired.

How will telling John to shape up or be fired lead John to change his actions? What specific advice does the respondent have that will make a compelling argument that, in effect, if you threaten to fire someone he will alter his actions?

Advice	Problem
Be clearer about what Bill means by an "atmosphere in which we can work constructively."	She could not produce it with Bill.

In the following, the advice given to Bill is abstract but the sender thinks it is concrete:

Advice	Problem
Should "express confidence in John's abilities and suggest that John narrow his priorities."	What leads the respondent to believe that if Bill expresses confidence, it will help John to change? What leads her to believe that by suggesting John narrow his priorities, John could do it?

Advice	**Problem**
If John develops more self-confidence, the hope is that he will be looser and more comfortable in dealing with people.	Yes, but how can Bill help John develop more self-confidence?

To summarize, when respondents were asked to diagnose a situation that was difficult because it required Bill to communicate potentially threatening information to John, then the following happened:

1. The reasoning processes they used to diagnose the situation contained evaluations and attributions that were never tested and, if communicated, would have created feelings of defensiveness in Bill that they were telling Bill he should not create in John.

2. After becoming aware of that puzzle, the respondents varied in their responses. Some agreed that they might have been inconsistent but that if they had, it was in the name of organizational health. They had to be candid and forthright. It is the responsibility of the superior to say the difficult things. In all the scenarios these respondents wrote, they did create immediately the defensiveness that had led Bill not to listen as effectively as they wished he would. If the reason to be direct and forthright, in the manner used in these cases, was to enhance the organization's health, I could find no evidence that this indeed did happen.

The majority of respondents eased in. In effect, they took the position that one executive once used: "I'm not foolish to say what I think. I will, of course, translate my thoughts in ways that are more palatable to the other."

Whether they succeeded or not depends upon the meaning of *palatable*. For instance, we saw that easing in created difficulties in understanding and trust. Moreover, all the cover-ups became undiscussable and the undiscussability of the undiscussable was also undiscussable.

This covering up may make the easing-in approach more palatable for reasons I suspect were not in the respondents' minds. Helpees may prefer the easing-in approach not as much because they feel understood and helped but because it is easier to cover up their frustrations and doubts. If they decided to cover up their reactions, then they could hold the helper responsible (after all, the helper was withholding). If the situation reached the point that the helpee was fired, he or she could blame the organization for the injustice.

3. Respondents often gave advice that was abstract and difficult to figure out how to implement (for example, help John gain self-esteem). These same respondents advised Bill to be more specific in his advice. Respondents also advised Bill not to perform certain actions, but they then performed precisely those actions in the scenarios they had written. For example, they would advise patience and listening, but after the first interchange, they would begin to tell.

4. No matter what approach was taken, all respondents did some very important self-censoring and did it covertly. They tended to withhold their negative feelings about Bill, their attribution about his overidentification with John, their tests to ascertain how open and aware Bill was, and their strategies to be in unilateral control over Bill while acting as if this was not the case. The combination of unilateral control and secret testing made it difficult for the respondents to place their evaluations and attributions to genuine tests. By genuine tests, I mean that their ideas could be disconfirmed.

This is a recipe for escalating communication problems, defensiveness, misunderstanding, and mistrust. Part II discusses how to begin to overcome these problems. At this point I would like to emphasize that these findings are not unique.

Why do we find these same results in the United States, South America, Europe, India, Australia? Why do we find them among men and women, minorities and majorities, the powerful and powerless, young and old; rich and poor?[1] Indeed, the results we got were so consistent that for several years, I wondered if there was not something wrong with our procedures, that we were unknowingly causing these results, or that our ideas and theories were full of gaps that we did not see. I believe that we are discovering something that is valid and that deserves explanation in light of the data we have collected under so many different conditions.

Our explanations reside in the way our mind works and in what we are taught to think and how to act when dealing with other human beings on difficult issues.

EVALUATIONS, ATTRIBUTIONS, AND HIGH LEVELS OF INFERENCE

When respondents are asked to diagnose Bill's effectiveness, they evaluate his actions and explain them. The respondents' explanations ranged from Bill's being too dominant to being too sensitive and close to John and from using traditional managerial ways of dealing with the problem to not being traditional enough. All these are attributions about Bill, his motives and attitudes, that, if true, would explain his actions.

The trouble, of course, is that all of them cannot be true. Bill cannot be distant and too close, weak and dominant, vague and too specific. We need not judge which is true. We need to understand the way individuals reason, the way their mind works. What we can say with a relatively high degree of certainty is that the diagnoses were at a high level of inference and that they were rarely, if ever, tested publicly. It is as if the respondents felt that their diagnoses were concrete and so obvious that they did not need any further testing.

What is meant by a high level of inference? Figure 2.1 illustrates a ladder of inference that we all probably go through to make sense out of our world and to act. The first rung of the ladder is the relatively directly observable data — in our case, the conversations that Bill had with John and those the respondents wrote they would have with Bill. The second rung is the meaning we would impose on the conversation that would be culturally understandable. For example, it would not be difficult to get agreement, in our culture (and cultures similar to ours), that Bill was telling John that his performance was unacceptable. The next level is the meaning that we impose on the culturally accepted meanings. Thus, some respondents felt Bill was weak and too sensitive while others saw him as coming on strong and dominating. We explain these differences by hypothesizing that different individuals may have different theories about how to deal with John.

FIGURE 2.1 *Ladder of Inference*

4	The theories we use to create the meanings on rung three
3	Meanings imposed by us
2	Culturally understood meanings
1	Relatively directly observable data like conversations

Finally, there are the meanings that I am imposing on all of this or that any observer performing my job would be doing.

The first point to the ladder of inference is that in order for us to operate under on-line conditions, we must make inferences such as evaluations and attributions. The second point is that the inferences we make are probably learned early in our lives and, in this case, are related to what we believe would make individuals like Bill or John become defensive. The third point is that we do not test these inferences. We appear to act as if the inferences are concrete.

One explanation for not testing because of the belief that such inferences are obvious and concrete is that we are highly skillful at this kind of reasoning. The features of skillful behavior are that it is automatic, effortless, and it works when no one is paying attention to it. Indeed, if we were forced to pay attention to everything we were thinking and doing, we might slow down our action so much that we would accomplish little.

Hence, we have another puzzle. The human mind operates quickly and so automatically that we no longer are aware of all the inferences we make. If we call someone insensitive or dominant, that is obvious and concrete because we no longer have to pay attention to the inferences we have made in a matter of milliseconds. The difficulty, of course, occurs when individuals differ in their belief about what is concrete and obvious after looking at the same conversations.

If evaluations and attributions are necessary, what prevents people from testing them? If done well, testing should not take too long, and it could reduce the escalating difficulties just described. We have found two reasons for this behavior. First, the very feature of skillful behavior makes it likely that we are distanced from our reasoning process. Second, given the theory we use, we may also become disconnected from our reasoning processes as we are using them.

REASONING AND ACTIONS THAT LEAD TO DISCONNECTEDNESS

This case (written by Gerry Garnett Ward) illustrates the essential difficulties that subordinates encounter when dealing with a superior who is suspected of controlling the situation to his or her ends.[2] The dilemma facing the subordinates is that they would like to discuss the situation but they believe that the superior will protect his or her hidden interests at all costs. To speak openly is to risk the wrath of the superior. To withhold one's views violates one's sense of responsibility.

The writer of the case, the subordinate, chose to pursue the familiar path of not discussing his suspicion, focusing instead on the facts of the situation. "Inevitably," he writes, "that route leads to my feeling dishonest and being a partner in protecting the superior's hidden interests. However, the approach has some merit in that it may allow [the superior] to feel freedom enough to allow some movement toward my position." The description of the situation and the scenario of the case are quoted directly from the subordinate's writeup. Only minor editorial and name changes have been made.

At the time this dialogue took place, the director was aware that morale among his assistant directors had dropped significantly. He thus encouraged them at their annual retreat to consider means of creating professional growth and satisfaction on the assistant director level. He was fearful that the morale problem would reverse the success for which he and his staff had received credit over the past few years.

Tom, the director, had established an undisputed reputation with his staff as an autocratic administrator. In spite of the likelihood of Tom's negative reactions, the assistant directors made a proposal for a major change in office responsibility that would involve them in some of the associates' planning and research. Tom and the associates did not react with encouragement at the time of the initial proposal but chose not to dismiss it completely, perhaps being aware that an immediate denial would create further dissatisfaction among the assistant directors. The following dialogue is a reconstruction of one that took place in a subsequent meeting between the director, Tom, and Gerry for the purpose of further discussing the proposal.

Uncommunicated Thoughts and Feelings	Conversation
That's an insincere question. I know from our explanation and Tom's reaction at the retreat that he fully understood the essence of the proposal. He's asking me to describe details of the plan that we can't possibly have. Therefore, it will appear to be ill formed. From experience I know that Tom is much too defensive for me to say that. I'll simply explain the assistant directors' position.	Tom: Well, Gerry, what is it exactly that you and the other assistant directors had in mind concerning your proposal?
I'd better re-emphasize the fact that we're in need of a change and underline that it's necessary by alluding to our dissatisfaction. Otherwise he could completely dismiss this.	Gerry: We haven't formed any of the specifics of the plan since it will require a great deal of time and effort by a number of staff members — assistant directors and associates. We don't think that such an investment could be made without your commitment, at least to the theory of the proposed change.

**Uncommunicated Thoughts
and Feelings**

Conversation

The assistant directors feel that since all of us have been on staff for at least a couple of years, expanding our responsibility would allow us to contribute more and would be more satisfying professionally.

That praise is gratuitous. He's trying to prove that he appreciates us before he squelches the proposal.

He's avoiding the central issue: Will he commit himself to expanding our responsibilities? He's hiding behind the supposed need for specifics. He knows that, given the present schedule, many of the assistant directors aren't available and will be pressed with other work when they return. His strategy is to put us off, since in six weeks planning will be impossible.

Tom: I'm aware that most of you have done a good job and probably have something more to offer. But I can't give any commitment to the proposal until I've seen the specifics. I think that this proposal will have to be developed by the assistant directors as a group, and then we'll consider it.

I'll skip the judgment of his ultimate strategy and simply present our dilemma.

Gerry: The proposal is a major change and would require hours of meetings for the assistant directors and the associates to plan adequately. Such an effort

Uncommunicated Thoughts and Feelings	**Conversation**
	couldn't take place without an initial commitment from you. I don't think that anyone, especially the associates, would risk spending hours of time on something so tentative.
He's staying with his demand for specifics, knowing that there's little hope for us. He's also playing on professional responsibility and initiative, one of Tom's favorite ploys.	Tom: And I can't approve anything that's so tentative! Such a proposal, with its specifics, has to come from the assistant director level. You're the people who are proposing it.
I'll simply reassert my position and partially acknowledge his.	Gerry: I realize that we are the ones who are proposing it and therefore are responsible for the specifics, but the specifics are difficult to come by without time, effort, and cooperation.
He's employing his usual tactic of demanding his position and then concluding that we're irresponsible if we don't meet it. It's a great way to put me on the defensive and to protect his position.	Tom: Well, you know that if the assistant directors are really committed to exploring the possibilities for change, then they should certainly be willing to make the effort that's necessary.

Uncommunicated Thoughts and Feelings	Conversation
I'll counter his implication that we lack commitment.	**Gerry:** It's not a matter of the assistant directors' commitment to the effort; they are willing to work hard on this. But as I've explained, we can't invest so much with no positive indication from you that you'll accept it.
I'm repeating myself and sounding frustrated. He knows that he has successfully prevented our getting this proposal off the ground.	
He's creating the guise of remaining open but is actually closing the lid on the discussion and, in effect, is eliminating the proposal's chances. One more power play for Tom!	**Tom:** Gerry, as I said before, I'll consider the proposal when it appears in a fully developed form submitted by the assistant directors.

Gerry did appear to meet his intentions. He never mentioned his mistrust of his superior; he held back his feelings of anger and frustration (left-hand column) and dealt mainly with the substantive issues. Further, he maintained and reinforced his views of Tom as a person who connives, uses ploys, hides his intentions, and lies to maintain his position.

Let us examine the reasoning processes that Gerry used and the action strategies he took. They could be described as follows:

I (Gerry) am dealing with an individual (Tom) to whom I attribute several intentions: (1) to control the situation to his own ends, (2) to act as if he were not doing so, (3) to use his greater organizational power to accomplish 1 and 2, (4) to act as if 3 were not the case, and (5) to consider all these actions undiscussable.

This cluster of attributions becomes the premises that Gerry holds about Tom. They will guide his reasoning processes and his actions toward Tom.

In order to create these premises, it is necessary that Gerry know and believe these attributions about Tom. If Gerry is to know and believe these facts about Tom, they cannot be hidden to Gerry. Hence, the facts that he believes Tom is hiding are not hidden to Gerry. We can infer, therefore, that Gerry's premises (attributions about Tom) require an additional set of attributions:

1. Tom is unaware that his intention to hide these facts is not working.
2. Tom is unaware of the negative impact his actions and their undiscussability have on Gerry and the others.
3. To discuss the undiscussable would upset Tom and could lead him to become angry with Gerry, which in turn, could make Gerry vulnerable to Tom's greater power.

The scenario that Gerry wrote suggests that he never tested these attributions, that he acted in front of Tom as if they did not exist, that he therefore made them undiscussable, and that he acted as if they were not undiscussable. To maintain the premises that Gerry held about Tom, he had to reason and to act in precisely the way that he considered Tom should not act. These conditions can cause injustice and feelings of incompetence. Gerry's approach, then, not only makes it less likely that he will deal effectively with Tom but also creates conditions in which Gerry must hold himself responsible for acting unjustly and incompetently.

If we assume that people will not feel comfortable about being their own worst enemies, then it is rational to predict that they will blame others for the injustice and incompetence and will not test their attributions. Hence, we have Gerry describing Tom as "closed," "autocratic," "manipulative," and "punitive." If Gerry sees his superior as having these characteristics, he may understandably believe that it is necessary for him as well to become closed, autocratic, and manipulative in order to survive. His negative responses are caused by his interpretation of Tom's actions.

However, the degree to which Tom is closed to Gerry's influence may also be related to how Tom interprets Gerry's action. What if Tom senses that Gerry (and the other assistant directors) sees him as closed, autocratic, and manipulative? It is unlikely that he will feel understood and respected by the assistant directors or that he will take risks with them. He will probably create his own set of attributions about Gerry and the other assistant directors that will be as counterproductive to dialogue as those created by Gerry. Tom may indeed depend on his organizational power because that will make it likely that he will win in this relationship of minimal trust and understanding.

Returning to the dialogue, we note that Tom, like Gerry, focused on the substantive issues. He asked for more facts about the proposal. Gerry's reply was to argue that the details were best worked out by the assistant directors. In effect, Gerry's action strategy was this:

> When Tom asks me to work out the details, I will respond that his suggestions are inappropriate.
>
> I will also ask for a commitment to the theory underlying the change that I am proposing.

Gerry was using an action strategy that violated his own premises about Tom. Gerry saw Tom as unilaterally controlling the situation for his own interests and afraid to share influence. Hence, Gerry had now created a double bind for himself. If Tom accepted Gerry's suggestions, then Gerry would have to conclude that Tom's premises, his actions during the meeting, and the reasoning processes that he used to create both were distortions. If Tom rejected them, then Gerry would fear that he had lost or jeopardized his standing with Tom.

One way for Gerry to prevent himself from experiencing either feature of the double bind would be to reason and act in ways that identify Tom as the culprit. Indeed, Gerry made this strategy highly probable by the way he framed the problem at the outset. Gerry believed that he was caught between leveling with Tom and going along with him in ways that might "allow Tom to move toward my position" without Tom's realizing that Gerry was managing the movement. This is a heuristic commonly observed in everyday life. It is often touted as a great skill of leaders — namely, getting others to do what you want them to do in such a way that they believe they are following their own choice. Gerry thus becomes as manipulative as Tom.

In this connection, Gerry remarked during the discussion of his case, "Ironically, I believe that I still am on good terms with Tom." Why not, we may ask? He utilizes the same reasoning and strategy that he attributes to Tom and is very careful not to discuss the undiscussable.

Proposed Reply	**Analysis of the Reply**
I would like to design planning processes that would enable us to discuss our plans with you as we go along.	Suggests a joint process, with Tom periodically involved.
I'd like to have your ideas incorporated into the plan so that we don't end up putting lots of time into something that you believe is unrealistic.	Tom could see this as a potential trap, requiring time that he does not have and involving him in discussions that he wishes to avoid.

Participant 1 then asked Gerry to respond as Tom would "if he were being tough." Gerry said he would be glad to role play Tom using "the attributions I make about the guy of *really* wanting to protect his position, the suspicions that I have of him. . . . Is that what you want?" Yes, was the response.

Role Play	**Analysis**
Gerry (role playing as Tom): I don't have the time to really sit down with you people. Moreover, it really has to	Tom distances himself from responsibility to work with assistant directors by repeating his lack of time and focusing

Role Play	**Analysis**
come from you people. You're the ones who are proposing it.	on the assistant directors' desire to create and propose the new ideas.
Participant 1 (role playing as Gerry): OK. I'd like your thoughts on one potential problem. Developing a detailed plan would require lots of hours of work (without your help). The chances are greater that the plan would be unacceptable to you.	The suggestion that the plan might be better if Tom participates may not be relevant if Tom's intention is to stonewall the plan.
At the same time, those who have worked on it would feel highly committed to it.	Tom might feel that this is a risk that he would take because if the plan is not acceptable, then he may have put down such action for quite a while.
If we become highly committed to a plan that you find unrealistic, then we've not only wasted staff time but we've created a morale problem.	
Gerry: I understand the choices are difficult, but I am so swamped [enumerates] that I must take that risk. I do not have the time.	Tom continues by protecting his time, acknowledging the risk, and suggesting that the probable morale problem would be less severe if the assistant directors were committed and loyal.
And I really do think that it is your responsibility to come up with this. I know there's a risk involved, but it is a measure of your commitment.	
Participant 1: I can understand you're busy. I think it is unfortunate, but that is your decision. These are the problems I	Respects Tom's decision but is also clear that he has communicated the potential problems to Tom.

Role Play	Analysis
see, and I wanted to make it clear to you what I see going on.	

Then Gerry (speaking as Tom) said that he felt the assistant directors would now be "back to square one, . . . I think it would settle down to an impasse." Participant 1 agreed and added, "If I were an employee, I would not know what to do next." Another participant said, "It is almost an impossible situation." Gerry added, "Yes, that's the problem in the case."

However, there was one important difference between this role play and Gerry's scenario. In this role play, Participant 1 was able to state some of the views he believed were important. He did not collude in the same way as Gerry did (by talking about details). Hence, he may have felt that he had been more honest and had generated more valid information about the situation. Assuming that the role play produced more valid information about the dangers of Tom's not becoming involved, it also led Tom to maintain his position of distancing himself from any responsibility for the plan.

Participant 2 then asked to continue the role play, even though the situation appeared impossible. First he reviewed what Participant 1 had said.

Role Play	Analysis
Participant 2 (as Gerry): I'm sorry that you do not have the time. I hope that I have communicated to you that I can understand your dilemma. I also hope that I have communicated my belief that if we do not do something, we will con-	Reviews his judgment and informs Tom that he would not recommend either action because both would make the situation worse.

Role Play

tinue to exacerbate the morale problem, and if we do it the way you suggest, we will have a morale problem. I would not recommend that we go either way, and would say that to the assistant directors.

Gerry (as Tom): Look, I'm not totally shutting down the plan. You can still go ahead. I'll still look at the proposal when it is done.

Participant 2: You're saying that the assistant directors should trust you, that you're going to remain open but that they have no right to involve you. [It is difficult for them to feel trusted under those conditions.]

Gerry: I agree that this is not ideal, but we have no time for the ideal.

Participant 2: What is your view of the time frame that I am asking for?

Gerry: Meeting periodically with the assistant directors over the next four weeks.

Participant 2: What I am asking for is a one- to two-hour meeting at the outset. We would like to learn what your concerns are about such a pro-

Analysis

Tom does not want to be held responsible for shutting down the plan, but his actions do create a no-win situation for the organization.

Tom's position requires of Gerry unilateral trust when he and the assistant directors imply that low trust exists at the moment.

Again, time is critical.

Asks for a short period of time to establish criteria and guideposts.

Role Play

Analysis

gram. We could use them as guideposts in designing our plan or at least be able to tell you explicitly why we did not follow some of them.

Gerry stated that he believed that Tom would agree to one meeting of the kind that Participant 2 had suggested.

Why was it possible for two others to create a scenario that was acceptable to Tom, as role played by Gerry to be as tough and resistant as Gerry could imagine. A frequent response to this question is that the seminar members were not as emotionally involved in the situation as Gerry. This is a valid but inadequate answer. It is inadequate because it implies that if Gerry had been less involved, he might have acted more constructively. The difficulty is that involvement is inescapable when people are dealing with critical everyday challenges. Gerry and others require knowledge and skills to help them become more effective while being involved.

For example, Gerry appeared to reason as follows:

I, Gerry, diagnose Tom as closed, manipulative, and interested in remaining in unilateral control and not losing:

I, Gerry, am aware that I am behaving toward Tom in the same way.

Any time I act in ways that I assert are unjust and incompetent, my reasoning is faulty and the consequences will be counterproductive. Under these conditions, it is highly likely that I will interpret what Tom says in ways that will confirm my diagnosis. Because I keep the diagnosis tacit and the testing of it secret, I run the risk of generating self-fulfilling and self-sealing processes.

Such reasoning will not allow Gerry to design any scenario other than the one he did design. Gerry also cannot design a more candid scenario in which he moves the ideas and feelings from his left-hand column to his right-hand column so he can test the attributions. Tom has not asked Gerry to be his interpersonal consultant. Indeed, Tom gives Gerry clues that Tom does not wish to deal with such issues.

Reflecting on this case, we can now see that Tom (as described in Gerry's case) was distancing himself from dealing with the assistant directors and from those features of himself that related to subordinates' asking for more autonomy and influence. Although Tom never said to the assistant directors that he was distancing himself from them, they felt it. Gerry's approach was an attempt to help Tom become more involved with his subordinates.

To accomplish this involvement, however, Gerry used a strategy that also distanced him from the problem. He never told Tom that he (and the other assistant directors) sensed the distancing and the mistrust it implied. Moreover, Gerry was aware that his strategy was leading him to collude with Tom's strategy to keep the mistrust issue hidden, but Gerry became detached from his reasoning processes. He diagnosed the problem as being Tom's fault. He framed the dilemma as either leveling with Tom and being rejected or hiding his true feelings and views and acting as if he were not doing so. Gerry eventually placed himself in a situation in which he would have to become aware of his reasoning in order to test his attributions publicly. To view himself as a rational and just human being, he had to overcome his irrational and unjust reasoning.

GENERIC RESPONSES TO THREAT: BYPASS

The results presented in this chapter are consistent with the data we have been obtaining for the past decade in our research. There appears, therefore, to be a generic response to deal with threat — namely, to bypass its causes.

There are two major bypass strategies. One is to be directive and forthright. The directive and forthright approach is usually used in response to someone who has already acted in ways that are considered by the recipients as overly hostile or when the actor is trying to fulfill a stewardship such as being a superior in an organization, a parent, or a very close friend. "I just had to lay it on the line for her sake. I was responsible."

The problem with this strategy is not that the individuals should not strive to be honest. The problem is that individuals tend to be honest and candid in ways that come across as unilaterally judgmental, closed, and unchangeable. The actors may value honesty, but they express it in a way that makes it difficult for the other to be honest.

It is because neither the actor nor the recipient creates the conditions to encourage inquiry into the causes of the problem that the forthright strategy is a bypass. This is an important distinction because the common sense view is that "telling it as it is" is engaging and not bypassing. It engages, all right; it engages the defensive routines of both parties. Problems will not likely be solved effectively under those conditions.

The second bypass strategy is easing in. Easing in is not necessarily the opposite of being forthright. The opposite is to be quiet, passive, or to withhold. Easing in is a covert way of being active. The individuals may appear to be passive, but they are active; they may appear to be withholding, but that is only temporary and depends on how smart the recipient is to guess what they are hiding; and they most certainly are not quiet since they are talking. Easing in is a strategy to control others by making them think that this is not the case.

The tacit operating rules for easing in are as follows:

1. When I must communicate information that may be threatening, I must do it in a way so I cannot be held responsible for the receiver's defensiveness.
2. It is appropriate to say that I want to be helpful. Do not say that I am going to be helpful by protecting the others from their defensive reactions.

3. Face-saving strategies are helpful, but they require white lies. I cannot say that I am trying to save the other's face.
4. White lies require making undiscussable my attributions about what makes the other person defensive and the fact that my strategies are face saving.

We may now begin to see why mixed messages are produced: they are face-saving devices. Face-saving devices attract face-saving devices on the part of the other person; that is, the reasoning described in the preceding list is now used by both parties. This leads to distancing from each other. By distancing, I mean the individuals do not realize their responsibility for the defensiveness they are producing or, if they do realize it, they tend to hold the other responsible for the defensiveness.

The reasoning and the behavior are highly skilled. Skilled reasoning and actions are tacit and automatic — that is, we do not think about them; we produce them in a way that is second nature to us. If we combine this skilled action with the reasoning involved in face saving, then we have little need to reflect on our reasoning and action. Hence, we become, as we saw in Gerry's case, disconnected from our own reasoning; that is, we are not aware of the contradictions in and counterproductive consequences of our actions.

If distancing and disconnectedness are automatic reactions, then we can predict that they will occur automatically whenever there is an intention to protect others. Thus, the president of Corning (Chapter 1) automatically redesigned the resource allocation meetings to reduce the division managers' pain and in that way, I may add, to reduce his pain of having to feel responsible for the pain of the division managers. By all counts he was acting humanely when he designed meetings to be more face saving. The same is true for almost all the examples that are presented in this book.

Defensive actions produce undiscussability, undiscussability of the undiscussable, distancing, and disconnectedness. These conditions set the stage for escalating the defensive actions over time. Also, these conditions, combined with their escalation, turn the organizational defenses into routines that are ingrained in the organization. The fact that these individual-organizational defensive routines become ingrained is one of the most important causes of ineffective implementation of strategy and organizational change.

REASONING PROCESSES CHARACTERISTIC OF DEFENSIVE ROUTINES

The following lists the characteristics of defensive reasoning:

- The use of soft data (that is, difficult to accept as valid descriptions of reality by individuals with contradictory views),
- Inferences that are tacit and private,
- Conclusions that are not publicly testable.

Behind defensive reasoning lie the following factors:

- A tacit theory of dealing with threat,
- A set of concepts that are tacitly interrelated,
- A set of tacit rules of how to use these concepts to make permissible inferences and to reach private conclusions and criteria to judge the validity of the test.

First, little conscious attention is paid by the actors to the nature of the data described as objective or obvious facts. Those who felt John was too directive and those who felt that he was too weak came to their respective conclusions by reading the same dialogue. Although the words printed on the page were the same, the meaning readers inferred differed dramatically. One reason is that individuals often ignore or pass over certain words. Another is that they often read into certain words meanings that are not there. Whatever additions and subtractions they produce from what is on the pages, the result is a different set of facts. Actors using defensive thinking assume that the data as they have organized them are the objective facts, and they pay little attention to testing this attribution. The data, in their eyes, are hard and objective. The data, in the eyes of someone on the receiving end, are soft and subjective.

The second characteristic of defensive reasoning is that the actors pay little attention to the possibility that the sources of their judgments and attributions about what was said, about the correct meanings to be inferred, and about the correct conclusions to be drawn are the tacit and explicit theories they hold about whatever subject matter is being discussed. For example, in the John and Bill case, executives held different theories about strong and weak leaders. The president of Corning and his division heads held different theories about the appropriate pain that subordinates can take or the cost benefits of different kinds of pain. The executives educating the young executive held different theories about how to educate him than by making him responsible for his learning, and the superiors or subordinates of decentralized organizations who use mixed messages have theories about dealing with threat. Defensive reasoning exists when the actors believe or act as if they believe that their theories are correct or are so obvious that everyone holds them.

The third characteristic of defensive reasoning is that almost no attention is paid to testing publicly the inferences made when arriving at conclusions. The inferences and conclusions therefore become impossible to influence and unassailable except to those who make them because they assume that this is not the case, an assumption that is also not tested. The result is that defensive reasoning violates one of the basic canons of reasoning — namely, that it cannot in some mysterious way authenticate itself (Boothroyd, 1978).

In the world of management strategy, individuals often divide reasoning into soft and hard, subjective and objective. Defensive reasoning is usually considered to be soft and subjective. This division is usually made by the more analytically and tough-minded executives as well as strategy professionals. The point is that this is not a valid division; indeed, it may be a defensive routine.

Thus, the key features of defensive reasoning are the unawareness of the inferences being made, the lack of testing those inferences publicly, combined with the certainty that none of this is happening. Defensive reasoning is inflexible and unchangeable, not wishy-washy. If individuals using defensive reasoning appear to be vacillating or jumping around, it is because they have a rigorous program in their heads to pull off such fancy footwork.

These conclusions, we hope to show, can also be true of the reasoning used to formulate features of a strategy. The difference in strategy formulation, however, at least in some cases, is that there is a body of explicit theory, a set of rules about analysis and testing, that is held publicly as a standard by which to test the reasoning processes being used. We return to the differences in defensive reasoning after we explore further the question why so many individuals choose to use the same kinds of bypass strategies whenever they are dealing with threat, be it a technical or human problem.

three

INDIVIDUAL AND ORGANIZATIONAL CAUSES OF DEFENSIVE ROUTINES

The reason for action is to solve problems. Most of us face at least two major types of problems in everyday life. The first is to achieve a goal. We strive to produce a match between our intentions and actuality. The second problem is to detect and correct any mismatch between what we intended and what actually happened. Producing either type of action is more complicated than it may appear. It is important to understand the complexity if we are going to understand and reduce defensive routines.

Think of action like a conversation to influence someone to do something as the end result of the following process. First you determine what you would like the other person to do. Next, you invent a solution to how to get that done. Then you produce or implement the solution. Finally, you evaluate the results. You may discover a match and that ends that episode. However, you may discover a mismatch, meaning you will have to seek a new solution. This process of discovery-invention-production-evaluation is basic to much human action. It is also basic to strategy formulation and implementation. It is a generic learning process.

Two assumptions exist at the core of this learning process. First, we intend to design and implement matches rather than mismatches. Our sense of competence comes first from a good track record of matches and, second, a good track record of detecting and correcting mismatches.

The second assumption is that it is not possible for us to design and produce an error or a mismatch knowingly. If we design an action that we believe will be an error in a particular context and if we produce it correctly, then it is a match. This means that when we produce errors we probably were unaware that we were doing so. We can become aware as we are producing it or immediately afterward, but then we would be detecting and correcting an error.

The reason that it is important to keep these two assumptions in mind is that if unawareness is itself an action, then according to our view, it too must be designed. But what does it mean to say that unawareness is designed? One answer is that people must have a program in their heads that they activate to keep them unaware and that they are unaware of the program. The reason for being unaware need not be some unconscious factors. It could be, as we saw in Chapter 2, that the program is internalized and therefore tacit.

THEORIES OF ACTION: ESPOUSED AND IN USE

A program can be a set of rules or propositions in our head that can be retrieved to provide guidance for how to act. The action strategies that we produce flow from these rules.

The requirements of everyday life do not normally provide us the needed time we would like to design a particular action. The need to feel some sense of personal wholeness requires that there be an underlying consistency across the actions. These needs and actions combine to lead us to hold values that govern the kinds of action strategies we will try to implement. We come to a situation, therefore, with a set of governing values that helps us select an action strategy from one already in our heads or design a new one.

Whenever we act in conformance with our governing values, we will necessarily produce consequences. We hope they are the intended consequences. The governing values, action strategies, and consequences can eventually be organized into propositions — for example, if I act in such and such manner under such and such conditions, then I can expect the following consequences. These propositions form the theories of action with which we design and implement our intentions.

There are two not so obvious features of these theories. First, they are tacit because they are highly skilled. They are highly skilled because they have been learned early in life. Second, although these theories govern human action, when it comes to threat, they are most likely inconsistent with what is espoused to be our values and intentions. For example, the people advising John and the executives in the cases in Chapter 2 espoused beliefs and intentions that were thoughtful, concerned, not upsetting to others, fair, and just. However, they produced consequences that were counter to these values and intentions.

Thus, we come to a puzzle. We hold beliefs and values that are dear to us — indeed, we would defend our honor on them — but the explanation for how we act (when threat is involved) requires a different set of beliefs and values. Our research calls the theory that is espoused an *espoused theory,* and the theory that is used is called the *theory in use.* Both are important to understand. The theory in use, however, is the most powerful and the one that we are usually unaware of. We can get a clue of the theories in use that produce defensive reactions by reflecting on the actions described in the cases in Chapters 1 and 2.

Recall, for example, that the president of Corning tried to create an effective resource allocation process, that the president of Vick and the executives bypassed the managerial routines he had designed, and that the corporate and divisional people created mixed messages. In each of these cases, the individuals strove to be in control of the context in which they were operating. Each player also tried to win and not to lose. The individuals strove to minimize the creation of negative feelings in others or in themselves. They appeared to do their best not to upset others or themselves. Finally, individuals strove to be rational by having a goal in mind and trying to achieve it. These four features — (1) obtain unilateral control, (2) maximize winning and minimize losing, (3) minimize negative feelings, and (4) maximize rationality — turn out to be the four values that govern the actions of most of the individuals we have studied.

We have created a model of a theory in use that has, as its first component, these governing values (Figure 3.1). The second component of the theory in use is the action strategies. The two most common action strategies are (1) advocate your position and evaluate individuals' actions or make attributions about their intentions without encouraging inquiry into them or testing them publicly, and (2) unilaterally save your own face or that of others, and of course, act as if this is not the case.

Such actions lead to consequences, the third component, that are primarily defensive. This defensiveness results in miscommunication, mistrust, protectiveness, self-fulfilling prophecies, and self-sealing processes. These results make it less likely that errors will be corrected — indeed, it is more likely that errors would escalate. We could complicate the diagram by showing how the consequences feed back to reinforce the governing values and the action strategies. Under the defensive consequences, it is understandable that individuals will seek to gain as much control as they can over their context, to win and not lose, and so on.

We may now provide a possible explanation for the bipolar action we have found in many of the cases. Simply put, whenever we get into trouble dealing with threat, the only other skills we have are those that are consistent with the opposite of the theories that we are using. For example, if overcontrolling behavior is counterproductive, we may reduce our unilateral control; if we are too active, we may become more passive and vice versa (although the vice versa is more difficult to produce). Using the opposite behavior often leads to suppression of old skills rather than learning new sets of skills to deal with the complexity. The moment we behave in less controlling ways, we believe that things are getting out of hand and quickly revert to our original behavior.

Another reason for bipolar action is that we tend to condemn behavior in others with which we do not know how to deal confidently. If I cannot deal effectively with authoritarian behavior, and if I believe Bill acted ineffectively with John, then I will tend to see Bill as having acted in an authoritarian manner. If I am uncomfortable with executives who ease in and appear to be too close to their subordinates, then I will see these as the errors in the case.

Bipolar thinking and action will not make us very good at

FIGURE 3.1 *Model I Theory in Use*

Governing values	→	Action strategies	→	Consequences
Control the purpose of the meeting or encounter. Maximize winning and minimize losing. Minimize negative feelings. Maximize rationality.		Advocate your position in order to be in control and win. Unilaterally save face — own and others'.		Miscommunication, Mistrust, Protectiveness, Self-fulfilling prophecies, Self-sealing processes, Escalating error.

dealing with paradoxes that, as we have seen and will continue to see, are increasingly important consequences of defensive routines. Paradoxes contain contradictions, and holding contradictory views makes us vulnerable to criticisms of being vague or self-contradictory. For example, Barnes (1981) found the following:

Barnes's Observations	**Theory of Action Explanation**
Often executives fail to go beyond their initial reactions in order to look at deeper levels of the issue.	Do not run the risk of losing control and making yourself vulnerable — that is, losing.
Issues fall in opposing camps; hard data and facts are better than soft ideas and speculation.	Create win/lose dynamics. Seek hard data to win, to prevent losing. Abhor speculation lest you become vulnerable.

Model I theory in use is therefore self-reinforcing and not particularly good at self-correcting. We presume that since Model I theory in use is so pervasive, it must be taught early in life. Why is it so pervasive in so many different cultures? Indeed, if *I, Claudius* is valid, why was Model I so pervasive 1,000 years ago? The answer that we propose is not easy to describe in detail (I refer you to Argyris, 1982). Put simply, it is probably not possible to bring up an infant with any other model of action except one like Model I. First, parents are so pressured that they rarely have the opportunity to spend the countless hours that would be required to help the child to learn the complex skills of being competent and strong while simultaneously being vulnerable and less unilaterally controlling. How many of us have stated in exasperation, "Do it!"? This feature of our theory in use appears to be used with a vengeance, especially by adolescents.

The other and perhaps more profound reason is that, in order to develop the skills of inquiry, reflection while acting, vulnerability coupled with strength, we would have to know a language, to understand the ladder of inference as it applies to us, and to be able to articulate our theory in use. As far as we can tell, it is impossible for infants to learn a language and reflect on it in such a way that they can simultaneously make explicit their reasoning processes. It appears that we must learn and become acculturated through the use of Model I. Other models have to be learned later.

IMPACT OF THEORIES IN USE ON ORGANIZATIONS

Think of organizations as designed to fulfill their intended objectives. Recall also that the overwhelming number of organizations uses the hierarchy or pyramid as a structure. Why?

One reason is that the fundamental features of the hierarchical structure are consistent with the way the human mind works. I refer to the specialization of work, the coordination of actions through the use of authority given to superiors, and the use of information systems to help control and manage human behavior. Let us explore each of these a bit further.

At a minimum, organizations require employees that have the skills to produce a product or perform a service. How do we acquire and use these skills? A skill is acquired by remembering and using the answer to previously solved problems and remembering and avoiding previous traps. Developing skills even for a simple activity like riding a bicycle is an extremely complex process.

The capacity for information processing is quite limited in comparison to the demands of the environment in which it is found. We have learned a skill when the program necessary to perform the requisite actions is so much a part of us that performing the skill does not have to be conscious and explicit. We are then free to use our finite information-processing capacity for other kinds of problem solving.

Before we can use these skills effectively, however, the programs must be rigorously generalized and stored. Thus, workers not only make their skill programs tacit but also, once they do, must make them rigid and not easily alterable. Otherwise they could not be performed without thinking. Only when errors are made do the programs become explicit, but then their rigidity must also be dealt with in correcting the programs.

So managers are faced with the task of monitoring employee actions that are guided by programs hidden from the employee yet rigorously generalized and tenaciously held. For example, workers who have learned to use a machine have learned a highly complex program of skills. Once they have learned these skills, they must adhere to them rigorously or they will make errors. They cannot deviate from the program without getting into trouble. The manager is held responsible for the workers' performances, but neither the manager nor the workers has direct access to the programs that produce the performance. Moreover, if corrections are necessary, some employees will hold on to their programs and resist these corrections. The manager is then faced with a predicament. Errors will be charged against him, yet he (and the workers) may have great difficulty in discovering and correcting their cause.

The uncertainty created by the nature of human information processing is cumulated and expanded because managers are also finite information-processing systems. They, too, make their programs tacit and hold on to them tightly. Even with the capacity to make programs explicit, there is a limit to how much information they can cope with. Hence, the need arises to monitor managers.

Although managerial control is necessarily incomplete, managerial responsibility for results is not. We must find ways to reduce the probability of error, and one method is to simplify jobs. If a tacit and rigid program has to surface to be corrected, then it should be as uncomplicated and basic as possible.

Another method is to define production or work standards and what errors are allowable for achieving these standards. If performance errors exceed the tolerances for them, corrective managerial action must be taken. This strategy is called *management by exception*. At its core is the creation of gaps of knowledge about employee performance coupled with a continual sampling for errors. For example, the performance of employees is not monitored (hence, gaps of knowledge) until error is observed (hence, monitoring for error). Implicit in the effectiveness of management by exception is acceptance of the theory that managers need valid information only when workers deviate from standards. But since managers are finite and monitor the work of many human information processors, the data they obtain about the performance of their subordinates must be both comprehensive and manageable. Of necessity, therefore, they must also be abstract. The unique aspects of each situation must be ignored because they would make the data too complex to be useful.

So now we have workers with programs that are tacit, rigorously generalized, and difficult to control directly and managers who use information that is abstracted from the unique situation for which they are responsible (for example, the weekly or monthly budget and production figures). The managers create their own tacit programs and hold on to them tenaciously. These managers must, in turn, be managed, and the problems of tacitness, incompleteness, and abstractness become replicated.

The managers who are most distant from the local level have the greatest responsibility for what happens at that level. In order to manage effectively, they, too, must design gaps in their knowledge while being held responsible for these very gaps — hence, the need to assure themselves that they can institute programs to detect and correct error. One result is that power increases with distance from the local level.

So far we have developed the major features of organizational hierarchical structures by following the requirements of the human mind, but there may be additional reasons for the pyramidal structure. Indeed, the radical economists would say the hierarchy is a capitalist technique used to control people. I agree that the hierarchy is a system of control, but it is hardly the invention of capitalists and was used long before capitalism was created. It is also used, and often with great vengeance, in communist or other totalitarian societies.

The pyramidal structure is a structure of control that is consistent with Model I theory in use. For example, the hierarchy provides some superiors more unilateral control over subordinates. Policies are often designed to make sure the superiors maximize their winning and minimize their losing. Indeed, workers have often adapted to the unilateral control by creating their own organizations — trade unions — that also use the hierarchy.

Since the pyramidal structure is designed to satisfy Model

I governing values, it is possible to predict that when we act in accordance with its dictates, we will act using Model I action strategies and produce the same defensive consequences. It appears that we have designed organizational structures that fit the way the mind processes information and the theories in use we hold. Such a basic match guarantees that people will be available to staff organizations. It also guarantees that organizations will be predisposed to defensive routines.

We have developed a model of some of the defensive routines that will be produced in organizations as a result of this match. We call this Model O-I, where O stands for the organizational equivalent to Model I (Figure 3.2).

Before we describe the model, please note an important assumption in our logic. We are saying that it is individuals, programmed early in life, that cause organizations to have Model O-I systems. Once these programs are in place, they join with the other factors to create a circular self-reinforcing situation. Under these conditions, it is fair to say that organizations may cause defensive routines. However, it is not accurate, I believe, to see organizations as the initial cause.

Why fuss about this distinction since I have just said that causality is circular and self-reinforcing? The distinction is crucial when we wish to change these conditions. It is unlikely that changes in organizational factors will change our theories in use or the way our mind works. It is likely that a new theory in use that respects the way the mind works can, if learned, lead to organizational changes. Indeed, unless there are organizational changes it is unlikely that the new theory in use will last.

Turning to Model O-I, we begin with the notion that if employees are programmed with a Model I theory in use, they will create organizational environments consistent with their defensive routines. For example, we tend to act in ways that lead us to avoid threatening issues by making them undiscussable and by making the undiscussability of the subjects also undiscussable. This should lead to self-fulfilling, self-sealing processes and error escalation. The same conditions should lead to competitive win/lose group and intergroup dynamics as well as games of deception, cover-up, and protectionism.

Under these conditions, errors that are nonthreatening or

FIGURE 3.2 *Model 0-I Learning System*

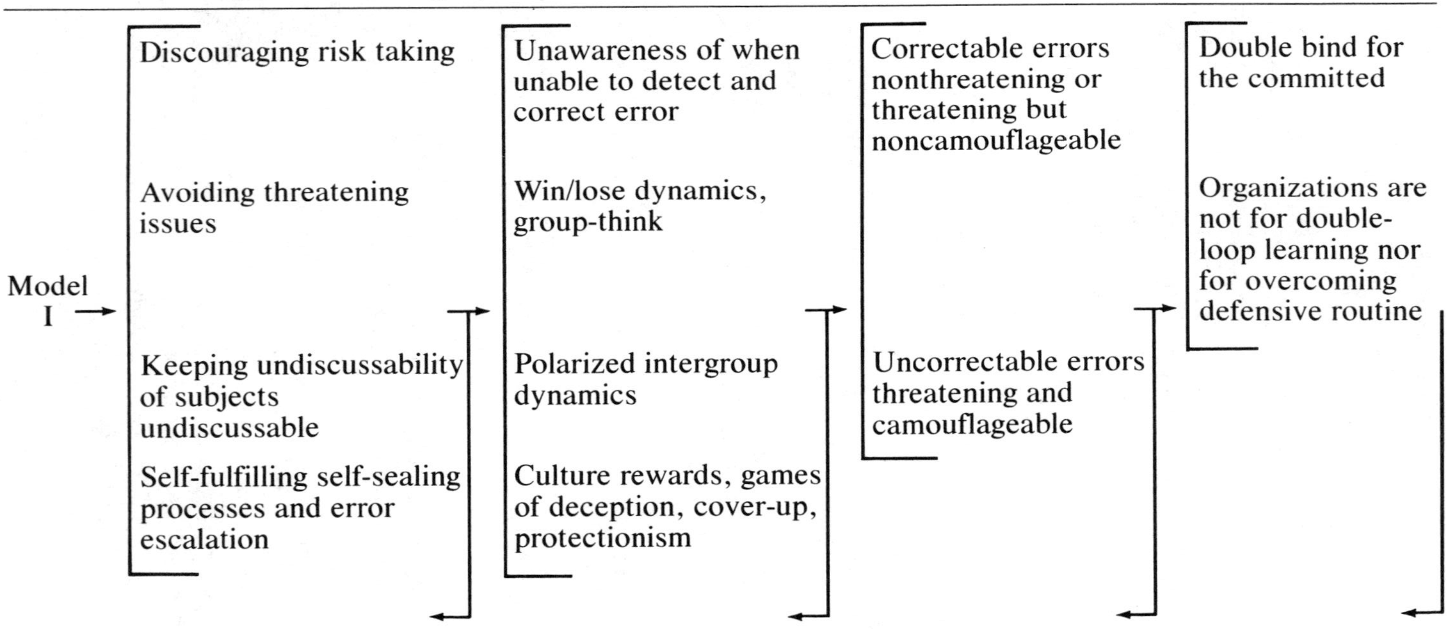

Model I →	Discouraging risk taking	Unawareness of when unable to detect and correct error	Correctable errors nonthreatening or threatening but noncamouflageable	Double bind for the committed
	Avoiding threatening issues	Win/lose dynamics, group-think		Organizations are not for double-loop learning nor for overcoming defensive routine
	Keeping undiscussability of subjects undiscussable	Polarized intergroup dynamics	Uncorrectable errors threatening and camouflageable	
	Self-fulfilling self-sealing processes and error escalation	Culture rewards, games of deception, cover-up, protectionism		

threatening but not camouflageable will be corrected. Errors that are threatening and camouflageable will not be corrected. All these conditions feed back to reinforce each other. The error-producing features that each represents will be reinforced and strengthened, and this tends to create a double bind for the employees who are committed to the health of the organization. If they see errors that are hidden and blow the whistle, they run the risk of bringing down the wrath of the entire system. If they collude to hide the errors, they will feel a lack of integrity. It is not surprising for individuals to adapt to this situation by developing an operating assumption — namely, that organizations are not for learning how to overcome defensive routines. Once individuals begin to operate consistently with this assumption, then they cut off the possibility of critical learning for the organization.

To sum up so far, we are programmed with a theory in use about how to deal with others that is predisposed to create defensiveness and error, especially when there is threat. Organizations are designed to give some individuals control over others, and the control is reinforced by information systems as well as reward and penalty policies. These systems and policies combine to place individuals in a state of continual potential threat. They could get in trouble if they do not get along with the individuals above them. The subordinates, at any given level, will protect themselves as best as they can by creating various kinds of defensive routines. These defensive routines make it more likely that indivdiuals will especially adhere to their theory in use to protect themselves.

The prognosis, therefore, is that defensive routines will flourish and that, as a result, organizations will become more rigid, compulsive, and ineffective in the way they deal with threatening issues. Some day the pollution caused by these consequences could spread into the area of nonthreatening, routine issues. It could become increasingly difficult to change even those routine and trivial issues. Defenses will be built whenever this occurs because it is more embarrassing to the players than when change is difficult because of threatening issues. Large corporations and governmental bureaucracies are especially subject to this danger because, in order to manage complexity, they tend to proliferate many rules about dealing with routine issues. The rules become so massive that there are rules about how to find the rules and specifications about how to deal with specifications.

The system of defensive loops, therefore, is not self-correcting; it is self-reinforcing. What probably prevents many more blowups from occurring is that the subordinates learn to take it; the culture rewards this action and reinforces it by norms that state this is normal and to be expected; layering is produced in organizations to distance people among whom a danger of blowups exists; policies are put in place to buy off individuals for the tension and frustrations they endure; and normal attrition, voluntary or otherwise, helps to reduce number of employees who are unable to take it.

Our analysis provides an explanation for two studies of interagency warfare and governmental regulation. In a story of the interaction among Secretary of Health, Education, and Welfare Joseph A. Califano, Jr.; Secretary of Labor Ray Marshall; and President Carter and his aides regarding welfare reform (Lynn and de F. Whiteman, 1981), the players used typical defensive routines. Califano kept secret for a long time his doubts of genuine welfare reform at zero cost increase. The president sensed Califano's doubts but apparently never explored them directly with him. When Califano said that he was working hard on a plan that Carter might be able to call his own, the president asked Califano for a plan that he would gladly call "the Califano plan." Califano's policy analysts were frustrated by his actions. They never said so, but they built up strategies to protect themselves. These strategies got them in trouble with Califano and a competing group of analysts in Secretary Marshall's office. This led to interagency warfare, a state in which positions harden and everybody looks out for Number One.

Reich (1981a) suggests that an entire industry is rising as a result of the self-fulfilling prophecies, self-sealing processes, and escalating error between private and governmental sectors. The new industry is composed of experts who deal with the difficult relationships of private business and government by:

- Seeking to achieve clear controversies in which the client's position can be sharply differentiated from that of its regulatory opponent,

- Exaggerating the danger of the opponent's activities,
- Prolonging and intensifying conflict,
- Keeping business executives and regulatory officials apart.

Regulatory agencies are also administered by similar defensive-reasoning processes. This means that the regulators will probably deal with difficult, threatening issues that are undiscussable by translating them into discussable, nonthreatening issues. For example, I have found that if regulators do not trust builders, instead of dealing with that issue, they create piles of regulation in an effort to prevent cheating by dishonest builders. However, these regulations may drive out the honest builders while they stimulate the dishonest ones to new heights of creative dishonesty.

IMPLICATIONS

We, as a society, hold a theory in use that is basically oriented toward unilateral control, winning not losing, and face saving. This leads to defensive consequences such as miscommunication, self-fulfilling prophecies, self-sealing processes, and escalating error. It also leads to defensive reasoning. Defensive reasoning is characterized by the use of soft data, by reasoning that is privately compelling and privately testable.

The theories in use and the defensive routines lead to defensive organizations and organizational culture (Figure 3.3). We

FIGURE 3.3 *Organizational Defensive Loops*

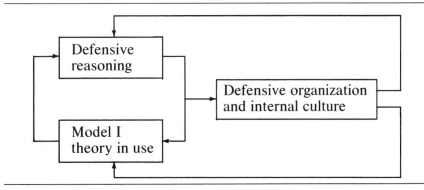

thus have a massive defensive loop composed of theories in use, defensive reasoning, and organizations that contain defensive groups, warring intergroups or coalition groups, as well as defensive cultures. Each part of this loop feeds back to reinforce the other, creating a circular system that is difficult to interrupt and correct. The result is that this circularity is often taken for granted and thought to be as natural as day or night. People do not expect to change it. They expect to adapt to it, and the biggest adaptation strategy is to bypass it.

four

SEEKING HELP: THE LITERATURE AND CONSULTANTS

In Chapter 2, we saw that individuals were able to give sound advice to Bill about how he should have dealt with John but that no one was able to produce this advice when they were given the opportunity, that those doing the producing were unaware of the gap, and that the observers and the recipient of the advice had no difficulty in observing or experiencing the gap. These are not isolated or unique results. They happen routinely whenever individuals are advising on issues that contain threat. The gap and the blindness are caused by the theory in use and the defensive reasoning that accompanies it and by the wider culture that supports the first two factors. The results are defensive loops where learning to solve problems that contain threat is inhibited, if not blocked, but is taken for granted because that is the best any of us knows to do.

We are now going to see similar defensive loops in two domains to which individuals may turn for help on implementing strategy and change. The first is the advice in the literature on how to implement strategy when dealing with threat. I believe that the writers are unaware of the contribution they are making to the defensive loops, that some readers may be aware of a gap between the advice and implementing it, and that other readers are not aware of the gap and believe it is useful and helpful. No matter what the group, the end result is that the advice will not be implemented effectively because it requires skills to engage defensive routines that most individuals do not have. To engage defensive routines is to confront them and make them discussable. Indeed, they have skills that are counterproductive coupled with skills to keep them unaware of their counterproductivity.

The second major domain for help on implementation is internal or external consultants. The situation here is a bit different, but the ultimate consequences are the same. As we will see, consultants are able to identify client defensive routines. They know what kind of advice they would give. For example, they would encourage open discussion about the undiscussables. They also know that such advice is dangerous. One reason the advice is dangerous is that it violates the ideas in good currency about dealing with undiscussables, which is to bypass them. Another reason is that if the client agrees that defensive routines exist, it is highly likely that the consultants do not have the skills to teach the clients how to engage them. Both result in the consultants' dealing with defensive routines by addressing them obliquely if not by clearly bypassing them. Whatever bypass strategy is used, the consultants will act as if they are not bypassing. The result is the familiar cover-up of the cover-up.

In the interest of fairness, I remind the reader that everything that I just said about consultants is true about line executives, workers, professors. Almost all those that we have studied use bypass routines to deal with defensive routines.

THE STRATEGY IMPLEMENTATION LITERATURE

The literature on strategy contains a puzzle. On the one hand, there is an increasing emphasis on the importance of defensive routines. For example, Hermon-Taylor (1984), Ansoff (1982), and Naylor (1978) point out that organizations have defensive routines against changing the status quo. Gluck, Kaufman, and Wallick (1980) report that in their consulting practice, the two most frequently encountered barriers to effective strategic planning and implementation could be illustrated by two comments: (1) "We did not feel comfortable with the decision at the time, but it was Joe's program and we didn't want to vote against Joe," and (2) "We didn't really have a choice." Tichy (1983) concludes that the political system in organizations is the least talked about openly, yet it is frequently the major absorber of senior management time and resources. Day (1982) recommends that it is time for strategic analysis no longer to postpone, evade, or overlook the key issues by making tangential arguments whose tangentiality is frequently recognized but is undiscussable.

On the other hand, I could not find any systematic discussion or advice in the literature on how to engage defensive routines or prevent them from arising. What little advice is given is, as we shall see, abstract and difficult to tie to concrete actions. Indeed, much of the advice is actually bypass routines.

Gaps in Advice

What kind of advice do the professionals provide about how to overcome defensive routines? First, we are advised to be open, encourage diverse views, reward the competent, surface hidden agendas carefully, and so on. Those who would agree with the advice would have the problem of how to produce such advice in a real situation that contains threat. Others would agree and believe that they could implement it.

Another example is the advice to create genuine participation, beginning at the lower levels and working upward. For example, Bourgeoiss and Brodwin (1982) recommend the crescive, or growth, model for strategy formulation and implementation that involves genuine involvement of people at the lower levels who are not held tightly accountable for successful implementation and who are led by a leader who defines the premises and who is able to compromise to a second-best strategy if necessary, to maintain the openness of the organization to new and discrepant information, to utilize a general strategy to guide the firm's growth, to manipulate systems and structures to encourage bottom-up strategy formulation, to intervene in the logical incrementalist manner, and to adjust structure and staffing to minimize morale problems.

I agree with these ideas. The questions that arise, however, are how is genuine involvement obtained when defenses are strong? How do defensive individuals or groups manipulate leaders who are not held tightly accountable and can use a second-best strategy? How is openness maintained when closedness is preferred and covered up? Finally, how is a genuine bottom-up strategy implemented when individuals will use it to salute instead of to take personal responsibility for overcoming their and the organization's defensive routines?

The advice in the literature uses what might be called a microtheory of implementation.

If the readers understand what is written,
If they wish to implement the advice,
If they are free to implement the advice,
Then they can implement the advice effectively.

This microtheory of implementation is valid when the individual-organizational defensive routines and the bypass routines are weak. It is not likely to be valid when the defenses are strong. An assumption used in this theory of implementation that is like the one found in most football plays. Each is designed to lead to a touchdown as long as there is not formidable opposition. The difficulty, in our case, is that the opposition is formidable and is often composed of the very individuals who are seeking to implement the strategy and change. To compound the difficulty, the individuals are often not aware that they may be their own worst enemy.

One approach to strategy formulation and implementation is concerned with implementation and emphasizes participation and involvement at the top levels of management. Quinn's (1980) study of how strategy is formulated and implemented in several large, successful organizations is one of the best examples. He has called the approach *logical incrementalism*. The reason why it is instructive to single out this approach is that it encourages open discussions among the actors rather than defensive routines. However if our research is valid, then the actors will not be able to produce the advice, especially when they are dealing with threat.

If we examine Quinn's (1980) carefully documented examples, we find few examples of threat and defensive routines. One possible reason for this is that these data disconfirm our view. There are several reasons why this explanation may not be valid, however. First, the overwhelming amount of data presented were from interviews, and interviews produce primarily espoused theory data. There were very few quotations from the executives and illustrations of how they acted.[1]

Second, some quotations that were presented do suggest the existence of defensive routines. For example, there are descriptions of how CEOs did not pay much attention to the formal planning paperwork that flooded their desks, how they attempted to keep their views submerged until the others had spoken, how they often shaped the discussion subtly (in their eyes) to help the group come to the conclusion they had reached, and how, at times, the CEOs acted in ways not to snuff out differences but to prevent those differences from creating too many difficulties.

Quinn (1980), I believe, might suggest a different explanation. Because it is possible to take more time to deliberate at a less hurried pace, there may be less competitiveness or fewer misunderstandings. Logical incrementalism may create conditions that reduce the negative consequences described here. For example, Quinn identifies four important features of the logical incremental approach: (1) Begin the planning process with broad goals and policies that accommodate a variety of views, and (2) provide the conditions under which different views can attract supporters, which would lead to (3) less politically charged conditions since the proposals are only proposals and there is time to discuss them, thus creating (4) the conditions that encourage innovation or that kill unwanted alternatives with less political exposure (p. 52).

The logic in these views is that the abstract quality of the broad goals plus the time available to discuss them plus the expectation that progress will be gradual reduce the probability of creating politically charged interactions because no hard choices have to be made immediately and people can think about their differences more constructively. As the discussions mature, it will be easier to encourage or discourage the ideas so that the end result is in line with the preferences of the CEO. This may be true as long as there is no reason for the organizational defensive routines to be activated.

Wilson's (1982) study is relevant to the point being made. He studied an important strategic decision over a period of 4 years. During phase one, the major thrust of the strategy formulation was consistent with the formal, rational planning model questioned by Quinn (1980). However, during phase two, the issues took on a threatening meaning that did not exist before because of political maneuverings. At that point, the organizational defensive routines began to become prominent.

There are quite a few ifs built into the description of the effectiveness of the logical incremental process. It will work as suggested if users can specify (1) how broad goals and policies necessarily accommodate a variety of views, (2) how supporters can be attracted if the differences in views are threatening, (3) how proposals are necessarily less threatening, and (4) what conditions can encourage innovations and kill unwanted proposals with less political exposure.

A different scenario could be written that focuses on the phrase "less political exposure." In a world where defensive routines are strong, acting in ways to reduce political exposure is crucial. If individuals learn that the CEO begins with broad goals and slowly narrows the options to reduce political exposure and conflict, then they can learn to play the game. They will differ up to a point and submerge their differences to remain within the acceptable limits of the CEO. The defensive routines are then driven underground. The CEO is not aware of the group-think he may have helped to create, and hence, when CEOs respond in interviews, they do not include these issues because they are not aware of them. Unfortunately, the data available do not permit us to rule out this scenario. There are enough references to the subtle manipulation of the group by the CEO to suggest that some of the defensive routines could have been operating.

If the defensive routines were operating more powerfully than the respondents suggest, and if they were not knowingly distorting their description; then some of the assertions about the positive features of logical incrementalism have to be modified by, at least, adding the unintended consequences like the games people play to remain within the theory of minimal political conflict found in this approach. This modification is not only necessary if a complete picture is to be developed of what goes on when the top people meet. Equally important is to develop an accurate and complete picture of what goes on below the top group as subordinates plan for and have dry runs to brief their respective superiors, the members of the top group.

There is another reason why it is important to be able to rule out the scenario I have presented. Quinn (1980) faults the more formal approaches to strategy as focusing unduly on the measurable, as underemphasizing the vital qualitative dimension, and as becoming rigid, cumbersome, and routine. These conditions, in turn, could drive out the creative dimension and cause counterproductivity.

The operative words are *unduly* and *underemphasis*. From our perspective, these are both errors. Recall that errors cannot knowingly be designed and implemented. If they exist, it is because individuals are unaware of producing them. Presumably, the logical incrementalist will say that the focus on the formal, quantitative, and analytical can lead to those errors. It can and it cannot. Individuals who use formal quantitative analysis not only can be as aware of these errors as anyone else but also might be able to create conditions that overcome the difficulties that exist in the logical incremental approach. The work of Hermon-Taylor (1983) and the strategy consultant that is described next illustrates that adhering to the measurable and analytic does not necessarily blind individuals to the vital human and qualitative dimensions.

This leads us to the deeper issue involved. It is possible that the logical incremental approach is infected by the scenario described previously. If so, this approach also can become rigid, cumbersome, and routine when dealing with threatening issues. The difference is that most of the cues will be driven underground. Logical incrementalism may also drive out creativity, not because the players intend it but because they are programmed to do so, and they are unaware of this possibility.

The advice, therefore, contains gaps, some of which are recognized and some of which are not. Even if the gaps are recognized, I am suggesting that many readers will not be able to implement the advice and will be unaware of this fact, especially if they are dealing with business issues that are intertwined with defensive routines. Recall the John and Bill case. The respondents had little difficulty in formulating sound advice. The big difficulty they had was to produce their advice even in the relatively supportive and pressureless context of a classroom. The unrecognized gap is built into the way we think about and act to deal with defensive routines.

If the respondents had used the reasoning processes that they probably used to produce their technical advice, then they would have seen the gap. For example, the literature advises that the analysis be based on hard data, that the inferences made from the data be explicit and tested rigorously, and that evidence can be amassed to show that the recommendations are realistic and sound. Thus, when advising readers on how to reason about strategy formulation, writers use publicly compelling and testable reasoning to minimize gaps and inconsistencies.

Mintzberg (1979) raised the possibility that this very type of reasoning could be a major cause of ineffective implementation. He begins his argument by questioning whether implementation activities are the underlying cause of ineffective use of policy analysis. He notes that most writers explain the causes of ineffective implementation as (1) the managers do not understand the analysis or are not sold on it, (2) the analysis lacks support of top management, and (3) the solutions are blocked by individual-organizational defensive routines. Mintzberg believes the problem is in the formulation of policy analysis. For example, managers do understand the analysis and believe it is unrealistic, full of gaps, and so forth. Top management does not support the plans for good reasons like the analysis ignores many important but not easily quantifiable factors. Finally, planners may create counterproductive defensive routines to protect themselves and build their empires.

Professional planners are aware of this possibility. For example, Bowman (1983) and Hermon-Taylor (1983) have cautioned against planners' becoming disconnected from the line by formulating policies independently and by using reasoning that is different from that used by some line executives. There is much truth in this position: witness how often line people use pejoratively the metaphor *techie* to describe professionals who produce formulations that are rigorous by their standards and not useable by line.

I have studied situations that would confirm these views and others that would not. For example, I have observed cases in which managers understood the analysis but did not support it. However, they covered up their true feelings by bypassing the issues and thereby activating defensive routines. I observed other cases in which the managers did not understand the analysis, not because of flaws in the analysis but because of flaws in their competence to reflect and to think rigorously and abstractly. Under these conditions it was the planners who bypassed these issues by activities such as upping the level of proof or describing their view in a way that was experienced as patronizing by the line. Both groups activate defensive routines that are undiscussable, with the result that implementation suffers.

Mintzberg's (1979) analysis appears to group operations research (OR) and strategic planning together. This may be one reason for our differences. I too have studied OR professionals and found them more "techie" oriented because the models they use are highly quantitative and they assume a reality that even some of the leaders of OR believe is much too simplified. Strategic planning, in contrast, has as its base economic theory (finance, marketing, and so on). Some models are narrow while others are much more comprehensive. Moreover, sophisticated practitioners use the models in ways that are consistent with Mintzberg's plea for the inclusion of softer but critical variables.

Mintzberg's diagnosis appears to focus on the defenses of the planners and OR types more than on the defenses of the line. If these defenses could be made explicit and discussable, not only may they be reduced but also the more profound issues of what is sound formulation could be explored by the parties involved.

When providing advice on dealing with people issues, however, researchers do not hold themselves to the same standard. Some authors may respond that the people side is not their forte. Fine, but that does not preclude them from identifying the gaps and inconsistencies in their advice. I am not implying that the writers have nasty intentions. I believe the reason the gaps go unnoticed is that the writers are as human as the rest of us. They also are influenced by the same defensive reasoning when dealing with defensive routines as is taught to all of us early in life.

There is an important lesson for advice givers. Advice is

complete when the writer illustrates how to produce the solution with a set of rules and action strategies that are useable by individuals. This lesson is taken for granted in many professions — for example, an accountant who recommends a particular kind of analysis and then can produce it.

The Advice Recommends Structural Changes

Another characteristic of the advice in the literature on strategy implementation is the focus on what I call *structural features*. Individuals are advised that if they want effective implementation of a strategy, they should define the tasks, the jobs, and their reporting relationships clearly; that is, define a clear-cut structure. Moreover, a valid information system should be developed with which the strategy implementation can be monitored. There is also the advice to hire competent individuals and reward them fairly. Finally, the CEO is advised to support the strategy.

This advice makes sense, but as we shall see, it does little to eliminate the defensive routines. For example, Overmeer (1983) reports that general managers have ways to say no during the resource allocation process that are unilateral and indirect. They do not say in a direct way that they are not interested in the project, and they do not encourage discussion of their conclusion. The indirect no combined with the subordinates' feeling left in the dark lead the subordinates to conclude that the issues are not discussable. This conclusion reinforces the feeling of being left in the dark as well as the sense of being unable to influence the CEO. Again, none of these issues is discussable. Overmeer suggests that the following error-inducing loop may be created:

1. If somebody produces a plan, don't tell him why you don't like the plan. Hence, the person doesn't know what he has done well or wrong.
2. The person starts after a few times to imitate the same behavior toward his subordinates.
3. Hence, neither he nor his subordinates learns.

4. The information presented in plans becomes increasingly un-reliable, and the drafting of plans becomes a ritual for subor-dinates, as the approval of plans is based on criteria other than soundness of information.
5. The above is exacerbated by a time pressure on subordinates.
6. The use of sophisticated techniques (elaborate computer pro-grams, for example) may be used as a way to patch up the unreliable information and to impress others.
7. This is a reinforcing cycle, and the longer it goes on, the less likely it is that the plans are sound and that it becomes dis-cussable. The whole pattern has to be discussed. Hence, one resorts to like or dislike and all kinds of devices to express that evaluation.

These defensive loops are often created by CEOs who be-lieve that divisional heads must be convinced that it is important for them to participate in the resource allocation process because participation is the basis for proper business decisions. This is hardly a process to encourage genuine participation.

We have found that some of the world's leading strategy professionals have the same bypass routines as anyone else. We have observed mixed messages in corporations whose structure followed strategy and where the jobs were defined clearly. We have observed CEOs and senior strategy professionals, who sup-ported the strategy enthusiastically, deal with threatening issues by bypassing them.

In these ways, individuals who use defensive reasoning keep private the logic that makes their argument compelling to themselves. If they test any of their inferences and conclusions, they do it privately. The result is that their reasoning is inacces-sible for examination and inquiry by others who are involved. This is a recipe for trouble, especially when there are genuine differ-ences around an issue. It is a recipe for deep trouble if defensive routines are also involved. The "best" result is often distancing and bypass. This is the type of reasoning that is found in the ad-vice of strategy implementation.

What is even more concerning is that readers of the liter-ature who use the same kind of reasoning may not see that the advice they are getting is full of gaps, oversimplifications, and inconsistencies. The advice makes sense and they recognize it as a good idea. The difficulty is that they may be unaware of their inability to produce the best features of the advice, and they may be unaware of why they are unaware.

This dilemma is not limited to the literature on strategy. It is true for most of the management literature that deals with defensive routines. For example, let us examine some of the work of Drucker. He first describes one of his most important contributions to management as the quest for responsibility that he defines as the individual making himself or herself capable of performance and contribution. Second, he believes that he has put forth a perspective on management that is demanding. He then adds, "In some ways, this has been the most successful and most effective contribution I have made" (1985, p. 8).

I agree that Drucker has focused on responsibility, demanding standards, and uncompromising, exacting behavior with integrity. I believe this is true for much of his stance on management except for those aspects dealing with individual-organizational defensive routines. In this domain his writing is informed by defensive reasoning. For example, his writing contains several important references to defensive routines: "Organization structure will not just 'evolve.' The only things that evolve in an organization are disorder, friction, and malperformance" (Drucker, 1973, p. 523). Although Drucker has much to say about reducing the probability of disorder, friction, and malperformance, he has little to say how to diagnose and reduce those problems when they already exist. I could not find an analysis of the processes of evolution that he was referring to, but they are central to his point.

Next, Drucker gives advice that probably feels right to thoughtful executives but if they thought about it carefully, they would see that it contains gaps that make intelligent application to defensive routines difficult. For example, "organizitis," which is a self-inflicted hypochondria, should be avoided. "Organizational change should not be taken often and should not be undertaken lightly. . . . A certain amount of friction, of incongruity, or organizational confusion is inevitable" (Drucker, 1973, p. 549).

An executive may ask How can I tell what is "often" and "not often enough"? What is "taking it lightly" or "not lightly enough"? How much friction, incongruity, and confusion are inevitable, and how can I tell what is inevitable and what is not? It is important to know the answers to these questions not only to take effective action but also to know when the defensive subordinates or superiors are not rationalizing away a needed reorganization or pushing for an unneeded one or protecting themselves by saying that friction, incongruity, and confusion are inevitable.

Another illustration of defensive reasoning is the pattern of what appears to be oversimplification and polarization. The pattern I refer to would probably not hit the readers between the eyes unless they were interested in using publicly compelling reasoning on defensive routines. For example:

> One can either work or meet. One cannot do both at the same time. [Drucker, 1973, p. 403]

> The only thing that is proven by a man's not performing in a given assignment is that management has made a mistake by putting him in. [p. 457]

> If executives spend more than a small fraction of their time on human relations problems, on feuds, on frictions, then the work force is almost certainly too large. [1966, p. 43]

This advice could be correct, and it could be wrong. First, meetings can be unproductive, especially if they are full of defensive routines. But why not find ways to reduce the defensive routines? I have seen quite a few executives who were given the right assignment and who later were ineffective for reasons that were not predictable and none was the fault of the organization. Third, it is true that overstaffing is a source of organizational problems. Indeed there is some fascinating social science theory on what I call *optimal undermanning* (Argyris, 1964). The executives interested in being responsible and tough must ask themselves how the overstaffing arose in the first place.

Drucker understands that defensive routines exist. Discussions of concepts such as "safe mediocrity" and "conscience decisions" illustrate the point (Drucker, 1973, pp. 457–458). The difficulty with his advice is that it bypasses the routines or assumes they can be knocked down by a decisive blow on the part of the superior. Drucker knows that this is unlikely. He gives an example of Harry Truman wondering what Ike thought after sending down an order and finding out nothing happened. By the way, this is a good example of what I am proposing. I believe it is time that we take seriously the fact that nothing will happen because of defensive routines whose only future is to intensify and shackle.

HELP FROM CONSULTANTS

During the past 10 years, I have interviewed many consultants about the way they deal with threat. Many of these consultants are members of several leading management consulting firms. During the past 5 years, I have also had a chance to observe consultants of two firms and several inside corporate consultants as they dealt with client defensive routines. I illustrate what I have found with four cases.

Case A: The Hesitation of an Outside Consultant in Dealing with Defensive Routines

This case illustrates the dilemma often faced by consultants who work with decentralized companies. In this case the consultant has diagnosed a mixed message problem in a large decentralized firm.

During a feedback meeting, the consultant had just been complimented on his work by one of the senior clients. He reported to me that he appreciated the feedback but was concerned that one reason the clients felt good about it was that they had not engaged some key organizational routines.

Consultant's Thoughts	**Dilemma**
Consultant: [Up to now] we have been tacitly manipulated	Dilemma: I can improve the quality of the casework and

Consultant's Thoughts	**Dilemma**
by them; we have not engaged them about their behavior. So far we have not broken any major frame about how to think about the business and its competitive position.	run the risk of blowing the client. If we give them the quality of help we can give them, they may not be as happy because we would ask them to discuss issues that are presently undiscussable.

This is a familiar dilemma to consultants and line executives. One management consulting firm advises its professionals to deal with these problems by using the so-called art of the possible. In effect, the rule is to be as honest as the client permits. If an issue is genuinely undiscussable, then do not violate the defensive routine. The difficulties with this strategy are: it remains within the client's defensive routines, it reduces the probability that the client will become aware and solve some of the major causes of the problems, it places the consultant in the role of colluding with the client's way of reasoning and dealing with threat, it makes it necessary for the consultant to act as if this was not the case, thus feeding back to reinforce the client's defensive routines.

The consultant was aware of these possible consequences and was trying to find ways to engage the client's defensive routines rather than to bypass them and to do so without jeopardizing significantly the client relationship. As it turned out, he was willing to take risks as long as he could do so in ways that expressed his views about the situation so that if the client became upset, he (consultant) could, in good conscience, say that he had done his best.

Chris: Could you say something like this: "I appreciated the positive evaluation you gave us the other day. We value you as a client and want to do our best.

"In this connection, I would like to describe a dilemma and get your advice. I believe that we have analyses to present that may not be easily digestible by the organization. We do not want to hide information from you, but neither do we want to upset our clients."

Consultant: That would help. It certainly would make me feel more comfortable. But it isn't going to be easy. The way they charge themselves for . . . [describes financial procedures] is counterproductive.

Chris: What do you think will surprise them about that?

Consultant: I think it will embarrass them.

Chris: Do you think they know it?

Consultant: That's hard to answer. They are very much prisoners of their procedures. . . . It will embarrass them because they will have to act [in a way that is not easy for them] or cover up.

Notice that the sources for the hesitations are created by the ability to sense and empathize with the client. Thus, the consultant worried less about explaining the errors in the financial policies than about the sense of embarrassment that it may cause plus the potential for a cover-up. The latter two problems were undiscussable. Note also that the consultant was seeking to design an intervention that would work and, at the same time, that was riskless.

This particular session ended with the consultant promising to give the issue more thought. Over the next few weeks, he had several further conversations with me. What became increasingly clear to him was that the undiscussability of the bad financial policy was part of a larger problem — namely, the relationship between the division and corporate. He collected several examples to show that one reason bad policies existed was that the subordinates would not usually communicate all they knew to their superiors in order to minimize inviting the superiors to meddle into the management of the divisions. This is an example of the general scenario described in Case A in Chapter 1.

The consultant decided to begin to engage rather than bypass the defensive routines. He raised the issue by describing how the different functional areas in a particular division acted when they had serious and conflict-laden differences among them. We join the discussion as the consultant said:

Consultant: It appears to us that the way the differences are solved is to kick them upstairs [gives examples].

CEO: Basically what you have given is an example that I recognize. But I would say that our record is as good as anyone's in this business.

There is always going to be a certain amount of people protecting their own job and turf, reluctance to give in or give up something.

I think that is not unusual in any company. . . . I think we are a long way from coming apart at the seams or having a situation that is getting out of hand. I don't say that you are inferring that.

The CEO's first reaction was to confirm the existence of the problem and then to assert that it is normal and not serious. He even applauded the fact that the consultant had not said that it was serious — an accolade that could make it more difficult for the consultant or the other members of the management team to disagree with the CEO.

Later, the CEO asked if the consultant had any plans for showing the slide to the executives of the holding company:

CEO: I don't know what you plan to do with this. I'm not saying don't make your point.

Consultant: I don't know if that slide will be shown to anyone else. I wanted to be explicit about this.

CEO: I understand. [By the way] it is not embarrassing to me. It does demonstrate some of the concerns that many of our people have had. I just want to make sure that it is in perspective.

Vice-president I (client): I guess he [consultant] is telling us that our people still have an inability to communicate upward — for example, with people like myself.

CEO: Communication: I recognize that it is not one of our strengths.

Vice-president II: People I work with are easy to communicate with — where is our problem? I don't detect a smidgeon of it. . . .

And what I have said is not really in conflict with what the consultant has said. [Several other vice-presidents say yes-yes.]

CEO: All this is very important, but time is passing by. How much more do you have to present? Let's get on with it. Okay?

Here is a situation where a vice-president agreed with the consultant that there was a communication problem. Another vice-president disagreed completely and almost in the same breath asserted that what he has just said was not inconsistent with the consultant's views. Several vice-presidents immediately supported that view. The CEO followed up by saying that the discussion was interesting but that time was short and they should return to the presentation.

Note the escalation of undiscussables. The consultant began by exploring the problem of people at the lower levels passing the responsibility upward when the issues are conflict laden and potentially threatening. The CEO responded by agreeing that this was a problem in all organizations but not an important problem in this organization. He added to the problem of undiscussables because another one may be that the vice-presidents did not disagree with the CEO when he made such statements. When one vice-president respectfully disagreed, he was neither encouraged to discuss his views nor supported by anyone — another undiscussable. Finally, those who questioned the validity of the consultant's views also said that their disagreement was not a disagreement. That, too, became another undiscussable. It is difficult to confront individuals on such obvious inconsistencies. Indeed, the obviousness of such an inconsistency may be a clear message to the consultant and the vice-president to change topics. Finally, that hypothesis cannot be checked because the CEO admonished the consultant to get back to his presentation, thereby implying that this discussion was a deviation. The CEO was correct. The consultant had included this point as part of another presentation to protect himself from what just happened.

Case B: The Dilemmas of Professionals Coping with Defensive Routines

This case describes the experiences that three professionals (two working within two different large organizations and one working in a management consulting firm) had with line executives. The first two professionals are judged by their professional peers (in other firms) as being bright, very competent, and one of them, as probably the best in the country. Both report that their respective CEOs are analytically oriented and ask tough questions but are fair and willing to be confronted. It is not likely, therefore, that the concerns described now can be related to technical incompetence or fears about their superiors.

The first problem that the consultants described was, to quote one of them, "the perennial one" of dedicated line executives who value strategic planning but do not possess the analytical know-how to think as rigorously as would be required for the quality of strategic analysis to which they aspire. The problem is exacerbated by the fact that these same line executives often do not appear to be aware of the gaps between their abilities and their aspirations.

As I heard these attributions about the line executives, I wondered how their validity could be determined. How do I know that these judgments are not defenses of the two professionals? The tack that I took to get answers to these questions was to ask them to describe what cues they use to make the judgments. Both professionals were able to describe actual conversation they used as cues. For example, the line executives might state generalizations about strategy that were not supportable by data, but they implied that they were. "Our analysis of the data indicates clearly . . .," when the data do not indicate clearly and they did not make their analysis explicit.

In another example, a line executive finished a presentation to the top group with a slide that read "Conclusion: We are following the correct strategy and are on the right track." The difficulty was that the presentation never made a compelling argument about why the strategy was correct. "It was one statement of assurance after another. He was telling us in effect, 'Don't worry, everything is fine.' The CEO said to the line executive what I was thinking. 'I realize that you believe that we are on track, but I do not know the reasoning behind it.' " No one stopped to explore the validity of the CEO's conclusion. If the CEO was correct, no one explored why the line executive kept his reasoning private.

The other strategy professional described an episode in which he tried to surface the gaps and inconsistencies in the reasoning of some line executives by being as diplomatically straightforward (a contradiction in terms?) about substantive errors. Their responses were abstract and very high on the ladder of inference. They were empty answers, but the line executives thought they were giving concrete replies. The strategy professional sensed their blindness. Not wanting to embarrass the line officials, he backed off and acted as if he were not covering up anything. The line executives apparently felt good about the way the situation was handled because they reported that no major disagreement had occurred during the meeting. Thus, we have, in the interest of not alienating a client, a bypass routine that covers up a critical problem — namely, how top line executives reason about strategy.

The dilemma faced by the consultant is that by behaving according to the ideas in good currency about how to deal with threatening issues, he is using the same types of defensive routines that are being used in the company and that often inhibit genuine learning. In the case just cited, I learned that some of the vice-presidents have held confidential talks with their CEO about other difficult business issues that involved other group members. The CEO listened attentively and promised to maintain confidentiality. In so doing he reinforced these actions and may have created the question in the minds of those vice-presidents, I wonder if any of my colleagues are doing what I am now doing? Also, in one of the cases, the vice-presidents realized that they were being grilled (their term) by the internal strategy professional. Of course, they did not discuss this with him but dealt with the issue by describing him privately as "bright but a bit of a smart ass."

Case C: A Professional Bypassing Defensive Routines

A strategy professional, extremely strong in formal, quantitative analysis as well as being predisposed to engage individual-organizational defensive routines, was faced with the following dilemma. The top executives of a large corporation were seeking a new strategy. More important, they were asking him to educate the divisional vice-presidents how to produce and implement more effective strategy. However, the corporate officers were part of the problem and were unaware of this fact.

During a discussion with the top management, the strategy professional pointed out that a focus on the corporate strategic planning process inevitably leads to issues of organizational structure, control and reward mechanisms, communication patterns, and individual skills and behavior on the part of the senior executives at corporate and at the divisions. The consultant ordered these issues inversely in terms of importance but the order in which he believed they would be heard. He thought the top management would have little difficulty in discussing organizational structure and most difficulty in discussing their behavior. He also believed that this was the order of discussion with which he would do best. The reason that he would have difficulty discussing top management skill and behavior was not that he did not have adequate data, that he was not confident of his analysis, or that he doubted that he could present his case clearly. He believed that he would have difficulty because if he presented the data and analysis forthrightly, he would threaten the clients. He, in turn, was not confident how he would deal with clients if they felt threatened. If he could not deal with these feelings effectively, then the clients could legitimately become upset.

I pause to point out two features of his decision. First, to repeat, it is possible for professionals who are highly competent in formal, quantitative analysis also to be aware of critical defensive routines at the highest level. Second, and more important, if one reads the literature that cautions against too much emphasis on the measurable and a greater emphasis on open, candid discussions among the top, one will not find much discussion of the problem faced by this individual — namely, that the behavior of the top is harming the planning process. However, management consultants report that this is one of the most frequent problems they face.

To return to the case, the consultant designed a presentation-discussion session. His major objectives were:

1. Identify top management's major reservations about the lack of effectiveness of the present planning process. They included the facts that plans are overoptimistic compared to performance, that some new ventures have been less successful than expected, and that divisions present incomplete information for top management to make decisions.
2. Identify the divisions' major concerns. They included the facts that corporate does not have a strategy, that the roles and expectations of the divisions are unclear, and that corporate emphasizes budgets more than strategy.

The consultant began by describing, in the form of a mini-lecture, the important features of effective strategic management in any corporation with illustrations of weaknesses on the part of the client corporation. The material used to illustrate points 1 and 2 preceding required 2 slides. The material in the following discussion required 16 slides. The point is that the emphasis placed on the discussion by the new material could make it possible for the clients to distance themselves from discussing 1 and 2 as well as the defensive routines implied in these presentations.

The consultant also pointed out several weaknesses of the compensation scheme — for example, good/bad performance was not defined, feedback on performance was either inadequate or nonexistent, and bonuses were unrelated to performance. He then noted that such a compensation scheme implied that corporate believed that divisional management did not know what the goals of their business were and that strategic and budgeting objectives were not reinforced. Division's reaction, in turn, was on being noncontroversial, not rocking the boat, and maintaining the status quo. He concluded that the corporation must move toward a management compensation system that rewarded the attainment of previously agreed upon goals.

Next the consultant focused on why the divisions tried to avoid controversial subjects. He suggested several possibilities including the meetings may be too large for top management to ask tough questions, limited time for preparation results in reactive styles, meetings are polite with little challenge, follow-up is limited, and operating issues are often confused with strategic issues. The consultant ended this segment of the slide presentation by asking, "Are not divisions aware of this or is it that they believe the top expects 'onward and upward approach' and/or they fear reprisals for unfavorable forecasts?"

If we examine this material, the consultant presented many important issues that are related to the organizational defensive routines. However, he did not create the opportunity for the top to discuss these issues. Instead of stopping and encouraging discussion on these issues, he moved ahead to a section on suggestions for action steps.

The action steps included:

1. Reallocating top management between budget reviews and strategy,
2. Requiring each business to articulate its strategy for the next 5 years,
3. Specifying that these documents be formally accepted or rejected by the top,
4. Holding short annual strategy review meetings,
5. Implementing a compensation scheme (specifying the features),
6. Making sure the executive committee is better prepared to discuss strategy alternatives.

These steps imply more corporate staff work — specifically, posing questions prior to meetings, follow-up after meetings, and smaller meetings.

Note what has happened. The consultant raised questions about defensive routines. He avoided giving all the data that he had lest that upset the clients. He did not encourage discussion of the questions as he was raising them. When he arrived at his suggestions, he focused on structural and administrative processes as did most of the authors in the literature cited previously. The advice such as posing tougher questions ahead of time or holding smaller meetings can be implemented in such a way that the defensive routines do not get addressed.

The consultant's ambivalence is evident by the fact that he identifies the defensive routines and then bypasses them when recommending actions. Also, he never discusses the skills and actions of the top officers (corporate and divisional) that are causing the defensive routines he identified.

The consultant recalled that he went into the meeting with trepidation. He wanted to focus on difficult issues that strategy consultants are not normally expected to deal with. Being concerned about the possible negative reaction, he used the easing-in approach. The easing-in approach also led him to down play the defensive routines at the top and act as if he were not down playing them. Part of down playing them was not to present as rigorous and complete a map of the defensive routines and their consequences as was available.

The consultant's approach made it less likely not only that the clients would bypass important defenses but also that he could help the clients use some of the errors to begin to learn how to learn. For example:

The Executives Learned	They Should Also Learn
They were too soft.	What individual and organizational factors lead them to reason and act in soft ways?
They should hold smaller and more frequent meetings.	What prevented them from reaching this conclusion by themselves?
They should develop a more sophisticated planning system.	How aware were they of the gaps and the errors in the planning process? What prevented them from beginning to close

The Executives Learned	**They Should Also Learn**
	their gaps and correct the errors?
Division executives saluted corporate.	What factor leads division executives to believe that saluting is necessary? How do they hide it?
Strategies are often overoptimistic.	What factors lead planners to design strategies that are overoptimistic? If they know they are overoptimistic, how do they hide it? If they do not, then what does it say about their competence?

Answering the questions on the right-hand side accomplishes several important types of learning. First, the organization identifies the causal factors that inhibited the original learning as well as the factors that inhibited the executives from identifying the causal factors in the first place. Second, such causal factors are usually finite in number but almost infinite in their impact on the total functioning of the organization. Hence, identifying the factors that may inhibit learning related to planning will provide rich and relevant data about the organizational defensive routines related to other important topics. Third, if the clients are able to deal with the factors that inhibited their learning, they will increase the probability that they can be masters of their destiny.

Recently, I participated in a study of CEOs and other senior line and planning executives regarding ways to enhance strategy formulation and implementation. In most cases the executives (especially the CEOs) agreed with the importance of learning to learn. As one CEO stated it, "If consultants could help us do that, their value would be significantly increased." However, the same executives expressed concern about how this was to be accomplished. They saw learning to learn as a very difficult process to create and as a potentially dangerous one in the sense that it could upset long-standing defenses. That is not only understandable but also predictable from the perspectives described in Chapters 2 and 3. Therefore, many executives have an ambivalent reaction toward learning to learn. They want it but they fear it. They fear it because it means that the defensive routines must be engaged rather than bypassed.

It is also important to point out that many executives said they doubted that any consulting firms could provide skillful assistance in this area. As the discussions continued, it became increasingly clear that some of them would take the risks (and willingly incur the extra costs) if they felt confident in the consultants' abilities to help them achieve such learning. Many line executives noted that most of the consulting firms were at their best in producing the art of the possible, which meant that they rarely engaged the defensive routines and acted in this way out of deference to the top clients' defenses.

This is not necessarily true, some readers may say. After all, this consultant did surface some of the defensive routines, which is an important step forward. The underlying problem, as we shall see, is that the consultant behaved toward his clients the way he was asking them not to behave toward their subordinates. He produced this strategy because he never tested the attributions he made about the clients regarding what they could take and could not take. If he had tested his attributions, he might have found out that his clients were more willing to discuss some of the undiscussables than he had originally thought. He might have also learned that their willingness to discuss the undiscussable was also related to how confident they felt their consultant was in discussing these issues.

To summarize, the consultant was afraid; hence, he eased in. The clients were afraid, and they too eased in. The consultant reinforced the clients' fears when he also eased in. The clients then shied away from discussing the undiscussables. This, in turn, proved to the consultant that he was correct in easing in. The proof could have been a self-fulfilling prophecy in a self-sealing process. I now close the loop by examining what happened to a senior consultant who was trying to get some of his colleagues to think differently about their practice and who encountered some defensive routines.

Case D: A Strategy Professional Attempting to Deal with Colleagues' Defensive Routines

Bill is the senior professional in a corporate strategy department. During the past two years he had studied the activities of the strategy professionals in the corporation and concluded that not enough attention was paid "to building better bridges with the line executives in order to enhance commitment and implementation." Bill's diagnosis of why this happened included the following:

1. We overanalyze instead of talking with clients.
2. We go into a presentation prepared with a rigorous analysis that we believe should make us heroes with the clients.
3. Because we do not talk enough with our clients, we do not know if and where problems may exist during the presentation.
4. We rely on our confidence in our analyses and on our ability to react quickly to questions about the validity of our analyses and, if necessary, to raise the level of proof.

Bill's diagnosis contains several causal microtheories and views of what actions to take.

Causal Problems	**Suggested Remedies**
We overanalyze and talk too little with the client.	Reduce the analysis and talk more with the client.
We expect that a rigorous analysis will lead the clients to feel good about us.	Reduce reliance on the rigorous analysis and on the desire to be heroes.
We are blind to the gaps and difficulties with clients during the presentations.	Become aware of gaps and difficulties during the presentations.

As in the case of the literature, the diagnoses and advice are at a very high level of inference. They combine to hide the gaps that have to be filled if the advice is to be implemented. Bill is doing to his colleagues what he is complaining they are doing with the client. For example, Bill recommends that the strategy professional should interact more with the clients and depend less on highly rigorous analysis to make them heroes.

Let us start with the advice to interact more. Let us assume that Bill believes that whatever should be said, it should have positive effects. Let us also assume that the strategy professionals know how to implement the advice for the easy, routine problems. But what about the problems that involve organizational defensive routines? The probability is quite high that under those conditions the strategy professionals will activate their bypass routines. This could make it more likely that they will produce more and not fewer difficulties with the clients.

Next, let us examine the advice not to use rigorous analysis to create hero relationships. Recall, again, that no one can knowingly design errors. If the strategy professionals use rigorous analyses to become heroes, then they are either unaware of their error or they are aware of what they are doing and are willing to do so because it makes sense to them. Under what conditions would this strategy make sense? One possibility is, as we shall see, that strategy professionals (that we have studied) are prone to feeling vulnerable in a client relationship when the latter become upset or are not laudatory about the analyses. This vulnerability can upset them so much that they lose their cool. Losing their cool, in turn, reinforces their vulnerability. One personal bypass routine to prevent this loop from occurring is to be a hero. The dilemma is that being a hero in the eyes of the client will simultaneously distance the professional from the client. It is difficult to be close, relaxed, and feel equal with heroes. By the way, it is not necessary to seek to become heroes with line management who understand formal analytical procedures because they can understand and value first-rate analysis. Under these conditions, it is the client who chooses to applaud the professional and can do it without creating counterproductive distancing. It is not surprising that strategy professionals call these clients "smart," "excellent clients."

Moreover, if the strategy professionals chose this bypass routine, they must also program themselves to be unaware of what is going on. If they were aware, they would realize that striving to be a hero is a defense; hence, it is a sign of weakness and not strength. One way to become unaware is to place a great deal of emphasis on the importance of high-quality rigorous analysis and to believe that this is in the client's best interests. We are now back to Bill's formulation of the problem. It is not difficult to believe these ideas if the strategy professionals have spent many hours in classes in business school where they are taught to believe in the primary formal analysis by faculty who live in a world where they get promoted by being heroes in their respective fields.

Senior professionals often begin to examine the counterproductive features of these bypass routines because as they become senior, they also become responsible for maintaining a department or keeping a consulting firm busy. This is the reason that Bill began to re-examine the practice in his department. The difficulty is that the advice is not easily implemented.

I have had the opportunity to observe a few senior professionals who were superior at formal analysis and at creating effective relationships with clients. For example, one such senior professional realized that the presentation a subordinate colleague was making, which he had approved the day before, was not going well. He interrupted the presentation and said, "May I interrupt for a minute? I'd like to repeat what [my colleague] is saying in somewhat different words. It can be boiled down to the following. The firm is caught between the devil and the deep blue sea. [Explains.] One way to solve the problem is to place your bets on. . . . If you do not, the chances are . . . [that the following will occur]."

The CEO's eyes lit up and he said, "Good, that is what I thought you people were saying, but . . . if that is your view, I want to challenge it." The consultant responded, "What are your doubts?" Note that in helping the client understand his view, the consultant also made himself more vulnerable. His willingness to be vulnerable and to deal with the confrontation that followed led the CEO to call him "my kind of consultant."

Let's get back to Bill as he was discussing his analysis with his colleagues. Most of them reacted positively. "It is a sound study," "Good ideas," were typical comments. Then, one of them said, in effect, that they were aware of such problems and wondered if Bill understood this. Bill responded, "Of course, there is probably little that is new in this memo. I just thought it might be of value to draw the problem to our attention." They responded, "Of course."

Does that sound familiar? It is the same response that the previous consultant received from his clients when he tried to communicate some doubts he had about their effectiveness. Bill's response was also the same in that he withdrew from following it up lest he alienate himself from his colleagues. He could have asked, for example, for illustrations of how they dealt with the problem. Or he could have asked, "How could the analysis be correct and they understand it, but the problem continues?" Bill's automatic response was to bypass. His colleagues' responses were the same. The clients in the previous case were the same. All probably left their respective contexts feeling good. However, these are the very bypass routines that cause the problems in the first place.

SUMMARY

We are programmed to deal with others' or organizational defensive routines by bypassing them and acting as if we are not. The others tend to collude because the bypassing behavior is usually seen as being thoughtful and civilized; no one will be embarrassed. The collusion is reinforced by the culture of the organization as well as the larger culture in which the organization exists. That is one set of defensive loops that reinforces each other.

The next set of loops is related to the professionals who are supposed to help the clients overcome the defensive routines. As we have seen, the management consultants (internal or external) often use the same bypass routines when they deal with threat. Thus, the professionals collude in creating another defensive loop.

Finally, there are two other defensive loops to reinforce the first two. The literature on implementation is replete with advice that makes it possible for readers to continue their bypass routines. The internal workings of management consulting firms or strategy units also deal with threat by using bypassing routines.

FIGURE 4.1   *Defensive Loops: Organization, Consultants, and Strategy Practice*

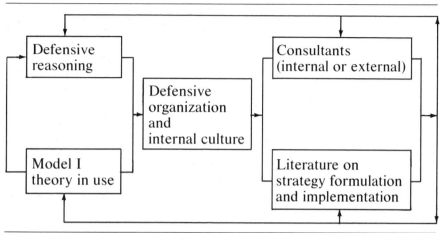

Hence, they are unlikely to reflect on their practice in a way that will lead to genuine changes of the status quo.

The primary lessons in this chapter are that the two most powerful sources for help to deal with defensive routines around strategy formulation and implementation — namely, the strategy implementation literature and consultants — tend to reinforce unintentionally the causes of the defensive routines (Figure 4.1). The third powerful source for help — namely, business schools and executive programs — also do the same. I studied a three-week senior executive program that was led by the superstars from the elite business schools in the United States. With two exceptions, the faculty bypassed whenever the executives used defensive reasoning in class to deal with emotionally charged issues, or they bypassed discussing the defensive routines of the organizations as described by the executives. One of the exceptions was a faculty member whose field was organizational behavior; but still he dealt with those issues; as he said, cautiously. The other exception was a faculty member who did question defensive reasoning and who asked the executives to reflect publicly on it. He was never invited back, although he was judged to be first rate in his field (Argyris, 1980). The reason given to me (and not to him) was that he required more maturing.

It is fair to conclude that there exists a worldwide set of loops, beginning with individuals and moving to groups, inter-groups, organizations, and finally to the larger culture, that creates, reinforces, and sanctions the use of defensive routines and bypass routines to deal with threat wherever it occurs. The challenge is to engage these loops. Unless we do, they will eventually pollute the world to the point that they would be impossible to change.

INTRODUCTION TO PART II

Divide problems into technical, business, or organizational on the one hand and individual-organizational defensive routines on the other. The focus of Part II is how to identify, reduce, or better yet, prevent defensive routines no matter what are the technical or organizational problems in which these defensive routines are found. The theory, methods, and competencies that I present hold for dealing with any type of defensive routine.

In Chapter 4, I noted that the professionals claim that the biggest barrier to effective strategy formulation and implementation are defensive routines. In practice, however, the clients rarely identify the defensive routines; they usually present the problem as being technical or organizational. For example, the top management often report that they have problems with the planning process. They cite such symptoms as no new ideas, irrelevant paper work, unnecessary meetings, and poor results. They ask for someone (insiders or outsiders) to take a hard look at the planning process and design one that is more efficient or effective.

So far, I have not met even a mildly competent professional who has difficulty with this request. The technical features of this problem are, to many of them, simple. The issues that worry them are the individual-organizational defensive routines that are found in the planning process. How do you deal with top management who give cues that they dislike conflict yet are unaware when they do so and who are uncomfortable with creative ideas that require risk yet keep espousing innovation, with subordinates who have learned to cover themselves by saluting and acting as if they are not doing so, with top executive groups who believe that they have developed a pretty good decision-making process when a serious examination does not support this view? These are the kinds of problems that plague the executive or strategy professional or anyone who is trying to improve performance where the aspiration is excellence.

As we saw in Chapter 4, the current ideas about implementing strategy include finding competent employees, defining their roles correctly, developing an effective information system, and providing those employees with genuine rewards. All these are good advice. The problem is, as we shall see, that planning processes and management information systems are often ineffective, that the rewards are counterproductive, and that all the players know it and have the competence to change it but see themselves in a straight jacket created by various defensive routines. For example, subordinates know they salute, know the planning process is ineffective, and know that they are producing a mountain of irrelevant paper. Many work hard at covering up these features because they would see it as understandable if the top took drastic action. Indeed, many report to outsiders like myself that they wonder what is keeping top management from taking action. They often report that top management is responsible because they do not want to see a vibrant planning process even though they say they do.

Top management, conversely, also know that the planning processes are ineffective but, as we shall see, often skirt the defensive routines involved. It is not unusual for them to deal with these problems by leaving divisional planners alone and, at the same time, creating corporate planning staffs to get the help they need. These corporate planning staffs are often hamstrung by the same defensive routines as well as new ones created by the divisions to protect themselves from corporate.

The objective, therefore, is to identify, reduce, and prevent individual-organizational defensive routines. This objective cannot be achieved without also identifying, reducing, and preventing the defensive routines that exist to bypass the first set of defensive routines. These bypass routines include the trained unawareness mentioned previously, face-saving rules that lead to mixed messages and the cover-up of the mixed messages, and rules that make all these undiscussable and their undiscussability undiscussable, coalition and interdepartmental warfare, throwing the dead cat into the other guy's yard, building a fire to create a crisis in order to move an uncooperative department, and budgetary politics where padding the budget is as creative a skill as producing the budget.

Organizations have a generic response to deal with poor performance. It is composed of three strategies:

1. Correct performance by changing and inhibiting factors that either do not involve defensive routines or that bypass them.
2. Bypass those technical and human factors that are relevant to the problems that cannot be corrected without disengaging the defensive routines.
3. Stay away from focusing forthrightly on defensive routines unless performance is so bad and so obvious that responsible stewardship means they cannot be ignored.

These strategies can lead to certain features of the technical problems to be corrected. But if the defensive routines plus their counterpart bypass routines aren't dealt with, the technical solutions will eventually be undermined.

There is a simple test for the existence of defensive routines and the bypass routines that protect them. Any time you hear words that imply unrealistically low or high performance promises, any time people do things that are patently counterproductive, any time people act obsessively, then defensive routines are probably the key causes. For example, Peters and Waterman (1984) identify some organizational factors that inhibit excellence:

Peters and Waterman	Meanings that Identify Defensive Routines
Organizations . . . pay obsessive attention to habitual internal clues long after their practical value has lost all meaning (p. 6).	Obsessive attention to the wrong factors.
Exclusively analytic approach runs wild, leads to an abstract heartless philosophy (p. 45).	Run wild.
People analyze what can be most readily analyzed, spend more time on it, and ignore [important features] (p. 44).	Do not pay attention to what is known to be difficult.

In a detailed study of the swine-flu affair, Neustadt and Fineberg (1978) identified the primary factors that caused the problem:

Neustadt and Fineberg	Meanings that Identify Defensive Routines
Overconfidence by specialists in incompletely validated theories.	Overconfidence in poor theories.
Advocating ideas based upon personal agendas and acting as if this were not the case.	Personal agendas and cover-up.
Premature commitment to unnecessarily early decisions.	Premature commitments.

Neustadt and Fineberg	Meanings that Identify Defensive Routines
Insufficient questioning of positions taken.	Insufficient questioning.

Peters and Waterman (1984) give an example where a well-meaning set of rational people with clean motives and dedication to sound performance designed an organizational process to launch a new product that had 223 linkages. Each linkage made sense, but when taken together, they stultified innovation. From our point of view, it is important to emphasize that the players knew that the process was counterproductive and either felt helpless to change it or hid behind it for protection.

The characteristics on the right-hand column and the example of the 223 linkages are not rare; they can be found in most organizations operating much of the time when some combination of individual-organizational threat is involved. Indeed, as Peters and Waterman (1984) report, their biggest surprise was how often individuals reacted to their examples, not with disbelief but by producing an example that topped theirs. The focus of this book is how to reduce these defensive actions and do so in such a way that the reduction holds true for dealing with any technical or organizational problems in which defensive routines are involved.

Finally, there is a dilemma that I face as an author. How do I describe what action to take? I do not want to repeat the error that the authors made in the strategy literature reviewed in Chapter 4. I could describe the what-to-do-about-it with some interesting stories that for the sake of economy of presentation are at the same level of inference as used in those books. The problem is that even if you agreed with me, my description would help you to see neither the extent to which your organization could not produce what is being recommended nor the skills that may be lacking.

I have made several choices to try to deal with the problem. First, I use transcripts from tape recordings or notes from observations (along with interviews) to provide the most directly observable data available. I also connect these data to my concepts. In doing so, I hope to make public my reasoning processes so that you can judge for yourself what is going on.

Second, I include examples in which the people involved in changing the organization were facing the same problem I face in this book. For example, consultants are faced with the issue of how to communicate their findings without glossing over the defensive routines. I present the reasoning behind their solutions as well as the solutions.

Third, I present transcriptions and observations of how the consultants fared when they met with top management, including the latter's reactions and how the former dealt with the reactions.

Fourth, whenever I am focusing on what actions people take, I point out what I believe were errors as well as correct responses. Whenever I identify errors, I present other strategies that might have been more effective. I identify patterns of effective actions that emerge and state the theory as well as the rules that underlie them.

Chapter 5 begins with advice on how to diagnose defensive routines and the self-reinforcing patterns they create, which I call *defensive loops.* Chapter 6 illustrates defensive routines associated with management information systems. Chapter 7 shows how a routine discussion on the meaning of financial numbers can be utilized by a skillful inquirer to diagnose a massive set of organizational defensive routines around strategic planning and management information systems. Chapter 8 describes how a feedback process can be designed to show the top where and how the defensive routines of the organization exist, to facilitate their taking the next step of involving their immediate reports, and to set in motion simultaneously a process of organizational change. We up the ante in Chapter 9 by illustrating how it is possible to help an executive group choose to examine the defensive routines in their decision-making processes and begin to make step-by-step progress (as well as to make a more informed choice if they decide not to go further). Chapter 10 describes some difficulties the consultants have in learning the new action strategies to deal with defensive routines. Chapter 11 describes the essential features of an organizational change program. Chapter 12 reviews the major findings, relates them to activities beyond business organizations; and suggests responsibilities that consultants have to build and manage their non-organizations with minimal defensive routines.

five

DIAGNOSING DEFENSIVE ROUTINES RELATED TO STRATEGIC PLANNING

Diagnosing defensive routines is a challenging task. I have selected several techniques, which have proved successful (to me), that executives or consultants can use. Before describing the techniques, a few words are needed to define a good diagnosis. The primary feature of a diagnosis is understanding the problem. The test of understanding is that we can use the diagnosis to design solutions and implement them. Solutions that flow unambiguously from the diagnosis also help test the diagnosis as well as help the organization to solve the problem.

I hope I have made the case by now that defensive routines can act to distort reality without our being aware of the distortion. If the action that is taken is based on a diagnosis that is unknowingly distorted, not only will an incorrect solution be implemented but also we may have reinforced and strengthened the defensive routines. Effective diagnosis, therefore, always addresses the question How do we know that we are not unknowingly kidding ourselves?

The second feature is that the diagnosis can be conducted in a way that does not require too much contrived attention. The more likely a diagnosis can be carried out without interfering with daily routines, the more likely it is that we will get genuine cooperation and, therefore, better data about the routines. The examples in this chapter rely heavily on observations of meetings and encounters as well as tape recordings of them. Whenever we use a case, it comes from an actual problem facing the firm. An officer meeting with his case team to reflect on how they could have provided even higher-quality value than had been given is one example that is included. Or, when we use a prepackaged case like the John-and-Bill case format, it can be done in an hour or less, and it can serve as the basis for a workshop to help the players examine the difficult problems in their organization, the way they engage or bypass the defensive routines, how their actions reinforce the defensive loops or reinforce the defensive norms of the culture, as well as to generate new ways of resolving these problems.

These factors lead to a third characteristic of an effective diagnostic method — namely, an intimate connection between diagnosis and action. A diagnosis should produce understanding of a problem that can be used to act to solve the problem. Not only does the action provide a test for the diagnosis, but it also reduces the dangers of using diagnostic methods that are not intended to be tied to action. One danger is that the respondents may not take such methods seriously and hence unknowingly distort or withhold data. The other danger is that it can overprotect the individuals creating the diagnosis. If they do not feel some responsibility to connect diagnosis with action, then they could get lazy about thinking through precisely how understanding and action are connected in the particular problem they are studying.

The fourth characteristic is that when diagnostic methods are used correctly, they should not produce knowledge that is necessarily counterproductive. This may sound odd to you. Why would anyone use diagnostic methods that produce recommendations that, if implemented correctly, can be counterproductive?

The explanation gets at the heart of an important dilemma in diagnosing defensive routines. Oversimplifying somewhat, the dilemma is that the ideas in good currency about what is a rigorous diagnosis are consistent with Model I. For example, the rigorous strategy analyst prefers to be left alone to come up with an empirically valid conceptually elegant model, and the designer of the new information system strives to get at the heart of the problem whether the players see it or not. These points lead the diagnostician to take a relatively autonomous stance from the clients, albeit a temporary one.

The first difficulty with this consequence is that it creates distancing. Gerry, as we have seen, became so distanced that he was disconnected from his own reasoning and was unaware of it. In the past, strategy formulators have produced rigorous analyses and, in the process, have become distanced and disconnected from their clients. The distancing and disconnectedness are not new. They lead to defensive routines that have to be eliminated because it is unlikely that you can produce a valid diagnosis of defensive routines with defensive routines.

The second part of the dilemma is that knowledge that is produced using a Model I theory in use will require the same conditions when it is being used elsewhere. For example, as a result of some famous social psychological research, people were advised that, if they wanted to influence the audience in a particular direction, they should advocate one view if the audience is not so smart and several views if the audience is smart. No one, I believe, in his or her right mind would state this to the audience ahead of time in order to be effective. The advice has to be kept secret just as it was during the experiment. It is an example of a socially acceptable face-saving technique that is consistent with the theories in use that create the defensive routines that we are trying to reduce in the first place.[1]

In the examples that follow, I start with interviewing because it is often used by executives or consultants. Next, I illustrate two kinds of observation schemes. The first is consistent with the more accepted modes of diagnosis. I therefore take time to show how the scheme can be used to connect it with action that is relevant to the organization. The scheme can also be used to generate information that is applicable to settings far beyond the one in which the data were obtained. This is important if the learning is to be generalizable, and generalizability is necessary because knowledge that is limited to a specific case can immobilize individuals. The challenge is to develop knowledge that is generalizable without losing contact with the uniqueness of the situation being studied. This requirement presents an age-old tension — namely, that it is unlikely that we can know ahead of time all that exists and all that is relevant. There will always be a place for gap filling. We provide a way for the executive or consultant to use the gap filling as an opportunity to involve the individuals that increases the probability of gaining the involvement needed not only for gaining valid data but also for effective implementation.

Let us now turn to the diagnostic activities. Assume that the problem is as follows:

> We are not satisfied with our strategic planning process. It has become cumbersome and often dominated by paper and what appear to be irrelevant numbers. Often the ideas produced are either not new, or worse yet, illustrate a "techie mentality" and not one of general management.

Let us suppose that your task, as a line officer or a strategy professional, is to diagnose the planning process so you can correct it. How would you do it?

INTERVIEWS

One early step is to interview some of the relevant players. I have found the following seven questions to be helpful.

1. Are there any problems with the process of planning that you believe are critical but not likely to be dealt with effectively?
2. What gets people in trouble when they deal with planning?
3. If you could change one thing in the planning process, what would it be? How would you go about doing it? What would you predict would be the biggest barriers to be overcome?
4. If you could hang on to or strengthen a particular feature of the planning process, what would it be? How would you go about doing it? What would you predict would be the biggest barriers to be overcome?

5. We have found in most organizations issues that tend to be undiscussable or discussable but unchangeable. Are there any such issues in this organization? If some are mentioned that do not appear to relate to planning, then ask if there are any undiscussables related to planning.

6. If the respondent says there are no undiscussables, then ask, "Would you please help me to understand what is it about this organization that does not lead to undiscussables?"

7. Recalling the defenses that you have identified, how aware are people in this organization that they exist? If they are aware, what leads them to continue? If they are not aware, what hunches do you have about the cause of their blindness?

I have also found it helpful not to begin with these questions. A more effective place to begin is to focus on the technical features of the planning process and to go to these questions later. The first reason is that the clients expect to be asked about the technical issues. These are the issues they believe are important and that are, at the outset, more closely related to their sense of stewardship.

Another reason for beginning with the technical issues is that they can provide a window into the defensive routines. The logic is:

Identify the technical errors, inconsistencies, or gaps	→	Ask what causes them or maintains them	→	That will lead to defensive routines.

The more competent and knowledgeable the consultants are about the technical issues, the more they are likely to discover nontrivial errors in the technical area, and unfortunately, the more likely that the clients may become upset when they do so. The last reason for beginning with the technical issues is that if the clients become upset, they are more likely to deal with their defenses if doing so can be related to producing a better planning process.

Technical errors such as too much paper and ideas that are not new are a fertile ground for exploring the factors that encourage such problems. For example, too much paper or humdrum ideas are negative evaluations. Recall the ladder of inference (see Figure 2.1). The first step is to ask the individuals to illustrate their evaluations with examples. The second step is to help them to make explicit the reasoning they used to arrive at the evelation. That may seem obvious, but often we find that the connection between the data and the conclusion is not so obvious. Individuals may reach different conclusions from the same data. If so, the third step is to ask them how each goes about testing his or her conclusions. What data do they see that lead them to believe they are correct? If the interviewer believes that another explanation is possible, he or she can say, "How would you respond to someone who says that the explanation is . . . ? What reasoning is being used that you question?"

The answers to the questions about their reasoning and the reasoning of others will not only provide a possible validity check for the evaluations but also insight into the theory that the respondent has about the subject matter. For example, if the top says, "We get a lot of unnecessary paper" and that the reason is that the planners are too "techie oriented," they are beginning to give us an insight into the theory they hold about planners. They are also unknowingly providing insight into the way they deal with this problem. For example, in most of the cases to be described, top management do not state their evaluations to the relevant people. "What good would that do? That will only upset them" is a frequent comment. The difficulty with that response is that often the planners know the top feels this but hesitate to discuss it because the top do not. Hence, we have a defensive loop that reinforces the problem.

Defensive loops often are surfaced when some individuals say, "Our planning process has always been that way," or "It is unlikely to change." These statements are cues of organizational errors that the respondent believes exist and that are unchangeable. The next question would be, "What, in your judgment, prevents them from being changed?" The answer to this question usually provides additional insights into the organizational defensive loops.

Once we begin to create maps of these loops, we are creating our own evaluations and attributions about the organization, and these require testing. The testing can occur during a feedback session designed to keep the executives up to date. For example, the map of the loops is presented, and the executives are asked to react to it. We should encourage individuals to express their different views. The differences in views become in-the-session inconsistencies that are worthwhile to explore. If, however, there is a lot of agreement, then the map can be used another way to further learning. We may ask, "If there is this degree of agreement, what prevents individuals from taking action?"

The answers to these questions will help not only to fill in the map but also to give us insight into individual bypass routines on the part of the respondents. For example, they may say, "The reason we cannot change things even though there is agreement is that the CEO would be upset." Again, an attribution that should be tested. We ask the respondent to illustrate, for example, "What do people believe he would say or do that inhibits them from trying to change the planning process?"

This could be followed up with another test of the validity of what the respondents are saying about the CEO's defensive routines as well as their personal bypass routines. "Assume for a moment that you had a meeting with the CEO. If you had your druthers, how would you begin this meeting? What would you say?" After the response say, "What do you believe the CEO would say?" And later, "Thinking back on these conversations, are there feelings or thoughts you might have that you might not communicate for whatever reason?"

All this usually is easier to see as a theory than to implement in a real situation. A lot of questions occur in peoples' minds when they think about implementing this approach. We deal with those questions concretely in Chapter 6. Once individuals learn to use these skills in an on-line manner, they will have developed the theory and the competencies required to design interventions for any defensive routines.

OBSERVATIONS

We have found two different modes of observations helpful in diagnosing defensive routines. The first is a method that gets at the quality of the problem-solving and the decision-making processes in the group being observed regardless of the issues being discussed. The second method is useful in understanding a particular situation like when a group is trying to diagnose how effectively it operated.

Method A

One set of categories that can be used to study any kind of two-person, group, or intergroup activity is related to Models I and II (see Chapter 9). For example, a simple matrix can be used as an observation sheet (Figure 5.1). On the horizontal plane are the categories of advocacy, evaluation, and attribution. On the vertical plane are illustration, inquiry, and testing. It is possible to score conversation in terms of whether the individual is advocating a point of view, making evaluations or attributions, and whether or not those are combined with illustrations, inquiry, or testing. The latter are indications of Model I and the former are indications of Model II.

Our experience, to date, is that individuals, with the help of a coach, can learn to use the categories in a matter of hours. Also, small variances in precision about the numbers for each of the categories is not detrimental for diagnostic purposes. The correct diagnosis of defensive routines comes from identifying the entire pattern — that is, whether the actions are consistent with Models I or II. Thus, if several observers differed within each model, it will not throw off the results or the action recommendations.[2]

Practitioners who wish to reflect on their practice so they can change it do not require a detailed and complex quantitative analysis. Indeed, the finiteness of the human mind to process information and the pressures of everyday life mean that they require maps that are complete enough to begin the process of

FIGURE 5.1   *Behavioral Strategies of Models I and II*

Model I	**Advocacy**	**Evaluation**	**Attribution**
No illustration			
No inquiry			
No testing			
Model II			
Illustration			
Inquiry			
Testing			

engaging defensive routines. An example of such a map is Figure 5.2.

The first column contains those action strategies that were observed to be frequent and infrequent. Frequent actions included individuals advocating and selling their ideas; individuals evaluating each other's ideas and agreeing or disagreeing, which were often followed with attempts to correct the other's views; discouraging the expression of threatening issues; and trying out new ideas to get the job done better.

The action strategies that were infrequently observed were providing feedback about the impact on other positives or negatives; expressing emotions and feelings, especially negative ones; encouraging the expression of threatening issues; and experimenting with ideas that questioned underlying policies and practices.

FIGURE 5.2 *Action Map of Top Management*

Action Strategies		Interpersonal and Group Dynamics	Consequences on Problem Solving and Decision Making
Frequent	**Infrequent**		
Articulating, selling ideas	Feedback about negative impact on others	Win/lose, competitive	Less effective when problems are important, difficult, and controversial
Evaluating others' ideas and agree or correct	Expression of feelings (especially negative ones)	Low trust, distancing	Management by crisis
Discouraging the expression of threatening issues	Encouraging the expression of threatening issues	Conformity, games	
Experimenting with ideas that get the job done better	Experimenting with ideas that question policies and practices	Group-think	Intergroup rivalries

The third column describes the consequences of the pattern of frequent-infrequent activities on interpersonal and group dynamics. For example, there were win/lose, competitive dynamics. The willingness to risk oneself was low, making trust low; distancing from dealing with difficult issues was high; and conformity and game playing were high.

These consequences fed back to reinforce the original pattern of frequent-infrequent behavior. Hence, we see a self-reinforcing loop. The consequences also fed forward (fourth column) to influence the quality of the discussions, especially those that dealt with difficult, threatening issues. Moreover, the consequences encouraged management by crisis and intergroup rivalries. These, in turn, would feed back to reinforce the previous consequences. We now have a second self-reinforcing loop. These loops combine to decrease the likelihood that the group will deal as effectively as it can with technical or defensive routine issues that are important and comprehensive.

In presenting the map, the consultants would illustrate each category and encourage confrontation of every illustration. Note that it is not necessary to attach numbers to the statements. The emphasis is upon understanding the pattern. Also, usability of the map will depend upon the degree to which the clients will confirm it. If they disagree with what strategies the consultants assert are frequent or infrequent, then they will probably say so. This discussion could provide an important validity check of the diagnosis.

If there is disagreement, the consultants could ask the clients to describe sessions in which different patterns existed. If such sessions had been observed and tape recorded, then the participants could go back and examine in detail one episode that the clients believed disconfirms the map.

The question of numbers is related to the more basic issue of rigor and precision on the one hand and the clients' abilities to use the knowledge to change on the other. When feeding back findings to help clients, it is possible to be too rigorous. An example would be using a level of precision and abstraction that is beyond client capacity to understand fully and upon which to take action. The challenge is to communicate complexity in ways that are understandable to the client. I have observed management, for example, conduct rigorous research and conceptualize it with elegant abstract, quantitative models. Then, instead of presenting these models to the clients, they presented metaphors that would communicate simply the essence of the meaning of the rigorous analysis. Once the clients understood the essence of the findings, then they could examine the more rigorous findings if they wished. Line executives do not usually ask for such presentations, but their technical staff do. Two different meetings could then be held.

The more difficult problems arise when we diagnose defensive routines, thus using soft data, and base the analysis on theories that have a more ideological than systematic framework, and use research methods that the clients would interpret as influencing the answers. Examples related to the research methods are, "Of course you found defenses. I too would if I asked such questions." "You probably interviewed more of the malcontents." "Don't you always find problems when you ask if there are problems?" The clients may attack the results because they mistrust the underlying theory and values of the consultants. For example, "Too much of human resources is overprotective of people," or "The personnel people with their theories never seem to face up to the realities of the organization."

There are two basic responses to these confrontations. The first is to deal with them as untested attributions. For example, if a client asserts that the questions produce defenses, the consultant would ask, "What is it about the questions that you believe triggers off defenses that are not there?" The consultants should not respond to the client's challenge by showing the reliability and validity studies conducted. These should not necessarily be excluded, but the first step is to help the clients learn to illustrate their attributions. Next, the consultants should test the validity of these attributions with their clients. As we show in the chapters to follow, there is often a wide variance in views among clients on these issues. This makes it possible for the consultant to reframe the problem from one of technical validity of the questions to one of helping clients educate each other. If later the consultants believe it makes sense to show the precautions they had taken to prevent the kind of distortion the clients were worried about, they could do so. Indeed, the clients may be more willing to listen and to appreciate these technical issues after they have dealt with the threat the data had generated.

The second response is to have a well-articulated theory about what produces defensive routines in individuals and organizations. This theory will help the consultants formulate the questions necessary to help the clients realize the defensiveness illustrated by their attributions. The theory also helps the consultants make explicit that for which they stand. Why do consultants focus on defensive routines? Are they making a mountain out of a molehill? Is it not possible to become too concerned about behavioral issues? What makes consultants believe that it is in the long-range interests of the organization to examine its defensive routines?

The clients should hold the consultants responsible for showing how the consultants would produce these results if the clients were to cooperate and what difference this would make to the operating effectiveness of the client organization. For example, the consultants could identify problems that the clients described as "central to the organization but unsolvable because of the defensive routines." They should be able to show that if the clients reduced the defensive activities, then the unsolvable issues should become solvable. For example, the management of a very large and distinguished newspaper that I studied had discussed a particular innovation for several years and never made a decision. After the defensive routines were addressed, a decision was made, by the same players, in less than one hour.

Method B

A second way to study defensive routines is to select an episode from a real-life situation that was transcribed. In this case, we focus on a meeting where the task was for the consulting team to examine its effectiveness in dealing with a client. If the session was not tape recorded, then the consultants could reconstruct it from their notes. If they do the latter, then it is important that they show it to several of the major actors in the episode to test whether or not the conversation recalled validly describes what the actors were trying to say. This should be done as soon after the meeting as possible.

Depending upon the clients' readiness to reflect on their behavior, two different strategies are possible. If the clients are ready to reflect, then the next step is to send them a transcript of an episode with a cover letter. The letter should ask them to think of themselves as consultants to the group. What is going on in the episode? Are there examples where individuals are hearing and not hearing each other? Are there errors or misunderstandings? How would they help the individuals examine these issues?

A session could then be held with all the players to discuss these questions. If possible, the sessions should be taped. Usually, the very way the players discuss the issues triggers off examples of the defenses that were found in the transcript. It is important for the consultants to point out these connections. It often helps the clients to listen to the episode if not immediately, then later on with or without several colleagues.

The fundamental assumption about using this approach is that we can learn from reviewing our conversations. Recall that although we are often unaware of our errors, others are not. Hence, others can help us to see some of the counterproductive features of our actions. If there are differences in views, so much the better, because that is part of the reality that we face.

Even we can recognize some of our errors if we can distance ourselves appropriately from our actions. Time is a good distancer. Reading a transcript or listening to a tape recording several weeks later can help many individuals see what they did not see during the session. The transcript takes on the role of a screen where the episode is projected. Then the individuals can deal with the episode at a distance (Havens, 1976).

To illustrate these points, let us provide an example. The vice-president in charge of a consulting team asked the five members to meet with him to reflect on their effectiveness as a team and on the service provided the client. He was interested in learning why a team of two very competent consultants and three managers, all of whom had successfully completed a similar project in another part of the client organization, did not produce the high-quality work expected by the firm and the client. The vice-president believed that self-reflection could strengthen the capacity of the firm, through its professionals, to detect and correct its errors.

First, I present excerpts from the tape-recorded conversation.[3] Next, I explore, step by step, the reasoning the participants must have gone through to produce the conversation. Next, I examine the causal theories involved in the conversations. Finally, I examine the reasoning processes the players used when they acted on their diagnosis. As we shall see, the primary action was a massive cover-up of which the actors were unaware while they were doing it but that they saw clearly when they reflected on their actions.

> Vice-president: One reason I called this meeting is because I don't understand [why we did not produce as good a product for the client as we could have]. This is probably as good a case team as can be put together. The people are good, the level of experience is good (for the most part), the client liked and respected us, our client skills are quite good [and finally, we had done a similar study for the client in another location].

The officer then asked the case team to be candid. He stated:

> I'll talk last because I do not want to bias what others of you say. I'll give my report [and I promise to be candid]. And I would say that we are all strong enough and big enough around here that we should be straightforward in our evaluations. I don't think that we gain anything by not being straightforward about all our roles, including officers as well as managers.

The vice-president then asked the persons around the table to give their views:

> Manager 1: I think we had a lot of chiefs and no Indians. Second, we never made explicit our internal [case team] organization. As a result of changing [client] conditions, redefini-

tion of the case, we ended up not being clear, and the changes over time caused a lot of resentment and were counterproductive.

Manager 2: Everybody had his individual piece, but people did not know what the others were doing.

Manager 1: And finally, there was some backbiting as well. Also, the vice-president had to change his time commitment [in midstream], and [Manager 3] was to compensate for his time. But I do not believe that was made explicit.

Consultant 1: I agree. We went into the field intensively, and once in the field, it was kind of irretrievable. [Later on, when new issues surfaced, we could not] go back to the field in a cost-effective way. So I think we could have done more thinking before we went into the field.

Manager 2: Also, since the order was to go out to do the market interviews, we had little time to interact as a case team. Nobody was really coordinating the case from a holistic point of view. [Provides detailed example.] The whole thing was basically out of control.

Chris: When did you sense that the project was out of control?

Manager 2: Between the start of the project and the first presentation.

[Another thing], we [rarely] met as a case team without the client so that we could integrate our work. It was always more of a "show and tell" presentation. We never had a normal case team meeting without the client and without the "show and tell."

Manager 1: We also needed you [vice-president] during the first presentation to the client. Just the fact that you weren't there in a situation where we were getting nitpicked to death. . . . I don't think any of us, and many of us tried, could stop [the nit-picking]. I think maybe you could have. I don't know why we couldn't stop [it]. I remember sitting there saying, "My God, we just killed ourselves for a week and I'm watching this presentation just get torn to hell for nonsensical reasons."

Chris: What could the vice-president have done that none of you could have done?

Consultant: Acted vice-presidential!

Manager 1: "Acted vice-presidential" is probably the perfect answer. It climaxed for me in [Consultant 2's] presentation. It wasn't one of his greatest, and it wasn't particularly bad. . . . The message didn't come through and they were nitpicking us on numbers that were their own creation. . . .

I remember sitting in that meeting and saying (to myself), "You have three choices. You can keep your mouth shut, and that wouldn't work. You can try to contribute when [the client is] getting off the point. Or you can try and stand up and say, Listen, you turkeys, you're being idiots. Stop the nonsense. Here is our message."

And I did not have the guts to do that.

Manager 2: Yes, that would have helped.

Manager 1: Which you [vice-president] would have done as a matter of course.

Chris: What would you have expected the vice-president to say?

Manager 1: [Roughly, he would say], "Today's session is an interim presentation. We are here to update you as to our progress. We also want to make sure that we're not getting totally off the track. I think the level of detail that you people are trying to explore *is* getting us off the track." Then he would give some examples and literally bring the meeting to a halt until that issue was resolved.

Chris: And you do not think anyone on this team would have done that with credibility?

Manager 1: I think [Manager 3] could try.

Consultant 1: I heard [another officer] once say to the clients in a meeting, "It doesn't matter what the number is. The point is, your performance in that area is lousy. It doesn't matter if it is 80 percent or 70 percent lousy. Once you're below 95 percent, it is awful. All right?" And he just totally shut the client up, and [the client's] boss kept a quiet approval. He can probably get away with it because officers have equal-level relationships with the client. And none of us would dare do it, no matter how senior we are. Or even if we did it, it wouldn't come off the same.

Manager 3: [I tried several times to do something like Consultant 1 describes], but there were so many levels of the client organization present — [client] was sitting there having a field day. It was a zoo.

I would like to put the mantle on you [vice-president] — and you probably could have pulled it off, but it was a difficult situation. It was difficult in a curious way because it wasn't particularly rancorous, it was just nitpicking.

Manager 2: [Returns to the issue that] we never had a chance among ourselves to say what the hell are we trying to accomplish . . . ? What are the issues, anyway?

[To another case team member]: I remember you said [such and such], and I sat there and I didn't even know what that meant. You made it sound important, but I didn't know what that meant.

Consultant 2: [Since there was a lack of coordination], I didn't know how to really pitch in and take the burden off [someone], because I didn't understand what we were doing as a whole, but I never said so.

And everyone was working madly . . . and the harder people work, the more frantic it is . . . the harder it is to tell anyone to do something or to give someone something to do.

Manager 3: I think I agree with most of what has been said. As I hear this, I have learned that probably I should have been a little more forceful [about the lack of coordination and who is the leader].

It was difficult to do so because I did not have the vice-presidential imprint so that I could say, "Now look, I want you guys to do this." And so I was listening to [the case team members] in a sounding-board sense rather than trying to take control. . . . Maybe that was a mistake.

I think the client was not easy [during the first presentation]. To this day, I haven't figured out whether we were talking at one level and hearing something back at a different level, or what the heck was going on.

As a result, [we created our own explanation. We decided] that they were crazy, not us, and you know, don't worry, we'll come around in the final analysis and we'll give them value for the money.

Finally, [because we had done this case before], there was an incredible fixation to come up with something that was different. And I think you [Manager 2] created a segment out of whole cloth just to try to satisfy yourself that in fact you had added something new and creative. Because I think that we were all disappointed . . . you know, this is a pretty boring business. I mean, there was nothing new under the sun. This was not my favorite assignment.

Oh, yes, and finally, I think in the final analysis we came up against a client to whom we were saying things that the client did not want to hear [illustrates].

Vice-president: OK, let me add a few more points. Our senior client contact, Jones, had just been made head of another outlet. They did not want their operation to report to the U.S. The old story of the U.S. overtaking. Hence, Jones was reluctant to force us down the throats of the client organization. That was why he asked for the most senior case team he could have so there would be lots of interaction with the clients. One reason we went into the market early was that Jones believed that his organization did not know what they were doing in the market. . . .

We have learned that it is difficult to have three levels of clients who all think they are clients. On the other hand, I do not think that we coped with it. We knew about this problem, and I do not think any of us, me especially, did a particularly good job. . . .

The case team meeting in May left me with the impression that you hadn't learned a damn thing. And not only that, you focused so explicitly on the businesses that they were in and so little on the peripheral sides of the business that [our presentation] would have been a disaster.

That is why I made the changes [that you described]. I said to myself that we can't show something that ignores half of the other guy's business.

And I think one of the major lessons here is that never through the whole case, until the end, did I feel that I could turn to any one of you for a holistic view of what the client's products were. I felt that each of you knew your own little piece and you were all going to do your own little piece as well as you could do it, without getting your ass in gear.

Not only that, but each of you specifically thought the other guy was not doing his job. There were people saying, "[Manager 2] didn't do his job," and [Consultant 1] said, "Did you see [Consultant 2 is] going to get credit for what [Manager 1] did?" [and I could give more examples].

And so I had no one coming to my office and saying, "I think, in fact, we're not facing the real issue." I didn't have a single guy come in and do that. Not once in the whole study did somebody come in and say, "I think we're looking at this wrong." [Manager 3] and I did do that toward the end, which is why we finally wrote the report ourselves.

And look, I was guilty too, because I just left the scene, so I can't claim that I'm a great help.

We each had our own little piece, and we came in here and showed it, and they [the client] came in the next day and said it was terrible. They did it at every single meeting after that. [Manager 3] and I could fend them off, [and so we privately] reorganized the presentation so that it covered more of the whole.

I think that the reason the first meeting went bad was because we had bad stuff [data and analysis]. I do not think that it went bad because I was not there. I don't think if I had been there I could have done what many of you said. I'm very glad I wasn't there, because I would have had to stand up and defend you guys, and it was probably bad stuff. . . .

For example, we produced the wrong forecast, and that is serious. I do think that they picked the hell out of us, but they would have tried that with me there. It would have taken some amount of chutzpah to get us through the meeting, no matter what.

After that, I'm sure we made a mistake in having them there for the briefing. That was a terrible mistake. [However, it is working in another client situation because we are maintaining intimate ongoing contacts with them, something we did not do in this case.] . . .

If I were to state the generic problem, I think the Indians/chiefs is the real one. That's important because if we are to be successful, we will have to have a lot of Indians. [In the future], we've got to sell more million-dollar-at-a-whack cases, which means more cases like this one down the road. That's the way we've got to go.

We've got to learn to work together, each carrying the weight of our salary in our billing range. And that means we need to identify, keep the whole in place, and then be able to approach each other when the work isn't good enough.

[We also must] approach the person who is leading [the project] and say, "I don't think that we're addressing the big issues here" — instead of each guy looking like "All I have to do is just make sure I don't get my ass in a sling and I'm billable and then I'll be doing good work."

Manager 3: The vice-president gave me a lot of free rein, short of saying explicitly . . . you know, he said to me, "I'm going to be busy at another case, so I'm going to rely on you." I think that put me in a difficult position because that statement was never made explicit to anybody else. Nor did I make the statement any more emphatically to anybody else than you made it to me.

Maybe an error was that I didn't begin to behave in more of a general/admiral kind of fashion. I found it difficult to have two fellow managers on the case. It got difficult to go to you and say, "Look, damn it, go do that." In my experience around here, two reactions can ensue from that approach. One is "Go screw yourself, [Manager 3]." The other is "That's terrific, [Manager 3]" — and then all of a sudden it starts coming back through the grapevine [that the person] was really upset.

Let me ask, is there anything that I did that dissuaded you from coming in and telling me, "This thing is going wrong?"

Unidentifiable speaker: I didn't see much of you.

Manager 2: I guess there is really no good answer. We should have come to you. I know that I didn't say a peep, and I don't think that I heard much of a peep from anybody else other than the kind, you know, on the airplane. The question was asked, "Why are we doing this?" but nobody ever said, "Maybe we should stop right now and do something else." [Several persons say yes.]

Consultant 1: But [to return to your question], I didn't get the feeling that if I said something to you about it, . . . things would change that much.

Manager 3: What do you mean by that?

Consultant 1: If I have a feeling that we are poorly organized but do not have real hard data or facts, how is talking about it going to change what you are doing?

Manager 3: What do you mean by that?

Consultant 1: If I have a feeling that we are poorly organized but do not have real hard data or facts, how is talking about it going to change what you are doing?

I saw you [and others] busy. You were running around. I figured the last thing you're going to have time to do is sit down and spend a lot of time trying to figure out if something's wrong when the only reason I'm saying it is because I do not see much interaction going on.

The interventionist reported that Jones, the client, had said he was disappointed with the case team's performance and that he blamed the vice-president for it. Jones felt that a case team was as good as its vice-president. This vice-president, he said, was superb. The problem, as he saw it, was that the vice-president had become overcommitted. Jones had expected that the vice-president would pull together a case team report that was technically good, understandable, and communicable and that he would have the team working cooperatively with the client's inner group. The interventionist gave excerpts from Jones's conversation: "Regarding the vice-president, he is very bright. But more important, he can come alive and make something complex become clear. It makes it possible for us to understand him and also to question him. Without the vice-president, I wouldn't buy this. I don't think that I could have sold this case to the group."

Diagnoses

Factors that Inhibited Performance

As we have just seen, the case team members identified the following causal factors as inhibiting their performance:

1. There were too many chiefs and not enough Indians. Chiefs like to manage, and there was no one to be managed.
2. Not enough time was set aside at the outset of the project to think it through.

3. The consultants did their own work in ignorance of what others were doing and did not take the initiative to find out what the others were doing. They saw themselves as individual contributors rather than as team members.
4. Team meetings should have been held without the clients present.
5. Some backbiting occurred among consultants.
6. The vice-president withdrew from active management, and no one filled the vacuum.
7. The manager who was the logical successor did not take adequate initiative to manage the case team.
8. The team lacked a vice-president who could "act vice-presidential" at the first client presentation to stop the client's nit-picking.
9. Managers felt helpless in dealing with the nit-picking client and suppressed their frustration. The client reps escalated their counterproductive activities, infuriating the team members. The meeting was a disaster.
10. Parts of the case were so routine that some members overinvested time and energy just to come up with something different.

Reasoning Processes Involved in Inferring These Inhibiting Factors

The causal factors just listed are inferences made by the team members about what caused the team's below-par performance. The partial and complete transcripts show that all the participants confirmed the relevance of each factor. Factors 1, 2, 3, 4, and 6 were identified as important, with the first one, "Too many chiefs and not enough Indians," being the key factor. The existence of a strong consensus among the members is not adequate evidence that these were the only causal factors. The team members might unknowingly be ignoring other important factors. Indeed, I hope to show that they were.

The next step in the analysis is to answer this question: What were the reasoning processes used to arrive at the consensus? One objective of the meeting was for each member to state what he believed were the causal factors that produced the less-than-desired performance — that is, to make a diagnosis. Each person gave his views, illustrating them whenever possible by sifting through his experiences as well as he could recollect them. These conclusions become the basis for our analysis. For example:

Participants' Comments	Inference about What Team Members Experienced
Nobody was really coordinating the case from a holistic point of view.	Individuals recognized coordination problems but did not discuss them or take corrective action.
I remember you said . . . and I sat there and I didn't even know what that meant.	Members were reluctant to discuss issues if it meant stepping on each other's toes.
I didn't know how to really pitch in . . . because I didn't understand what we were doing as a whole, but I never said so.	
We went into the field intensively [too early]. . . . We could have done more thinking [about the case] before we went into the field.	The team members realized early on that they could produce a better product if there were greater clarity about objectives early in the case.
We rarely met . . . without the client so that we could integrate our work. It was always more of a "show and tell" presentation. We never had a normal case team meeting without the client.	Consultants experienced difficulty in case team meetings because client representatives were present.

Participants' Comments	Inference about What Team Members Experienced
The whole thing was basically out of control. . . . I did not have the vice-presidential import so that I could say, "Now, look, I want you guys to do this."	Once the vice-president withdrew, the manager who was the logical choice for second-in-command did not take charge.

The team members' experiences described in the right-hand column became the premises for the next step in the reasoning process. For example:

Team Members Reported	They Therefore Concluded
The managers and consultants recognized the coordination problems as they occurred, but they neither discussed them nor took corrective action. It seemed as if the managers and (perhaps less so) the consultants did not wish to step on each other's toes.	Too many chiefs, not enough Indians.
It was soon obvious that the experience of a similar case was not an adequate guide. Team members felt they would have produced a better product if objectives had been clearer at the outset.	Team leadership did not take time to examine the assumptions and directions of the case because they did not see these matters as important.

Team Members Reported	**They Therefore Concluded**
Consultants experienced difficulty in several case team meetings because client representatives were present.	Some team meetings should have been held without clients, but team leadership did not schedule such meetings.
Once the vice-president withdrew, the manager who was the logical choice for second-in-command did not take charge.	Manager did not wish, or did not feel free, to take charge.
Case team members felt helpless to control client's nit-picking during early sessions.	Vice-president could have blunted counterproductive behavior of client.

Responsibility for the Causal Factors

Under these reasoning processes is a second, deeper, level of causal factors. The team members place responsibility for the first-level factors on gaps in judgment, inherent limitations of participants, and unforeseen events. For example:

If	**Then**
Not enough time was allocated during the early stages to think the case through,	The responsibility was the officer's and we (managers and consultants) had better not question his judgment. He is highly skilled; therefore, he will realize when the case is not progressing and blow the whistle, and he knows how to deal with difficult clients.

If	**Then**
There were too many chiefs and not enough Indians,	The managers did not act as if they had the capacity simultaneously to be managers and effective case team members.
Each participant acted as an individual contributor,	Good team members need only to make their individual contributions. The vice-president's responsibility is to generate and maintain effective team interdependence.
We had too many meetings with the clients,	The vice-president must have known what he was doing by inviting the client to our meetings; we had better acquiesce.
The team lacked a vice-president who could act vice-presidential,	The vice-president was responsible for creating a gap that could not be filled by others.

These second-level factors fall into three categories:

1. Gaps in judgment. For example, the vice-president erred in not allocating more time to early case team meetings and in inviting clients to meetings.
2. Self-imposed limitations in members' actions. For example, Manager 3 did not exercise leadership so no one integrated the individual contributions into a whole until the end.
3. Unforeseen actions counterproductive to the team's effectiveness. An example is the vice-president's withdrawal.

We now see that we have two levels of factors operating to cause the poor team performance. The first and more manifest factors — that is, those close to the surface — are the ones the case team identified. The second and more latent factors — those below the surface — are those inferred from the reasoning processes that led to the first factors.

The two levels of factors give significantly different targets for change. Moreover, if the second level causes the first, then correction of the first level is no guarantee that the second will not continue to exist to create difficulties in another situation. To complicate matters, the first-level factors can be used to avoid examining the second-level factors. Therefore, there must be a tacit consensus, or group-think, operating among the team members of which they are unaware. What could cause their tacit consensus, and why are they unaware?

Primary Recommendation

To answer the question, let us turn to the primary recommendation made by the case team members. The recommendation is the change target that the members agree on, and their agreement is our first clue.

The overwhelming consensus was for a chief who could be tough and forthright and who could exhibit take-charge leadership. This consensus continued even after the team members read a draft of the transcript. For example, the vice-president said, "Looking backwards in order to deal with the future, I think that I would get mad at these guys sooner," and "I could have endorsed [Manager 3] more directly, but he is a senior and respected manager [and so] I did not believe that he needed the mantle."

Their target, therefore, is to create a clear chain of command under someone who is able to coordinate and give orders and to whom the team members can communicate their views. Unilateral power in the hands of a case team leader is the recommended solution.

This recommendation, however, has limited effectiveness. Holding meetings to set the objectives of the case and holding meetings without the client present could not be achieved solely by the appointment of a chief. The major requirement is that the chief sense, and/or the team members tell him, that such action is necessary.

The vice-president might have been willing to take such

action if he had been so advised by the case team members, although he expressed doubts about the advisability of excluding clients. One could add further reservations about the team's recommendation: Appointing a chief may not solve the problem if the chief makes errors but is not particularly confrontable. His effectiveness could be seriously compromised in a team where the trust level is low. Appointing a chief, therefore, is no guarantee that problems will be solved in a way so they remain solved.

A chief does assure, however, that team members do not have to focus on the errors in their own actions and reasoning processes. For example, the team members could have communicated upward information about the factors that were harming the team's effectiveness; they could have explored the reasoning processes that led them to place the responsibility elsewhere; they could have explored the implications of their lack of initiative. They could have done these and more, but they did not because in their minds their actions were not errors and their reasoning was not faulty. They sincerely believed that what they did was in the interest of the organization. The analysis that follows will partially support this belief. Hence, we have a paradox: Actions that are in support of the organization necessarily also harm it. But how was this paradox created? Who is responsible for such conditions?

Several individual and organizational factors combine to cause the problem. The professionals have developed a strategy to protect themselves from pressure and from feelings of failure, a strategy that distances them from any responsibility for the internal system of the organization. For example:

Team Members' Actions	Features of Distancing
They identified factors that inhibited the team's effectiveness and chose to act as if they did not see them and to hide the act of hiding. Thus, there was a cover-up and a cover-up of the cover-up.	Individuals distanced themselves from their personal causal responsibility for both the cover-up and the cover-up of the cover-up.

Team Members' Actions	Features of Distancing
They chose not to go public with the cover-up when the vice-president requested that they do so in the interests of individual and organizational learning.	Team members distanced themselves from cover-up responsibility by holding the vice-president responsible for breaking the cover.
They also chose not to go public about the cover-up of their cover-up.	And they distanced themselves from any responsibility for continuing the cover-up of their cover-up.
They chose to focus on the manifest (surface) factors and to continue to suppress the latent (depth) factors.	Members distanced themselves from their decision to hide the latent factors and to focus on the causal, manifest factors.
The surface factors could be altered by creating organizational rules that would reduce case team effectiveness.	They also chose to hide the personal responsibility for the latent factors.

The professionals report a high degree of pressure and tension related to client relationships. They accept these pressures as legitimate, but there is a limit to how much pressure they can absorb. Hence, they habitually distance themselves from what they call "unnecessary and illegitimate pressures." Issues related to administration are viewed as unnecessary and illegitimate in the sense that they take too much time or get mired in long, tedious meetings. This kind of thinking evolves from the same reasoning processes the team members used in this case.

What led the vice-president to make errors in judgment? One reason was that he had taken on too many assignments and was absent from meetings more than he should have been. But no one told the vice-president that the team needed him or why. Perhaps team members were afraid to communicate upward, being apprehensive about his reaction. (Although such apprehension happened not to be a problem in this situation, I learned from subordinates that they would be careful in communicating upward with certain officers. Such information runs counter to the advice that a chief in unilateral control will solve the problem.) However, this vice-president is one of the officers most concerned about human relationships. Indeed, the very act of holding such a meeting and opening up his own actions to inquiry illustrates his interest in personal and organizational learning.

CASE STUDIES

A third diagnostic mode is to develop short case studies related to the planning process. The format would be as follows:

1. In one paragraph or less, identify a problem with the planning process that you believe is important.
2. In a paragraph or less, describe the strategy that you used or would use to try to solve the problem.
3. Next, divide the page into two columns. In the right-hand column write a scenario of what you believe did (or would) happen when you met face to face with the individual(s) involved. In the left-hand column include any thoughts and feelings that you did (might) have that you did (would) not communicate for any reason. Do this for at least three double-spaced typewritten pages.

Note that these three requirements are consistent with the learning process described in Chapter 2.

From conversation, it is possible to infer the behavioral strategies with which individuals deal with planning problems. It is possible to infer the feelings and thoughts they tend to censor. It is also possible to identify the gaps among the espoused theory to solve the problem, the actual behavior, and the theory in use. Inferences could then be developed about the types and range of defensive routines that individuals create and the way they interrelate to form a self-maintaining, self-reinforcing pattern. Finally, these factors could form the basis for understanding the important features of the organizational culture as related to planning.

The reason for the conversation is to discover the reasoning processes that individuals use when they deal with the problems. This will uncover their theories in use, not simply their espoused theories. It is the theories in use that create the defensive routines, and it is the defensive routines that can inhibit the implementation of a new and more effective strategy and change. For example, in the case of the consultant team just described, it is unlikely that any one of the members would say he or she uses bypass routines of cover-up and cover-up of the cover-up, but these were the crucial routines that would help in the understanding of what led to the less-than-desired performance.

Chapter 6 discusses how to use the data obtained from a diagnosis to engage the defensive routines. In preparation for such a discussion, let us assume that by using the kinds of diagnostic instruments we just described, the consultants concluded, about the planning process, that technical difficulties exist with the planning process that, if corrected, could reduce some of the problems that concern top management.

The very fact that these technical difficulties exist means that defensive routines also exist to support their survival. For example, what is often found when examining the planning process is that the top management is as much responsible for its ineffectiveness as anyone. Often top management is not committed to rigorous analysis. Often top management deals with differences by smothering the conflict. In one organization, the cues that the conflict was becoming uncomfortable with the CEO was when he would say "Time is running out; let's get to [other] issues." In another case, a CEO had the habit of asking for a break or saying, "Let's go to lunch."

It is thus not surprising that subordinates learn to play it safe. They learn to salute, which is another way of saying they remain within the defensive routines of the top. Under these conditions, it is less likely that planning will develop anything new and innovative. Since it must legitimize its costs, the planning group may turn to producing numbers that indicate it is working hard. This leads to the very conditions that top management is trying to overcome. We have begun to construct organizational defensive loops.

One Loop

- The present capability to do analysis isn't good enough.
- Analysis is sometimes misused (or so people believe) and is mistrusted in any case.
- Organizational norms make it hard to confront anyone on the adequacy of his or her analysis.
- Operating organizations aren't held responsible for quality of analysis in any explicit way.
- Hence, there is little pressure to improve analyses.

A Second Loop

- The top-level decision-making process is not very explicit; hence, it is hard for junior managers to learn why initiatives are accepted or rejected.
- The stronger subordinates learn to push bosses until their logic becomes clear; weaker ones take refuge in seeing leadership as more autocratic than it really is and decisions more political and arbitrary than they really are.
- The overall result is to force decisions upward and to tailor initiatives to what you believe the boss wants. This confirms the judgments of seniors and encourages them to gather more decision making to themselves.

There are several important second-order consequences of the loops. First, the loops have important implications for management development. The loops are powerful educators of younger executives as to what actions will lead to success and which to failure. Second, the loops influence the sense of responsibility and trust. Senior line managers, for example, would not take responsibility for the analysis done by their subordinates.

Mistrust existed in the entire planning process, leading individuals to mistrust each other when we-they competitive dynamics developed.

Senior managers wanted juniors to take more initiative. However, since superiors had been known not to support juniors, the juniors attempted to support their cases with lengthy analysis that they hoped was impenetrable. The more tightly reasoned and impenetrable the logic, the more arbitrary in the mind of the juniors will be a decision to reverse their logic. Soon juniors learn not to propose anything they believe will not win. This, in turn, blunts initiative. The excessive analysis may lead to a debasement of formal planning processes.

The defensive loops are not the primary responsibility of top management. Often, we find that there is incompetence at the lower levels — that they prefer to salute than take risks and that they are no more capable of encouraging innovation and risk than anyone else. The problem is rarely who is right or wrong but how we can intervene and interrupt the defensive loops that make the situation worse. This is the problem for which top management is responsible. If they do not legitimize the interruption of the defensive routines, it is unlikely that anyone else will do so.

Indeed, it is foolhardy for anyone else to do so because he or she would run the risk of being clobbered by top management's defensive routines, which are not easily confrontable, especially if the top has personal bypass routines that keep them unaware of the degree to which they are responsible for the very problems they wish to overcome. Under these conditions, even the best new planning processes will probably eventually deteriorate, and the consultants will probably be blamed for any failure.

six

DIAGNOSING AND ENGAGING DEFENSIVE ROUTINES IN MANAGEMENT INFORMATION SYSTEMS

The session described in this chapter began with one client describing his diagnosis of certain economic issues. Within an hour, the consultant was convinced that the clients' diagnosis was full of serious errors, that the logic underlying it was flawed, and that the clients could harm themselves and their relationship with corporate if they acted consistently with their diagnosis.

If you are an executive, read the case as if this could happen in your group. If you are a consultant, think of it as happening with a client group. In either case, in addition to reading the story, ask yourself how you would have dealt with the problem. Would you have covered it up, as several consultant readers told us they would, or would you have tried to get at the issues, as some line executives said they would? However, the executives who said that they would deal with the issues were divided about how they would do it. The majority would use some form of easing in (or private meetings). The minority would deal with it head-on but admitted that they did not know how to do it without raising negative feelings — for example, showing they did not trust their subordinates.

Consultant: I began to realize that the information they [clients] were using was not very good. It was not going to serve our purposes. I also realized that there was little commitment on the part of the clients to their own numbers.

The consultant framed the task as follows:

Consultant: I wanted to find a way to demonstrate to them, using their own information and their responses to their own information, that their explanations lacked consistency and did not hold water. I also wanted to demonstrate that they were differentially aware of all this — that they either intended or felt that they could not do anything about it — and that there was a whole series of interfunctional and organizational games that made it difficult for us to work with them, for them to work with us, and for any of us to get anything accomplished between division and corporate.

The consultant also wanted to help his immediate clients (the division) explore their willingness to accept responsibility for poor economic performance caused by factors beyond their control. Why did they believe that being good soldiers enhanced their position with corporate headquarters? Why did they not believe that such defensive strategies were not only counterproductive for the client firm but also that they could lead the divisional executives to expect the consultants to follow the same strategies? This could place undesirable constraints on the innovativeness of the consultants.

Consultant: [At times, I was saying things to defend and protect us.] We were asking them to pick apart their financial results. If part of their losses is due to their relationship with headquarters, I know I can't do much about that.

So I established that I work with my clients [the division] to fix those things we could fix. I made it clear that I couldn't fix things over which we have little control. I did not want them to expect us to stay within their constraints of how they thought about these economic issues. We had to be free to give them the best and most honest economic analysis that we could provide.

The officers then proceeded to produce what might be described as a series of probes. With each probe the clients could be helped to produce data that made it possible to discuss defensive routines that inhibited effective economic management of the firm.

FIRST PROBE: IDENTIFYING INCONSISTENCIES AND GAPS

During the first hour of the presentation, the consultant made notes of issues that he believed the clients must face:

1. [The clients] were excluding analyses of supply and demand, elasticity, and impact on prices; it was subsumed and not made explicit.
2. They had not reconciled their own financial statement to see what are the pieces of it [and how well they did or did not fit into a consistent whole].
3. They . . . made excuses about all sorts of factors . . . which will never make any money for anybody.
4. I think that top management may well order them someday to do something worse than what I would encourage them to do. . . . I would encourage them to identify the external factors over which they had no control and those over which they do, . . . then they should accept responsibility for the factors over which they have control and not for those they do not.
5. [If they are not careful, they could get into deep trouble with corporate because] they appear to accept responsibility for losses over which they have little control or influence but simultaneously expect others to believe that the losses are not their responsibility . . . . in addition, they act as if they are not doing this and depend on the good graces of other people not to confront them with it.

The consultant framed his first intervention in terms of three rules the clients seemed to be utilizing in the analysis of their economic performance because, by identifying the rules that drove the strategy, he would help the clients focus on how they framed the strategy rather than on their differences about specific economic features.

Please note that double-column format of "Conversation" and "Inferences" will be followed throughout.

Conversation	Inferences about What Is Going On
Consultant: There are three different ways that I hear us simultaneously describing ourselves. I would like to highlight three of them and get your reactions:	Consultant realizes that his three rules are actually attributions about propositions in the clients' economic theory in use; hence, he tests them publicly.
1. To hell with the rest of the world — what is causing us to lose money?	
2. How do we compare with the industry at large (which is diffuse)?	The rules are in the form of questions, each rule highlighting the view held by some client subgroup. Stating these theory in use rules in the form of questions and in nonformal language, communicates to the clients the consultant's intent to empathize with and to understand them.
3. How do we compare with the performance of those competitors we get antsy about, especially when they seem to be doing better than we (and we do not like it)?	

SECOND PROBE: REFLECTING ON THE MEANING OF THE DIAGNOSIS

The clients confirmed that the three rules were valid. The consultant then asked which one they felt was the most important. Several clients responded, each with financial numbers to support his or her particular choice. Their responses were windows on the different views and strategies that each functional group held in dealing with the economics of the firm. The next step was to get the clients to look through this window. The consultant achieved this by asking them to define the meaning that the numbers had for each group.

Consultant: My problem is that these are numbers you know. I guess everyone in this room knows these numbers. [I would like to know what these numbers mean to you.]

Consultant asks the clients to define the meaning the numbers have for each of them. This intervention accomplishes at least three things:

1. It alerts the clients that the consultants will question meanings the clients may take for granted.

2. Doing so differentiates the consultant's thinking from the clients' and at the same time integrates it with the clients' since the differentiation is in the clients' interest.

3. It sets the stage for a discussion of the clients' failure to reconcile financial figures. If they give different meanings for the numbers, they will have to explain why. Their explanations will surface their respective economic micro-

theories and the cultural factors that influence their micro-theories.

Client 1 (the client superior) responded that it would not be easy for them to agree on the meaning of the numbers. In explaining why, Client 1 began to surface the reasoning processes of various players as they generate and use financial numbers. Other client representatives chimed in with their views.

Consultant: What [some of] you are saying, in effect, is that the industry cost structure is driven by a set of positive factors that are less available to you to influence? [Several individuals say yes.]

Consultant tests his attribution about their view of the industry cost structure. He also surfaces his attribution that the clients have little control over the factors that drive the cost structure. If this is true, what is the function of all the economic and financial analyses they make?

Consultant: What I am trying to drive towards is [how our competitors can make two decisions in real time: (1) where to take losses as they occur and (2) when to buy (raw materials) and do it better than we are able to].

THIRD PROBE: CONNECTING THE DIAGNOSIS WITH POSSIBLE CORRECTIVE ACTION WHILE DEEPENING THE DIAGNOSIS

Some clients provided explanations that their colleagues considered were inadequate or incorrect. The consultant attempted to focus again on what they could do, what corrective action they could take.

Consultant: What we are driving at is that there are a lot of things in the world that are impractical. If I could have had the best imaginable last year, would I have made a fortune or still have lost X dollars?

A test of how bad things are in an industry is, in the best circumstances that we can imagine, could we have done better? [In other words], how much of the problem is related to operational managerial decisions, and how much of it was due to factors beyond our control?

In addition to the previous comments made about identifying the factors, the consultant said that he hoped his comments would begin to establish a concept of what is important.

The clients discussed the issues the consultant had raised. In doing so, they presented information that confirmed their poor financial performance but that focused on variables that neither they nor he could do much about.

Consultant: If I said that all this is helpful for me to understand, what do you recommend that we do now?

Client 4: Well, obviously we need to [specifies].

This intervention places responsibility on the clients to design remediable actions and simultaneously provides insight into the actions the clients would recommend and, thus, their reasoning. The con-

Consultant: But that will still leave us with an *X* dollar loss.

Client 4: Yes.

Client 3: All we were trying to do with this idea is justify Client 4's idea.

sultant also felt that it would move the clients away from the "Woe is me!" attitude.

Several other members of the client group attempted to justify their analysis. Their justifications provided further insight into their reasoning processes. In the consultant's eyes, they were confirming that their focus was on factors over which they had no control.

Consultant: Would the [idea that was mentioned] lead to corrective action? Is that something we can do anything about? Or what are some of the things that could be done after we wash out all the other items?

[Client 2 answers. Client 3 disagrees with him. They discuss it at length.]

Client 3: Until we upgrade our systems, we will have to live with [these inadequate numbers].

Consultant: What I would like to have clear in my mind is, after we clear up [all the questions about the numbers], how badly off would we be? If we

Again, the consultant asks the clients to start designing corrective actions.

Consultant again tries to get the clients to focus on those insights that would make genuine correction possible.

cleared up all this stuff, would we still be losing X dollars?

I'd like to have a baseline so that I can say, "Blame me for factors that I can do something about, but not for those that I cannot, because I cannot change those." Measure me off reality. That is why I am concerned about defining reality.

He repeats that he would be willing to be held personally responsible for the factors over which he does have control.

FOURTH PROBE: HELPING CLIENTS TO ACCEPT RESPONSIBILITY FOR THEIR ACTIONS AND TO IDENTIFY THOSE RESULTS FOR WHICH THEY SHOULD NOT BE RESPONSIBLE

The consultant recalled that he wanted to help the clients go beyond complaints about how constraining their system was and also to show empathy for their situation.

Consultant: I would prefer to help them become less prisoners of their system, but if they chose not to do so, I would understand [and we would strive to help them anyway, as best we could].

What they are doing is accepting responsibility for way more [than they can deliver], or they are relying on hope that everyone knows that they could not be responsible for all of it. In fact, what baffles me about what they are doing is that top management criticizes them for losing X dollars, and they say "Fix it!" The clients respond, "Yes, sir, we'll sure try." And they don't have a chance of a snowball in hell to fix it.

The clients continued to elaborate on the difficulties they saw in overcoming the financial losses. The problem was that they did not all consider the same figures to be valid. The consultant asked, "What do we know about [the amount] that is remaining?" Several clients conversed, trying to answer his question. The consultant then asked, "Are people comfortable with these numbers?" Again, more discussion within the group, capped by Client 2 saying, "I think that what we are saying, in essence, is that we need three sets of numbers." [Explains.]

Consultant: I have a problem with that answer . . . in that [I could be placed in the position of having to use numbers whose validity is doubtful to many of you].

The consultant is unwilling to accept Client 2's assurances because if he does, his analysis will be based on figures that are distorted due to organizational factors, factors the consultants are trying to correct.

The clients responded by assuring the consultant that they would come to agreement on what figures to give him so he would not later be faced with argument from one of them that the figures were not valid. Their response showed they had missed the point. The consultants did not wish to collude with the defensive aspects of the system but wanted instead to provide a service of genuine help to the clients. The consultant repeated that his goal was to provide analyses and models for everyday decision making that did not contain distorted numbers, even though the clients were willing to accept and validate distorted numbers and were in the habit of doing so.

FIFTH PROBE: BEGINNING TO RELATE ORGANIZATIONAL FACTORS TO ECONOMIC FACTORS

The consultant related this acceptance of invalid numbers to an organizational issue that was probably a primary cause of them — namely, cross-functional differences and rivalries.

Consultant: May I restate what you are saying? Our prior experience [with you] was that we got data easily from individual functions. But when we tried to mesh these into a coherent single whole that was explanatory, we had lots of problems. [Illustrates.]

In our last study, we took on the responsibility to reconcile the figures, . . . but now we are in a different situation. It is our task to help you find the best way for you yourselves to reconcile the figures.

Client 1: The best way is for you to tell us [about any problems you may have with our numbers], and we will get resolution and sign off . . . so that you get an agreed upon number.

Client 1 did not appear aware that his solution could force the consultants to collude in the very activities that were causing the problems they were trying to resolve. Client 2 did appear to understand and said, "The point is, they don't give a damn about the numbers; we do. They're trying to help us make sure that our communication [to the top is accurate and effective]. [Illustrates.]"

Consultant: [Building on Client 2's example] [We want to help you understand] how you get to the reality before negotiations [about the numbers] as opposed to . . . after the negotiations.

Client 3: I'll make it more complex. Even after we negotiate with each other for numbers that we will sign off on, the numbers will change.

Clients now begin to unpeel layers of organizational factors that can cause number distortion.

Consultant: Despite all that, isn't there a number that . . . [is cut off]?

Client 2: Yes [there is such a number]. But I warn you, in the real world, it won't happen.

Clients express a sense of hopelessness about effecting the changes that the consultants imply are needed.

Consultant: I can understand if you are telling me that the meaning of the numbers depends on which glasses you look through . . . I can buy that. What I do not understand is why it is not relevant to know the best judgment of this group [about the numbers].

Consultant empathizes with the fact that different departments may wish to have different figures. But he asks why he can't request an overall figure that is the best judgment of all concerned.

Client 1: We will give you a number that has consensus. [But I warn you], it will be high. It will be optimistic. [I promise that it will be based on a consensus of effort of the total team.]

The client who previously promised the consultant consensus numbers repeats this promise but now adds that the numbers will be systematically distorted!

Another client promises that the consultant will receive consensually validated data whose distortion is also consensually arrived at.

Client 2: [We may give you some figures on which you build a study that shows . . . .] The first time you present that, they [headquarters] will tell you the problem has been handled and [not to worry about it]. [Other agree and give additional illustrations.]

The clients report that they often unwittingly work on problems that are no longer of concern to the top. Part of the problem may be that the top no longer trusts them; hence, the top often assigns busy-work problems.

SIXTH PROBE: INTRODUCING HERE-AND-NOW ISSUES INTO THE DISCUSSION WHILE SIMULTANEOUSLY DEEPENING THE DIAGNOSIS

As the consultant was helping the clients to explore their diagnoses and actions, he was also creating in their group a learning system that he hoped the clients would use after he left. Whenever an example occurred in the group that illustrated what inhibited or facilitated the learning, he used it to help them to reflect on their defensive routines.

Such reflection also produces another payoff because the clients see the consultants modeling their own theories. For example, if the consultants recommend that the clients learn to reflect on their actions, then the consultants should do the same. To the extent that they do it well, they will teach the client that such reflection need not inhibit or delay effective action.

An example of an opportunity to explore here-and-now issues occurred when a client differed with the consultant's suggestion to re-examine the meaning of the financial numbers:

Consultant: I see you shaking your head and suggesting [this] doesn't make sense. I would like to know why.

Client 2: We battled over [these numbers] for 18 months. Finally we got some movement. They are not without fault. [Continues, identifying certain factors in the organization that, in his view] protect us enough, so let's get on with it and not let your question cause us to start over again.

Another plea that the consultants use the figures that contain known systematic distortions.

Consultant: What is it that you heard me say that leads you to believe I don't find what you are saying understandable?

Client 2: [Appears taken aback] Well . . . eh . . . uh, uh . . . [silence]. I guess my worry was "why worry about it?"

Consultant responds to the feelings of the client, empathizing with his problem and indicating he can work within it if necessary.

Consultant: I'm not.

Client 2: Then I really misunderstood your emphasis.

Let us pause for a moment and suggest an additional intervention. The consultant did express empathy, but he might have also expressed the idea that consultants must be free to provide the best possible ideas to their clients even if that means upsetting some agreements recently arrived at by the clients. For example:

Consultant: I can certainly empathize with your desire not to upset any progress that has been made after many difficult meetings. We will do our best to work within your constraints.

I do ask, however, that we feel free in this room to explore possible ways to keep pushing back the barriers of the system that you have described. We would like to push them back in order to give you the best possible product. However, we are interested in pushing them back when it can be done without an undue cost or pressure on you.

Returning to the transcript, Client 3 did take the opportunity to dig into possible inconsistencies in their practice:

Client 3: If we knew the market value of *X* was [this], why did we agree to sell it at a lower price? Were we bludgeoned into that?

Client 1: I'll give you an answer.[He does so.]

Client 3: I still do not understand.

This question ups the ante as to the issues the clients are willing to discuss. Indeed, this question may bring up a topic that was hitherto undiscussable in client meetings. If so, the consultant is already producing organizational changes.

The fact that Client 3 can tell Client 1 that he still does not understand is also a sign of progress since Client 1 is the superior.

There now takes place an animated discussion on the part of the clients about what they can and cannot do, about top management actions that produce dilemmas and errors for them, and about their astonishment at certain top management decisions. In addition to providing further rich evidence of the organizational difficulties, the discussion introduces another important theme: the sense of placing the blame on others. The clients feel they have little control over their own fate and that their only means of adapting is to complain and feel helpless.

Consultant: May I rephrase your question [about being bludgeoned into it]? However we got there, we all realize that we came up with [a poor result]. The question I have is how do we know we won't do that again when we are making such decisions in the future?

Client 2: Hopefully, we will [much laughter].

Client 1: I don't think that this will happen again [others laugh] because in those days we had centralized decision making.

Consultant: Are you saying in effect, now that we have profit centers [the problem is largely solved]?

Client 1: Yes [we can now refuse to take certain actions if we think they are wrong].

Consultant acknowledges that all agree that an error exists and tries to focus on the issue of how to correct the factors that produced the error so it will not be repeated.

There is a discrepancy between the optimism now expressed by the senior client official and the hopelessness of the others, as well as a discrepancy between his present optimism and what he said previously.

Consultant might have asked others to comment. In doing so, he could have upped the ante even further by discussing the undiscussable — that is, by encouraging responsible disagreement with a superior.

This is only the first session, however. Such a step would have required more time than was available. Also, the client superior might have felt that the consultant was fueling the openness of the meeting and that it was reaching a danger point.

The consultant could talk with Client 1 later to get his reactions. The intent would be not to collude with his anxieties as much as to get them out into the open and to help him design ways to overcome them. As we will see, the consultant accomplished this. I believe that some subordinates interpreted Client 1's preceding comments to mean that the discussion had reached the limits of what it was appropriate to discuss.

Client 2: I promise to give you good numbers. [Explains.]

Consultant: May I summarize? My understanding is that we can put on a piece of paper [such and such].

Client 3: There are accounting numbers and economic numbers. [Illustrates.]

Client 4: Yes. We will give you numbers that everyone will agree to [I think].

Client 2: We have to [laughter].

The clients return to the issue of getting good numbers.

SEVENTH PROBE: REFLECTING ON AND CONCEPTUALIZING ECONOMIC OPERATING PRINCIPLES

Consultant: Let me construct a theory that I will call "first principles" and ask you if it fits. In effect, corporate policy has been "We are not going to argue about price. We will honor our agreements."

Second, one way to cover the problem of earnings is to reduce inventories. [Elaborates on this.]

The point is that is a sequence of events that is logical but costly.

A question that I would like to explore with this group is how much did I spend in order to do things that made sense but that simultaneously hurt my bottom line?

It is not surprising that the two client comments that followed were further examples of their bewilderment. The consultant returned to his question.

Consultant: The point is, if you think that my story is sensible [then we can begin to identify what we can and cannot take responsibility for].

I would like, therefore, to get closer to those policy issues with you [silence from the clients], assuming this makes sense? [All respond "Yes, yes."]

One interpretation of the clients' silence is that they had arrived at the end of their protective rope. Up to this point, every time the consultant asked a question, they responded with rich illustrations of their trials and tribulations. Their silence seemed to indicate they had reached the end of their tales of misery and now had to consider constructive action. Their silence was broken when they began to identify features of their practice with which they would have to deal if genuine progress were to be made.

EIGHTH PROBE: DIGGING MORE DEEPLY INTO THE WAY CLIENTS PROTECT THEMSELVES

Client 5: We drew a position less than four months ago that did not allow for any inventory change. We promised not to change that.

The clients present further evidence of how they unknowingly escalate error.

We also promised that we were going to sell X amount. When our purchasing people saw these projections, they understandably ordered more raw materials.

Now business has gone a bit sour. We now want to reduce inventory. Then purchasing will say no because they've ordered all this material. [Others disagree with Client 5's description.]

Consultant: [May I ask that we focus on this question:] What kind of knowledge do we need to minimize the likelihood of this happening again, recognizing that sometimes it is inevitable?

Again the consultant tries to get the group to think about designing corrective action.

Can we identify the theory and the logic we used [to produce the wrong forecast] so that we can construct future plans that are [less subject to these errors]?

Consultant asks for the reasoning behind the clients' poor forecast.

NINTH PROBE: BEGINNING TO INTEGRATE ECONOMIC AND ORGANIZATIONAL FACTORS

The clients described their reasoning processes as they related to their economic decisions. Their description surfaced another powerful organizational factor that the consultant attempted to identify.

Consultant: There is an implicit theory that seems to have been operating [in your actions]. Let me tell it to you and help me see if I am wrong: If our forecast didn't happen as predicted [in this quarter], act as if it must happen during the next quarter. Therefore, do not change our predictions.

Consultant states a possible operating principle used by the clients.

[The reality now is that] we have losses and are under great pressure to reduce them. We are now in a position where the predicted turnaround has not occurred, and we are going to have to recommend cutting back.

Consultant relates the unintended consequences of the operating principle.

Question: Have we changed our theory as to what is likely to happen? Because if we haven't, we may be doing the wrong thing.

Client 1: We have changed our theory. [We recognize the upturn will not come and the losses will get bigger and bigger.]

Consultant: I understand that. In my terms, what I hear you describing is a change in forecast and not so much a change in theory.

Client 1: Yes.

Client 3: Let me interrupt here. The top economists of this country did not predict accurately this recession.

Consultant: [Is that what led us to make the wrong forecasts — the fact that we used their predictions?]

Client 1: No, don't misunderstand me. We did not use the numbers Client 3 referred to. We used our own numbers.

Again, the consultant tries to use the client responses to identify the underlying economic theory they are using and to build for the next steps that might be taken.

Consultant: Let me see. The underlying theory on which all this is based is a general [economic] forecast but, more specifically, the effect of supply and demand on market volume and prices. . . .

Question: What kind of data do we have describing such relationships [elasticity of demand, etc.] under different degrees of imbalance? Or are we using our operating experience and intuitions, which aren't bad in a slowly changing market [but which aren't so helpful in one changing quickly]?

What kind of information can this group bring to the party with respect to [this problem]?

Consultant again focuses on what action the clients can initiate.

Client 1: I don't know that we have anything on [such and such].

Clients begin to identify gaps in their knowledge and modeling.

Client 3: We don't have the data base or modeling to predict what will happen. . . .

Clients identify organizational factors that impede progress.

We all gather in smoke-filled rooms and we huddle together and come up with an answer.

One client said that the problem did not lie simply with them but that the entire industry was thinking in the same way. The consultant accepted this hypothesis and again asked the clients to focus on what they can do.

Consultant: OK [you are saying that the entire industry was wrong]. The question is, is there anything in our firm that makes it more difficult for us to say that we made a mistake and to change than for our competitors?

The consultant again tries to turn the clients away from blaming others and to focus on their own responsibility for corrective action.

Client 1: We are slower than our major competitors.

Consultant: Could you describe that further? One thing that we might be able to do in this room is identify what may make us slower than our competitors.

The clients gave these explanations:

> "Management people are slow to take responsibility to act, even though they now have the authority."
>
> "Top management was brought up to manage by looking upward. Everybody looks upward."

Client 1: The problem is, when it comes to making economic decisions, the systems that we have are just pitiful. That is our fault.

And top management is well aware of that. They have little confidence in our ability to make these kinds of judgments.

The senior client officer blamed the management system and acknowledged that top management has doubts about the group's effectiveness. This is an important organizational issue that will have to be explored because, even if the consultant is able to help the clients produce technically sound systems, there is still the problem of credibility with top management.

Client 1 continued by saying that his group's ability to produce useful information within top management's time frames was poor. Client 6 agreed but said the trouble was that it took a very long time for competing groups to meet and reconcile the figures. Moreover, the groups then had to sign them off with many corporate staff groups. Another client said that once a plan is made, top management casts it in concrete and it is very difficult to change it.

The consultant asked what prevented the people in the room from taking up these issues with the top. No one responded directly. Client 1 simply said that they chose to communicate through the normal channels that he had identified previously as "cumbersome." The consultant finally role played a scenario to test how open the clients perceived top management to be.

TENTH PROBE: TESTING THE CLIENTS' DIAGNOSIS OF HOW TOP MANAGEMENT INHIBITS CLIENTS' EFFECTIVENESS

Consultant: Are you saying that you cannot go to the top and say, "I know you dislike changes in the plan. You can criticize me rightfully for not having foreseen what I am going to have to say now. On the other hand, this is what I think we must do. I think it is right because it will make more money than the original plan [for these reasons]." Are you saying they would find that logic unacceptable?

Client 1: No, not at all. It is the screens and filters built into our systems that manage to muffle these things.

The clients then described the rigidity of the organization's present systems. The consultant attempted to conceptualize their responses in the form of a double bind. If his conceptions are correct, he not only identifies the deeper issue but also helps the clients feel more genuinely understood.

Consultant: Let me reflect on what you have said. You are responsible for producing the plan but also responsible for producing revisions of the plan. But you cannot do both. Is that what you are saying? [Replies of "Yes, yes."]
   [And if I understand you correctly], there are four different pressures that you must experience. They are:

1. Pressures related to creating an internal consensus,
2. Pressures that come from what our division may do that could hurt other profit centers,
3. Pressures with your bosses and what they find to be acceptable,
4. Pressures — even if I have all the above lined up — that I can't get others to go along with them.

[Replies of "Yes, yes!"]

The consultant then pointed out that this analysis also described the feelings that corporate headquarters had toward the clients. Top corporate people did not have confidence in the division's plans so they, too, made decisions on the basis of gut feelings and self-protection. They wished they did not have to do this because they felt responsible for approving the expenditures that created these divisional departments. The more frustrated they became, the less they wanted to deal with these departments. They reacted by distancing themselves; by expecting only late, useless reports from departments; by getting angry when forecasts had to be changed; and by not bothering to keep the departments informed.

Consultant: [Maybe one way to begin is to focus on that last pressure.] How do we get along with the other staff departments?

Client 1: The same old thing: the more the staff, the more the paperwork.

ELEVENTH PROBE: EMPATHIZING WITH CLIENTS WHILE REJECTING SOME OF THEIR PRACTICES

Consultant: I can see more clearly the dilemma you must feel. If you know that you cannot have confidence in reconciliation, you are reduced to acting on the basis of gut feelings and self-protection. If you are held accountable for gut-feeling figures, it is embarrassing because you didn't want to do it that way. . . .

The problem: The less you can believe what you are looking at, the less you want to spend the time to deal with what you are looking at, and the more you are likely to wind up doing stuff that later on doesn't prove out.

Client 1: We don't have the wherewithal.

Client 7: Every department hangs on to its figures.

Client 4: Let me say that I don't think there is anyone in this room, or in the entire industry, who could have predicted the sharp drop. The planning was based on historical numbers that we all had a lot of confidence in. It appears that we are unable to react to what the real world turned out to be.

Consultant: And another thing I have heard people say is that after we discovered we couldn't predict, we solved that problem by simply increasing [the forecasts so we would match the plan rather than simply saying we blew it and facing up to the issue].

Client 1: Yes.

Clients return to a litany of their difficulties.

Consultant again focuses on the way clients inadvertently escalate error and probably reduce their credibility.

Consultant: Question that I would like to ask — two questions. We have all the functional heads here. Why is it that functional heads are willing to come in with numbers that are not reconcilable with those of other functional heads?

The second question: What are some of the things that we can do among ourselves in terms of how we look at information and how we develop and sign off on our policies in order to improve our ability to get our job done and not run into all the complaints that each of you has been describing? What is it that prevents *us* from doing something about ourselves?

Client 1: I do have some reservations about what has been said. I really have trouble with what I hear now. If all this occurs, I'm shocked.

Consultant: Yes. But we must find out what is really going on.

Client 4: [I'll answer that frankly.] I think that we do have a communication problem with our organization between . . . and . . . . What has to be done to reconcile that? The heads of the two areas

Consultant again focuses on the clients' responsibilities and the need for self-correction.

Client superior expresses shock at what he has heard from his subordinates.

Clients begin to identify departments that are creating difficulties.

have to sit down with their people [and solve these problems].

Consultant: I like what you are saying because I think what you are saying is that each of us has responsibility for departments and we must do something.

Consultant reinforces the clients' willingness to examine their responsibilities.

[May I ask you people around the table] what is it that makes each of you comfortable with numbers that you know are not reconcilable to other departmental numbers?

Consultant asks a question about responsibility that may be difficult for the clients to answer.

[Much overlapping conversation.]

Client 5: There has been some change, but it is evolutionary.

FLOWCHART OF THE ANALYSIS

It is possible to plot some of the major features of the diagnosis in the form of a flowchart (Figure 6.1). The flowchart describes what was learned as the consultant probed to identify and surface inconsistencies, helped the clients discuss with each other features of their management information system and their relationships with corporate that had been undiscussable, and identified the defensive reactions, the escalating errors, and the self-fulfilling, self-sealing actions.

Figure 6.1, with slight modification, could become the basis for development of a map of defensive routines and their consequences between the division and corporate as related to their information systems that, in turn, influence strategy development

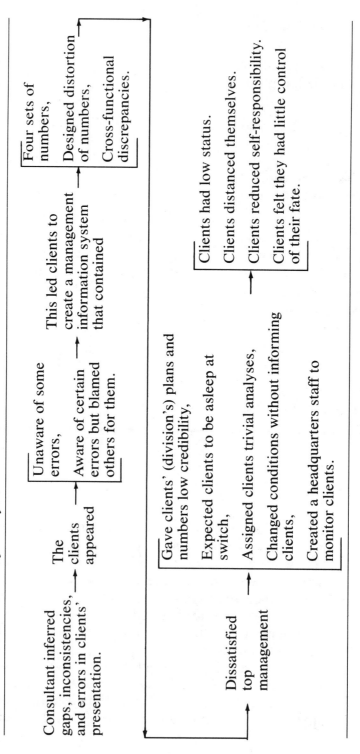

FIGURE 6.1 *Flow Chart of Analysis*

since strategy is formulated on the basis of the numbers provided by the information system. The map (Figure 6.2) begins with the inconsistencies that the consultant helped the clients to see during the meetings as well as their reactions to the gaps and inconsistencies. Next are the major responses the clients use to adapt, such as the development of several sets of numbers, distorting numbers by consensus, cross-functional barriers to communicating threatening information, and producing late plans partially because of all the bases that have to be touched within division before the numbers and plans are sent to corporate. Corporate management, in turn, is aware in varying degrees of all of these consequences. As a result, they feel dissatisfied with the divisional planners and their information systems. They assign low credibility to the plans, and they expect late plans and trivial and nonrelevant analyses.

Neither the division nor corporate players discusses these issues forthrightly. Moreover, they act as if these issues are discussable. Hence, we have the classic features of defensive routines: cover-up, inability to discuss the cover-up, escalating error, and dissatisfaction.

In this case, dealing with these defensive routines appears to be so abhorrent by corporate that they bypass them by creating their own corporate planning group to do not only corporate planning but also to monitor the quality of divisional numbers and exclude them from their plans. Corporate planning people follow the defensive routines and do not discuss forthrightly with division the problems the line executives have with them. The results are related to a low credibility of planning as well as poor plans.

Figure 6.2 describes what has gone on between division and corporate as well as what will go on. We predict that these defensive routines will not change unless they are dealt with directly. We would also predict that if a new planning process was designed by the outside consultants, it would get into difficulty. Some consulting firms have been known to promise that their new plans will not go astray if they are permitted not only to design the plans in detail but also to manage the new system for several months, thereby teaching the players exactly what to do. They also build in monitoring devices so that management can check up on the new performance.

FIGURE 6.2 *Management Information Systems and Learning*

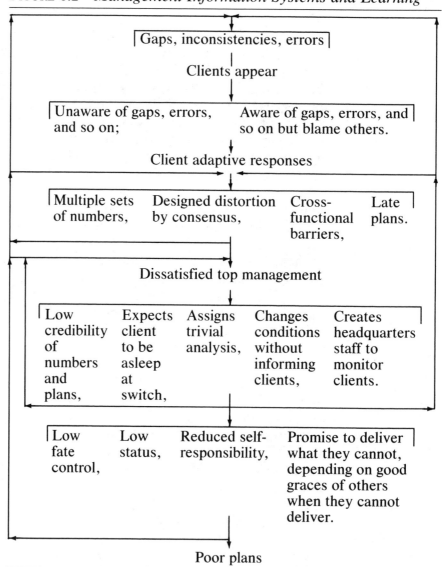

These strategies do work up to a point. Their basic flaw is that they bypass the defensive routines. The capacity of the players to build these routines is never addressed. The result is that the consulting firm becomes, for quite a while, an integral part of the organization. They are doing the managing. This, in turn, permits defensive players to distance themselves from feeling responsible for the difficulties. The organization, in effect, would now be paying two sets of people to manage these activities without creating in its people the capacity to learn how to learn to solve these problems.

These predictions can be tested by an executive or by the consultants. If the hunches are not disconfirmed, then the diagnosis is strengthened as a basis for taking action. Some possible steps for testing are the following:

1. Feed back the model to the client group. Ask for their confirmation or disconfirmation.
2. Identify any gaps or inconsistencies the group members develop, plus possible ways to generate data to fill in the gaps or test the inconsistencies.
3. Ask for clients' assessment of the degree to which the organizational actions described in the model are alterable. Identify the factors that they believe will inhibit or facilitate change.
4. Develop jointly actions strategies that will begin to change the situation.
5. Carry out these strategies and monitor the consequences.

Note that these steps can easily be translated into actions that provide clients with important learning and/or changes. Thus, the testing of the model can be integrated with unfreezing and changing the client system.

Another example of a possible test occurred when a meeting with the same client group was held a week later to obtain the economic numbers. If the model was correct, we would predict that in the second meeting, the following would occur:

1. The clients will have difficulty accepting responsibility for numbers or in producing numbers whose validity they will guarantee.

2. The clients will resist the responsibility for producing numbers they consider important to understanding the business.
3. When confronted with their inability, the clients will explain their difficulty by blaming others in ways that are consistent with the model.

The consultant tried to obtain a number that would express the real value of the product during a specific time period. There followed a 25-minute discussion in which the clients told war stories. None would provide such a number. The consultant then asked who might be able to produce such a number if given time. There was silence; the clients apparently were pointing to each other. Finally, the consultant interrogated each member of the group and narrowed the field to one individual. Once that individual accepted the assignment, he requested that it be put in writing. It took nearly 8 minutes to get agreement on a relatively short sentence stating his assignment. The following are examples of the dialogue that took place:

Consultant: Who would know this number?

Client 1: [So and so.]

Client 2: I don't know.

Client 3: Does anyone know?

Client 4: I think that I might have a few papers in my office where the number might be.

Consultant: Is that a good number?

Client 2: It *was* a good number! [Laughter]

Consultant: I'm frustrated. I keep hearing that this number is fine *and* that it is not.

Client 2: We need _____ to make the final judgment.

Consultant: [After much questioning and resistance] OK. Now we are saying that these two calculations will do it. Correct? [All reply "Yes, yes."]

Consultant: Fine! Now who is the best person to take on this responsibility? [Silence]

Client 3: Why don't we wait for _____ ?

Client 4: Sometimes we have to make a decision!

This meeting also provided examples of the counterproductive activities described in the model. For example:

- We go to meetings and all there is is talk. Nothing comes out of it . . . not a goddamn thing.
- We stopped [raising the questions] because [so and so] put out a memo not to appear as if we are bad-mouthing people.
- We can't even decide to treat customers like customers.
- We're slaves to information. We never have enough of it. And when we get it, we can't use it!

About a week after the meeting described here, the consultant had a discussion with the head of the group, Client 1. Client 1 focused heavily on the technical and analytical issues. When the consultant found a natural opening, he asked Client 1 his thoughts about the organizational issues discussed during the four-hour session

Client 1 responded that he was concerned about what had happened. He admitted that the participants had identified important issues. However, he felt that there was "a lot of griping" and that at times "they got into a group therapy session." He continued, "I suppose there is a role for that, but I think also it can be inappropriate." He then returned to a discussion of the technical issues.

Later during the discussion the consultant said, "Before you mentioned that some of what happened [in the four-hour meeting] was inappropriate. What was inappropriate in your eyes?"

Client 1: Well, maybe "inappropriate" is not the right word. But some people went out of line. I have always made it a rule not to personalize issues.

Consultant: Have you discussed it with the group?

Client 1: Yes, I had a meeting and told them my views [describes what he said].

The consultant expressed concern about the meeting for two reasons: (1) "Organizations are people and it is unlikely to have such discussions without identifying individuals." (2) "I am concerned about the effect it might have on your people. They acted in ways they felt were responsible and now they may feel this was an error. How are we going to begin to correct some of the organizational factors that the firm has asked us to correct?"

Client 1's reaction is typical of executives who have lived for years in firms where frame breaking about organizational issues is discouraged. This is why it would have been helpful if the consultant had flagged Client 1's expression of shock when the participants were being candid. They might have worked it through so that Client 1 would not feel so uncomfortable. Even if they did not, at least the group, including the consultants, would have had a more accurate picture of the barriers to be overcome. Actually, the individual whose comment upset Client 1 most did not attend the follow-up meeting. Client 1 asked that individual's superior to convey to him disapproval of his absence.

Consultant: Is it fair for me to say that you do not believe that such topics should be held in group sessions?

Client 1: I absolutely disagree with discussing such issues in the group. This should be said privately and the punishment administered privately.

The consultant pointed to two possible undesirable consequences of Client 1's position. First, those excluded would not know what went on during the private meeting and, hence, could conjure up all sorts of fears. Second, if they knew Client 1 disapproved of such group discussions yet did not state this openly, they might infer that he was weak.

The second consequence struck Client 1 because, as he put it, "I have been criticized for being a weak manager." After a little more discussion, he said, "I never would have believed that I would ever find myself questioning my beliefs about this rule." He smiled and winked. The consultant then said that neither he nor any case team member took the position of simply identifying faults: "I see you and the others as being ethical and hard-working people. You and your people are trapped in a system [that we would like to help you change]."

Client 1 responded that he could think of several people who might do better in his job, not because of technical competence but because of their ability to communicate. The session ended with the client thanking the consultant. The consultant reported afterward, "The frankness of this guy was incredible. All the time he was smiling, winking, smiling. I think he was saying, 'OK, you've reached me and no one here has ever done so.'" I might add that Client 1 could have said also, "And through your reaching me, I also reached myself."

seven

FEEDING BACK RESULTS THAT MAY BE THREATENING
(with Robert Putnam)

We are now ready to communicate to the clients the analysis of the defensive loops. This requires telling the clients (1) that they are behaving in ways that are counterproductive to the organization's effectiveness, (2) that they may be unaware of many of the consequences of such behavior, (3) that if they are not careful, the defensive routines could become so powerful they might lose control of the organization. To compound the difficulty, all this must be done with individuals who we know prefer not to deal with these issues forthrightly.

Clearly this is neither an easy task nor should it be if the diagnosis is correct. It also should not be bypassed because the credibility of the consultants' advice that the clients should engage the defensive routines will be tested by the clients by watching how the consultants apply their advice when they are in a difficult situation.

The methods used to engage the defensive routines can be used by line executives as well as consultants. A line executive would be faced with some of the same difficulties as the consultants. Indeed, some may argue that the consultants have more to lose because they could lose the client. Also, as you read the skills that the consultants used to deal with threat, please keep in mind that the skills can be used to deal with threat that surrounds any kind of business problem.

THREE UNDERLYING ISSUES

There are three generic issues with which consultants must deal during the designing and executing of feedback sessions.

- How can consultants design the feedback sessions by using the theory of change that they intend to recommend that the clients use in changing their organization?
- How can consultants deal with differences between clients and consultants in ways that join with clients rather than polarizing against them?
- How can consultants help clients deal with threatening issues?

The fundamental assumptions in these questions are that the feedback of the results is part of the process for change and that consultants should mirror their strategy for change in the way they feed back the results. The feedback of the results often does produce defensive routines on the part of the clients. Most of these, in my experience, are not overly strong or violent. Clients use the same defensive routines with their consultants that they use with each other. Thus, if the clients avoid conflict with each other, then they will avoid conflict with the consultants. If the clients are more directive and confrontational, then they will do the same with the consultants. The latter is not necessarily a sign that the consultants are failing, and the tranquility of the former is not necessarily a sign of success.

Designing the Feedback Session

Using Compelling Reasoning and Advocating Confrontable Views

The first rule is to design the feedback session in ways that illustrate what it means to combine compelling reasoning with decisive but confrontable action. One way to introduce these ideas is to design the presentation by using the concepts of compelling reasoning and the ladder of inference. Recall the rules that are found in the ladder of inference.

- Begin with relatively directly observable data (for example, comments from interviews).
- State the inferences consultants made from those data.
- Ask clients to give their reactions to the data and inferences, including more illustrations from the clients' experience that either confirm or disconfirm the consultants' inferences.

For example, the consultants could say:

- "During our interviews we heard comments such as . . . ."
- "From these we inferred conflict avoidance (or whatever)."
- "Before we explore the possible consequences, let's pause to see how much agreement exists about what you said and our inferences."
- "We would like to begin with your reactions, but eventually we must aim for implications."

It is important to begin with relatively directly observable data because then clients can understand what data the consultants selected and can judge for themselves the validity of the inferences. Also, clients are more likely to feel that they and the consultants understand each other and that the consultants will create situations in which the clients can feel competent in discussing their problems. These are the features that make it more likely that clients will feel internally committed to the diagnosis.

It is important to encourage clients to give their reactions because consultants can learn the extent to which clients confirm their views and because discussion helps build a sense of commitment to the diagnosis. Also, when clients discuss their reactions they often educate each other about the issues raised by the consultants. This reduces the risk of a we-they relationship between clients and consultants.

This approach can be contrasted with the talk-at-them style of presenting in which consultants have so many slides to present that clients have little opportunity to do anything but listen. This suggests some rules about what not to do when your intention is to create a relationship favorable to engaging defensive routines in order to reduce them.

> Do not come to the meeting with so many slides that little time will remain after the presentation for clients to discuss their reactions.
> Do not connect your sense of success primarily with telling the clients your ideas, but judge your success by the degree to which you stimulate client discussion of the data, issues, and ideas that you present.

Helping Clients Take Responsibility for Important Choices

Consultants often present their findings and implications as a package. They do so because they believe clients expect to hear both the findings and implications before a discussion is held. Another reason is that the consultants may feel secure if they have reported this information before the discussion is opened up to client reactions. They believe that some client defensive routines may be averted by first giving the total presentation. This belief is often true but it has costs.

The discussion may lead to important insights that would alter the implications. The consultants could then modify their presentation of the implications. If the clients feel more ownership of the diagnosis, they may be more willing to listen to implications and recommendations that may be controversial.

If the consultants control the presentation to minimize potential client defensiveness, they are beginning their presentation by using the same theory in use the clients use. If the clients misunderstand the results because they do not have the complete picture, the consultants can ask for a postponement of the discussion.

However, often the misunderstanding may be a symptom of the defensiveness the clients feel and the way they deal with the threat. The way the clients deal with the consultants and with the unsettling information provides real opportunity to learn more about the defensive routines and to give the clients livelier illustrations of these routines. It also provides the consultants with an opportunity to show how they would deal with the reactions. Modeling will help the clients test the credibility of the consultants' approach. It will also give them an idea about what they will have to learn to do when they help their immediate reports deal with the findings.

Dealing with Possible Client Misinterpretation of Consultant Strategy

It follows that if consultants have a choice in the design of the feedback meeting, then they should separate the presentation of the findings from the presentation of their implications. The clients should also be in on the choice. However, some clients may interpret a request for such a choice as weakness on the part of the consultants. One way to deal with the dilemma is for the consultants to advocate their preferences and encourage confrontation of them. For example:

• We prefer to present our finding with as much discussion as possible. Then we will present the implications as we see them. If you have another preference for this presentation, we are prepared to explore it with you.
• Our preference is to provide you with an opportunity to choose the sequence of the presentation. However, if you prefer, we have done our homework and are ready to recommend a sequence.

Some clients may conclude that the consultants have not fulfilled their responsibilities if they ask clients to choose. If the consultants were simply to respond, "Okay. We suggest starting with [whichever]," then the clients could conclude that they were right. Our recommendation, in contrast, communicates that asking the clients to choose was a deliberate action, undertaken for good reasons and not a sign that the consultants have not done their homework.

This intervention contains a message about the kind of relationship the consultants would like to create — namely, that the consultants intend to act as experts but that laying things out is not the only way to fulfill their responsibilities. Providing opportunities for the clients to make choices can also show expertise.

The intervention can be characterized by the following rule:

> If clients interpret an opportunity to choose as an indication the consultants are not fulfilling their responsibilities, then state that offering a choice was deliberate, and either offer to recommend an alternative or state why you prefer not to make a recommendation.

Similar rules apply to asking clients to provide illustrations that either confirm or disconfirm the consultants' diagnosis and to discuss implications of the diagnosis. Involving clients in these activities serves to educate both consultants and clients about the extent to which clients understand the issues, and it helps clients to build a sense of ownership of the diagnosis. However, consultants should have illustrations ready to supplement the ones that clients give and should have their map of implications in case clients have difficulty getting started. This suggests a rule about what *not* to do:

> Do not use client involvement as an excuse for not preparing your own position.

Consultants should come in well prepared but willing to hold some of their ideas while encouraging clients to choose where to focus, to offer illustrations, and to discuss implications of the findings.

Encouraging Client Involvement in Designing the Next Steps

Let us assume that the clients have accepted the diagnosis and ask what the consultants recommend as next steps. One strategy is for the consultants to present their recommendations and encourage inquiry. Another strategy is for the consultants to use the opportunity to provide the clients with more insight into their preferred strategy for dealing with defensive routines and changing organizations. For example, there are often several different kinds of next steps. The choice of which one to take depends upon the readiness of their organization. So far, all the consultants know is how ready the top is to begin implementing whatever they have concluded makes most sense for them. The next step is therefore to conduct a similar session with their immediate reports.

What if the clients ask, "Okay, your diagnosis of our problems makes sense. But what are we going to do about it?" The consultants could say, "There is a lot that we can suggest you can do. Much depends on your readiness and that of your organization."

This could be followed up with one of the following:

- If, for example, an organization is ready to deal with difficult issues, then we would recommend . . . . If it is not, then we would recommend . . . .
- I think the next step is to develop what is our view of how ready is the organization.
- Recalling the findings, which ones would you prefer to begin with?
- Recalling the findings, which ones do you believe the organization can digest best at this early stage?

The intention is to communicate that consultants feel responsible for helping clients to determine their readiness and for suggesting options but are not in control of what the clients should do or how long it will take. This depends largely on client readiness, which is a matter of both capability and willingness. Clients can successfully engage in reducing the defensive routines only when they are internally committed to them. By saying that "much depends on your readiness," the consultants communicate that clients should have responsibility for and ownership of the change program.

What if the clients say, "The diagnosis makes sense. Now tell us what to do"? The consultant could say:

Fine. Let's examine what has happened in this meeting. You have had a chance to question, confront, agree, or disagree, and when we finished you were ready to take the next step.

We recommend that the same sense of commitment be developed at the next level. The next step we recommend is a session with the enlarged top group to go through the same process.

One rule for this type of intervention has to do with the sequence of behavioral change in organizations, starting at the top and working down through the hierarchy. The rule is:

When the top group has discussed the diagnosis and has developed some degree of internal commitment to changing, suggest that the next step is to go through the same process with the next lower level.

If this next step is to work, the subordinates must see some credible assurances that they will not be harmed if they speak candidly. In one case, the consultants thought that it was important that the top line executives strike a balance between convincing the organization that they are serious about change and that the subordinates would in no way suffer by being candid and open. The consultants could say to the top:

One of the issues that usually arises in change activities like these is how seriously is the top committed to make the changes work. A second issue is how to design assurances that individuals will not be harmed by participating openly.

The consultants are responsible for raising these issues and helping participants to discuss them, but they are not responsible for resolving them unilaterally. Consultants do not have the power to insure that people remain deeply committed and that no one will be harmed. If they take responsibility for making such assurances, clients could hold them responsible for any unanticipated difficulties.

Both superiors and subordinates will have doubts about participating in the change process. The consultants' responsibility is to ask the clients to express their doubts so that they can be discussed and influenced. The client group may wish to stipulate limits and to work on procedures for both subordinates and superiors and to leave room for second thoughts about participating in the change process.

Notice that the suggestion is to say, "One of the issues that usually arises in change activities like these . . ." rather than simply, "How committed are you to make the changes work?" Thus, the consultant generalizes from the particular individuals in the room to what often happens in these situations. This is a way of making it easier to discuss issues that clients may find threatening. The rule may be stated as follows:

> When the consultant is aware of risks that may arise from choices clients may make in the future, raise these as issues to be discussed by clients.

If clients have difficulty talking about issues that should nevertheless be discussed, again introduce them generally as "issues that often arise in these situations" (assuming this is true). Consultants should not assume unilateral responsibility for resolving issues of risk and uncertainty that are part of the change program.

What if the consultants hesitate to suggest that the top group meet with their subordinates because the clients are not accustomed to sharing their uncertainties? The concern is that the top might not realize what they were getting into and that once they committed to genuine participation, it would be difficult to go back on the decision. The consultant could say:

> I believe that the next step should be to discuss this report with your subordinates. However, the way we do this — indeed, if and when we do this — should be highly influenced by how you feel about discussing your uncertainties with the group.
>
> It could be counterproductive to ask them to

participate in candid discussions that they infer should not be too candid.

The consultants are responsible for asking the top about their concerns (and if they had similar concerns with the subordinates, they should raise them in that group). They also have the responsibility to help either group be as clear as they can before they go into the meeting. However, it is not realistic for superiors or subordinates to guarantee ahead of time complete cooperation and no doubts. Again, the consultants should encourage discussion of these issues in the larger group.

The way in which clients deal with these issues is an important demonstration to members of the organization that the change program is not a fad that everyone is expected to go through but that individuals will have genuine choice about their degree of commitment. It also is a demonstration that the difficult issues involved in such a change program will be discussed openly and that all parties will be held responsible for the consequences of their choices.

Dealing with Differences Between Clients and Consultants

The way consultants deal with differences between themselves and their clients is important in the effective engagement of defensive routines. Four differences that consultants often experience with their clients are:

1. The degree of difficulties and problems in the organization,
2. The importance of dealing with behavioral issues,
3. The client's capacity to carry out something,
4. The consultants' competence to deal with behavioral issues.

The Degree of Difficulties and Problems in the Organization

For example, regarding this problem, the clients say, "Yes, what you say about our behavior may be right; but we really do this better than you say. This place is operating the way it ought to be."

A Consultant Suggested	Another Possibility Is
Well, that's really not what we heard when we interviewed individuals below you. They were able to give us illustrations [that perhaps we should now describe to you] of ways in which they felt things weren't working out as they saw fit. Now, maybe you can look at those data and decide that that's the way you want it to be. [But at a minimum, there seems to be a morale problem with the junior guys.]	This, of course, is not our conclusion based on the data that we obtained. It would help if you were to give us illustrations that lead you to believe that the issues we suggest exist do not. We would also be glad to share our illustrations.

The consultant's suggestion has several positive features. He states that he differs and proposes discussing the illustrations that have led him to his view. He indicates he would like to know how the clients interpret that data and that the choice is ultimately theirs. However, his first response to client disagreement is to defend his own view. This may contribute to a more polarized, win/lose interaction and suggests a rule about what not to say:

> When clients differ on the degree of difficulty, do not first present data to defend your view.

Notice that this rule does not say consultants should not defend their views, only that such defense should not be the first response. There is a second rule about what not to do that deals with the way consultants are likely to interpret client disagreement:

> Do not interpret differences as a necessary rejection of you but as an understandable defense of their sense of competence and stewardship.

Hence, rather than thinking "clients are resisting and inhibiting progress," consultants who follow this rule will think, "That's healthy. They are acting responsibly." If consultants are able to interpret differences in this way, they will find it easier to say what the interventionist suggests.

The key feature of the other suggestion is that the clients are asked to give illustrations to support their view rather than the consultants' giving more illustrations to support their view. This request communicates that it is not only the consultants who have a responsibility to illustrate their views but also the clients. Another feature is that the clients are involved in generating data relevant to understanding their problem. A third feature is that by illustrating their views, clients will have begun to act in ways that are more conducive to frame breaking and learning to learn in their organization. Finally, by looking at the illustrations clients provide, the consultants can learn what features of reality clients attend to and how they reason about what they see. This may lead to the point where the consultants can illustrate how clients are ignoring or distorting data. A rule that characterizes this intervention is:

> When clients and consultants differ on the degree of difficulties in the organization, involve the clients in generating information that illustrates their view, and encourage them to disconfirm the consultants' view.

If the consultant's diagnosis is right, then he or she should be able to show how the illustrations offered by clients are not disconfirmations. Indeed, it may be possible to show that the clients have unknowingly given illustrations that support the diagnosis. If so, then clients' sense of internal commitment to the diagnosis should increase. Alternatively, if clients do provide data that disconfirm the diagnosis, the consultants will have shown that they are genuinely committed to testing their views and to discovering the course of action that is in the clients' best interests.

The Importance of Dealing with Behavioral Issues

For example, the clients may say, "We asked you to look at the planning system. What we're getting into here is interesting, but it has very little to do with our planning system." The consultants could respond:

> You are correct. We came in fully expecting to work directly on your planning process. But our interviews and observations led us to conclude that there are several individual, group, and cultural factors that inhibit effective planning. Unless these are overcome they will inhibit the plan we or anyone else may suggest.

The rule here is:

> If clients question the relevance of behavioral issues and point out that the original contract was to work on technical issues, then confirm that the original issue was technical and explain how it is necessary to deal with the behavioral issues if the technical problems are to be solved.

If clients disagree that behavioral issues must be dealt with if the technical problems are to be solved, then other rules for dealing with differences between clients and consultants become relevant. For example, the consultants can ask clients to illustrate what leads them to believe that the technical problems can be solved even if the behavioral problems remain. The consultants can also offer their illustrations and ask the clients for their reactions.

The clients may say, "But do we *really* need to get into this behavioral stuff?" The consultants could say:

We are here to help you. We do not intend to press you to examine something you do not wish to examine. Yes, we believe these factors are important, and so do most of the people we interviewed. No, you will not be coerced by us to get into it.

This intervention responds to the clients' reluctance to get into issues that the consultants believe are important by joining rather than polarizing against the clients' reluctance while at the same time not backing down from what the consultants believe is right. This is accomplished by emphasizing that the choice of what to do remains with the clients, while consultants continue to take responsibility for stating what they believe is important. Hence, we can formulate a rule:

If clients express reluctance to deal with issues the consultants have said are important, then communicate that you intend to help, not coerce, and that the decision of what to do is up to the clients. Also communicate that you do believe these issues are important and that you will continue to take responsibility for stating what you believe to be in the clients' best interests while leaving the choice up to them.

Notice the sequence of the two parts of this intervention. When the clients express reluctance, the first response is that consultants intend to help and not to coerce and that the choice remains with the clients. This is followed by stating the consultants' advocacy position. If the first response were to advocate the consultants' position, there would be a risk of reinforcing the we/they polarization that is potential in the clients' expression of reluctance.

Clients' Capacity to Carry out Something

To illustrate this difference, for example, the clients say, "You tell us what to do, and we'll take responsibility for the next step. You give us the blueprint, and we'll take over." However, the consultant believes that clients cannot do this and that they are unaware that they cannot. This could be either a technical issue such as pricing a new product line or a behavioral issue such as dealing with conflict avoidance in the top management group.

A Consultant Suggested	**Another Possibility Is**
It is a natural reaction to want to get on with the program. And most particularly because you want to do it yourselves and show the junior guys you do not need help. And it is not in our interests to be around forever either.	I have two reactions to your wanting to implement this without help. First, it makes sense for you to be in charge and for us to leave as soon as possible. Second, in our experience this phase is difficult, and there is a role for an outsider.
We can tell you that this kind of stuff is really difficult to pull off. Without wishing to impose ourselves on you, there is almost certainly a role for the outsider.	However, let's explore your suggestion. For example, why don't we sit down and plan how you would manage the meeting? Let's design how you would begin, what you would say, what resistance, if any, you expect, and how would you deal with it? Then you may be better able to decide whether we may be needed.

The first paragraph of the right-hand column is a rewording of what the consultant said. The differences in the two versions involve rules about what not to say. The second paragraph is an addition that generates client involvement. This is a difference that involves rules about what more to say.

The biggest change in the first part is that no attribution is made (as the consultant did) that the clients' motivation is to show the junior guys they can do it without help. Two relevant heuristics are:

- Avoid attributions about motives.
- Avoid statements that, if they are to be accepted, hold attributions that must go untested.

An underlying rule is to state attributions in such a way that they can be tested. In the case of the attribution that clients are motivated to show the junior guys something, it is not clear that there are good reasons for stating and testing it. But the consultant is also attributing that clients are worried about the consultants staying around too long, and this is an important attribution to discuss. The difficulty is that both clients and consultants may have difficulty talking about this topic openly.

The rules about what to say that are illustrated in the right-hand column of the previous conversation may be stated in the following way. When clients assert they can do something that the consultant believes they cannot do, then:

1. Confirm what is valid in what the clients have said ("it makes sense for you to be in charge").
2. Advocate any view that may differ from what the clients have said that is relevant ("in our experience this phase is difficult, and there is a role for an outsider").
3. Inquire into the clients' view by asking them to illustrate what they assert they can produce.
4. Frame the task as a way of generating information so clients can make an informed choice rather than as a win/lose challenge to prove they can do what they claim they can do.

This fourth feature leads us back to seeing in the conversation the attributions, evaluations, and advocacies that have not been illustrated or open to test. For example, we see in the clients' statement the unillustrated and untested attribution that they have the competence to implement the consultant's plan. Also, the consultant advocates his or her view that implementation is difficult and there is a role for the outsider but does not illustrate this view or make it testable. The other design, in contrast, proposes a way to generate information to illustrate and test the competing attributions.

An important feature of the right-hand column design is that the clients are asked to illustrate what they would plan to say. This request will generate data that are relatively directly observable rather than more highly inferential statements like "We would encourage them to be open." Clients may be quite capable of giving an abstract description of what they plan to do but unable to implement their plan at the concrete level of what they would in reality do and say.

Asking clients to plan what they would say simultaneously involves them in planning what they can do about the problem and generates information about the degree to which they need help. Involvement is likely to increase their sense of internal commitment to doing something about the problem. Also, clients are likely to trust the information that is generated about the degree to which they need help because they are in control of what they say they would do. They will feel responsible for these data. If they discover they cannot produce effective interventions, they will become more committed to the diagnosis and to working with the consultants.

Consultants' Competence to Deal with Behavioral Issues

For example, the clients say:

> You have gone into some issues that I think are beyond your area of competence. You are not shrinks. You are strategy consultants. Quite frankly, you're a bit out of your depth here.

The consultants could say:

> You are correct. We do not see ourselves as shrinks. We are people who know how to integrate the peo-

ple and the organizational issues with the planning issues. When we feel we are out of our element, we promise to tell you.

For example, we have not asked individuals to analyze the causes of their preferences to avoid conflict. We are trying to solve it by relating it to the planning process.

If there are any times that you feel we are going in the other direction, let us know.

One way of thinking about the clients' challenge that helps consultants to respond is to place it on a ladder of inference. The attributions, "you are out of your depth" and "you are beyond your area of competence," are at a high level of inference. The lower-level inferences with which the client supports these attributions are, "you are not shrinks" and "you are strategy consultants." Hence, the consultant recognizes that the area of disagreement is in the reasoning by which the clients connect lower- and higher-level inferences. We can formulate the following rule:

When clients state a high level inference with which consultants differ and support it with lower-level inferences with which consultants agree, then:

1. Confirm the lower-level inference ("You are right. We do not see ourselves as shrinks").
2. Advocate the view that leads you to a different conclusion ("We are people who know how to integrate organizational and planning issues").
3. Illustrate what leads you to believe your view is valid and that tends to disconfirm the client's attribution ("For example, we have not asked individuals to analyze the causes of their preferences to avoid conflict").
4. Encourage clients to provide any data they see as disconfirming the consultant's view.

We can also think about this situation in a somewhat different way. Two meanings that can be inferred from the client's challenge are, "You are raising issues that would require the expertise of a psychiatrist to resolve, and you don't have that expertise," and "It would be inappropriate for this relationship to be one in which you act like shrinks." The response confirms the second meaning, thereby joining with the clients' definition of what is an appropriate relationship. At the same time, a definition of the appropriate relationship is proposed as one that integrates organizational and planning issues, thereby legitimizing discussion of the issues with which clients are uncomfortable.

Another way of thinking about this situation is to focus on the clients' concern that their consultants may not be competent. It is important that clients believe that they are in competent hands. The consultants' response reassures the clients that the consultants know what they are doing. Of course, it is critical that this reassuring message be valid. If clients get cues that the reassurance is empty, they will feel even more concerned. In this case the consultants' response is evidence of competence; that is, handling this challenge is an example of dealing with a difficult behavioral issue.

Helping Clients Deal with Threatening Issues

Dealing with threatening issues is a major challenge when engaging defensive routines. Four frequently encountered issues are:

1. How can consultants communicate information or get discussion on an issue that is both valid and one that clients may have difficulty talking about?
2. How can consultants discuss an issue in which there is a risk of violating the confidence of people or of harming people who might be involved?
3. When dealing with a CEO whom they believe avoids conflict, how can consultants both test their diagnosis and create conditions in which they can help the CEO learn to deal more openly with conflict?
4. How can consultants help clients discuss openly their responsibility for problems in the organization?

Communicating Information or Discussing Issues about which Clients May Have Difficulty Talking

Recall the previous case where the clients say, "You tell us what to do and we'll take responsibility for the next step." The consultant believes clients are thinking, "We don't like the idea that you are going to be around here for nine months" because they are especially concerned about consultants' trying to make a lot of money.

How can the consultants raise this issue? One way to initiate discussion is to ask forthrightly if this is a concern. For example, "Are you concerned that we might be here trying to create new business for ourselves?" This forthright approach communicates that the consultants are not going to avoid discussing sensitive issues. However, there are clients who might find the question both valid and embarrassing. It might be perceived as too direct. One approach consultants can take in this situation is to state the sentence in such a way that it can be looked at out there, as if on a screen, rather than directly to the people in the room. For example, "We find that clients are understandably worried that sometimes consultants appear as if they're just trying to pad their budgets or create business. Is this a problem for you?"

Clients might find it easier to respond honestly to the second approach. It is less personal because the issue is framed as something that often occurs in client-consultant relationships. This helps to legitimize the clients' concern. The legitimacy is reinforced by using the word *understandably.*

Also, with the more forthright question some clients might feel that a positive answer would mean, "you guys are doing something underhanded." The so-called screen approach reduces this danger both by generalizing to client-consultant relationships and by using the phrase *appear as if.* This is an easier attribution to confirm because the client can say the consultants appear as if they are padding without attributing that they are in fact padding or that they are intending to do so.

We can infer the following rules for implementing the screen approach:

Generalize from the particular episode in the room to "what often happens in these kinds of situations."

Communicate that it would be legitimate for the clients to have the concern that you attribute they may have.

Phrase the sentence in such a way that the clients can confirm it without attributing nasty motives.

Whether the consultant chooses the forthright approach or the screen approach, the point of the intervention is to create conditions in which clients can discuss the issue openly. This choice not only generates information to test the attributions consultants are making about this issue but also shows clients that the consultants are able and willing to help them discuss issues that are often treated as undiscussable.

Discussing Issues that may Violate Confidence or Harm People Who are Involved

The consultant is concerned about the value of getting two groups together who may not be willing to talk as openly as is necessary if the meeting is to be productive. In addition, the consultant fears saying this. It could get someone in trouble because it may involve telling superiors that their subordinates have told the consultant they hesitate to speak openly, or it could bring down the wrath of the superior on the consultant ("Not in my organization. All our people are open!").

For example, in the case of a conflict-avoiding top management group, the consultants hesitated to suggest a meeting between the top group and their subordinates. Based on their interviews with the subordinates, the consultants feared that they had been conditioned not to say things that the top might not want to hear. If, with encouragement from the consultants, the subordinates did say something controversial, the consultants feared that the top clients would give cues that this was unwelcome and that the subordinates would revert to withholding their views. If so, the meeting would be worse than useless because it would confirm subordinates' view that the wisest course was to say little and because their silence could be interpreted by the top as confirming the top's view that nothing was wrong. One way to deal with this issue is for the consultant to say:

> I would suggest the next step is to have a meeting with you and your subordinates so that we can get their reactions to the diagnosis and so that our project does not create a sense of we/they. However, one danger is that if the diagnosis we have been discussing is correct, subordinates may feel hesitant to speak. What do you believe is the danger they may not speak up? . . .
>
> I suggest that we take some time now for you to plan how you could encourage the discussion with the larger group. What would you say? What resistance would you expect, and how would you deal with it?

After giving reasons for meeting with the subordinates, the consultant states the attribution the consultants are making (that subordinates may not speak up) as an implication of the diagnosis that has already been discussed and asks the top for their assessment of the danger. If the clients say they see no danger, the consultants can explain how the diagnosis suggests the danger may exist, and they can also ask the clients to illustrate what leads them to believe subordinates feel free to speak openly. Hence, the attribution can be stated openly and discussed without saying, "Your subordinates have told us they hesitate to speak openly."

The second part of the intervention is to ask the top to plan what they will say to encourage discussion. This situation increases client involvement and generates information about the ability of the top to act in ways that encourage subordinates to speak freely. This might lead to the point where the consultants could illustrate to the top clients how they act in ways that contribute to the problem. In some cases, for example, if the top both says there is no danger of censorship and plans to act in ways the consultants believe would inhibit open discussion, the consultants might recommend the meeting not be held at this time. This would probably lead the clients to look more closely at illustrations of their behavior offered by consultants to justify the recommendation.

Discussing the danger that subordinates will not speak openly and planning how to deal with it serves to increase the awareness and discussability of the issue of self-censorship. If the top agrees there is a danger of self-censorship, they will be more alert to this possibility in the next meeting and will feel more responsible for reducing it. The role playing (when the top plans what to say) also creates an opportunity for the consultants to coach the clients on acting in ways that are unfamiliar. This would both increase the probability of having a useful meeting with the subordinates and begin to alter the behaviors that contribute to the problem.

Testing Diagnoses and Creating Conditions to Help Clients Deal Openly with Conflict

When the consultants discussed with the CEO what they thought was a pattern of conflict avoidance in the top management group, the CEO partially agreed, but he said that he had to act this way because of the relationship problems X and Y had with each other. He had concluded that although their relationships had become more amiable, it was unlikely that they would ever change. The consultants could say, "What experiences have you had that have led you to conclude that X and Y will not change?"

This question can provide insight into the reasoning processes the CEO uses to make these conclusions. His attribution that X and Y will never change may be part of the CEO's way of avoiding conflict. A relevant rule is:

> When someone makes an attribution about others that justifies his behaving in ways that contribute to the maintenance of a problem, ask him to illustrate what experiences have led him to make that attribution.

In another example, the consultants assumed that the CEO was thinking, "You may be right, but I don't know what to do with it." Two possible responses are:

1. What are your feelings and views about what we are saying?
2. Are you perhaps feeling that we may be correct and the question is what to do about it?

By raising the question the consultant tests his attribution and thereby models with the CEO how it can be done. The consultant also makes it less likely that he will get mired in the organizational culture and also avoid conflict. If the consultant avoids conflict when the issues are touchy, then he will have low credibility when he advises the CEO not to avoid the issues. A relevant rule is:

> When you are attributing that the other person is having a reaction to what you are saying and is not testing it, test the attribution by asking for his reactions.

The consultants had discussed with the CEO what they thought was a pattern of conflict avoidance in the top management group and had suggested a meeting with the CEO and his top reports. The CEO agreed but was somewhat apprehensive. The consultants now faced the problem of discussing candidly conflict avoidance with a group whose culture encourages conflict avoidance. In particular, it was likely that the CEO's automatic responses would be to act in ways that inhibited open discussion of conflictual issues. The consultant could say to the CEO while reviewing plans for the meeting:

> We would very much appreciate your help during the meeting in the following way. If some genuine differences arise among the participants, let us be responsible for handling them. It is our job to help them to see how they can overcome the problems that they identified. Another important task is to

help them see their responsibilities for changing their behavior.

If at any time you have views or concerns, we invite you to say so openly. We should be able to respond constructively. Indeed, it will give all of you an opportunity to see if we practice what we preach. It will give us the opportunity to show how, we believe, the differences can be dealt with more effectively.

The point of this intervention is to increase the likelihood that the CEO will allow the consultants to be in control of the meeting so that conflictual issues can be discussed more openly. In effect, the consultant is acting to bypass the defenses that inhibit discussing organizational problems. One of these problems is the very defense that is now being bypassed — namely, conflict avoidance. Hence, this is an example of a bypass intervention that increases the likelihood that defenses being bypassed can eventually be dealt with openly.

Asking the CEO to let the consultants be in control of the meeting is risky because the CEO may feel they are saying that he is incompetent. Several features of this intervention reduce the risk that the CEO will become defensive or apprehensive:

"It is our job to help them see how they can overcome the problems that they identified."	Defines being in control of the meeting as a legitimate responsibility of the consultants, and communicates they will focus on overcoming problems, not just surfacing them.
"Another important task is to help them see their responsibilities for changing their behavior."	Communicates that the consultants will not allow the meeting to become a complaint session that focuses only on the CEO's responsibility for problems.

We should be able to respond constructively. Indeed, it will give all of you an opportunity to see if we practice what we preach."	Defines their being in control as a test of the consultants' competence — hence, in the clients' best interests as a way of determining if the consultants can really be of help.

The features identified in the right-hand column could be reformulated as a rule. For example:

> When clients are apprehensive about allowing consultants to conduct a meeting to discuss conflictual issues openly, communicate that you intend to focus on the responsibilities of both subordinates and superiors.

An element of the screen approach is also illustrated in this case: The consultant says, "Help *them* see how *they* can overcome the problems that *they* identified" rather than "help *you* see how *you.* . . ." This approach distances the discussion from the CEO personally. Of course, it would not be appropriate to communicate that the consultants intend to avoid or prevent discussion of the CEO's role. Context is important here. In the case from which this illustration was taken, the consultants had communicated earlier in the conversation that they were focusing on the CEO's behavior as well as the behavior of his subordinates.

One of the interesting features of this intervention is that it is quite open on the one hand about the request to be in control and some reasons for it, but on the other hand it is not open about some of the attributions behind the request. For example, a key attribution was that the CEO's automatic responses would be to take control in ways that inhibited discussion of conflictual issues. The consultant did not recommend stating this attribution to the CEO. This is part of the bypass nature of the intervention. Stating this attribution might be upsetting to the CEO. At some point soon it will be necessary to deal with the CEO's being upset, but the consultant made the judgment that this was not the time. One consideration that contributed to this judgment was that the next meeting was likely to provide better data on the CEO's conflict avoidance. The consultants could use either illustrations provided by the top reports or the CEO's behavior in the meeting to illustrate the attribution. Hence, discussing the attribution was more likely to be useful in the next meeting than at the time the consultants and the CEO were reviewing plans for the meeting.

As we have seen in previous examples, consultants often automatically withhold attributions they are making. We have described instances in which it is preferable to state the attribution so that it can be discussed and tested, and we have described some rules for how to accomplish this. As this example illustrates, however, some attributions should not be immediately stated. It remains for future inquiry to identify rules for determining when attributions should be temporarily withheld.

Discussing Clients' Responsibility for Problems in the Organization

For example, the consultants wrote a report that focused on conflict avoidance issues, especially those created at the top. The top accepted the findings and agreed to a meeting with the larger management group. The consultants expected that the subordinates would like the report, but the top might feel that the consultants were focusing only on their actions. After the feedback of the results and the expected positive discussion, the consultants could say: "Okay, we must now fill in an important gap. The question is How do the executive and subordinates intentionally or unintentionally reinforce the features we have just described?"

This intervention will help both the consultants to produce a more complete analysis and the top executives to feel that they are not the only ones being held responsible. Also, asking subordinates to look at the way they may collude to reinforce the superiors' counterproductive behavior will make it easier for them to discuss why they feel forced to collude. It is important to identify the interactive responsibilities of all parties involved because only then can the consultants help clients to surface and deal with the dilemmas and binds they experience.

Relevant rules include the following:

> Do not focus only on the counterproductive actions
> of one set of actors.
>
> When clients identify counterproductive pat-
> terns in the actions of one set of actors, ask them
> to identify how others intentionally or unintention-
> ally reinforce these patterns.

We typically are aware of the counterproductive features of the actions of others and are unaware of those features of our own actions. If we become more aware of our contribution to the difficulties, we will both feel more responsible for doing something to improve matters and more tolerant of the errors of others. A related rule is:

> When inquiring into error, communicate that you
> do not make the attribution that people somehow
> intend to make errors or that they have nasty
> motives.

It is unlikely that counterproductive behavior is primarily caused by nasty motives, so this rule is partially aimed at increasing accuracy. At the same time, we commonly attribute that motives are the problem, and such attributions feed cycles of blame and defensiveness. Empathizing with and making explicit the good intentions of all parties can contribute to mutual understanding of the dilemmas we experience and to more useful discussion of corrective strategies.

CONCLUSION

In the relationships where the defensive routines are addressed, the clients, even those who are conflict avoiders, often choose to repeat the feedback sessions with their immediate reports. It is at this point that new problems arise. Subordinates may appear to discuss diagnoses more easily than to plan action steps because they may have differences with their superiors and are hesitant to express them. We now have a new condition of threat. The rules that we have just described to deal with threat would apply in this case.

Once the differences are worked through, then this enlarged group could begin to redesign the planning process. The consultants could provide their views, but the more important value added would be to help the clients redesign the process. One way to begin this task is to have the clients select a difficult and important strategic question. The clients and consultants could work jointly on formulating a new strategy. Periodically, they could reflect on their experience to redesign the planning process. The redesign would be examined by this group and other relevant players for possible errors and gaps. Finally, the consultants may help the clients generate a process by which the new planning process is monitored so they can redesign it as conditions warrant.

eight

UPPING THE ANTE

In this chapter, I tell the story of how the senior consultant of a team, skilled in dealing with technical planning issues and defensive routines, was able to help a group begin to examine undiscussable routines that had formed around an important technical issue. The story is told in three phases. The first one will be familiar to line executives and to planning professionals because it is the story of the first feedback session. The purpose was not simply to inform the clients but also to engage them in questioning, reinterpreting, and if necessary, redesigning their work activities. This, in turn, might facilitate the second purpose: to create a culture within the top group to question themselves, to discuss any defensive routines, and eventually to ask tough questions of any new strategic plan.

In the second phase, we see how the consultant, with the help of the clients, makes explicit some important business errors. While exploring the business errors, the consultant was able to help the clients express some of their fears. Once the clients expressed their fears, the consultant took the next step, which was to ask, in effect, what factors exist in this group or in the organization that inhibited the full discussion of the fears about the business decision. This leads to phase three in which the CEO was identified as one factor and, in turn, the immediate reports were also identified as an important factor.

By the end of the three phases, the consultant has helped, using an incremental process of inquiry, to surface business errors and defensive routines that had led to errors and further defensive routines that had helped to cover up the errors. The story ends with the clients and consultant ready to deal with the technical issues and defensive routines. The clients are positioned to go beyond detecting and correcting business errors and defensive routines. They are positioned to learn how to detect and correct errors, meaning they, as individuals and as an organization, would have been helped to learn how to learn and perform more effectively.

THE FIRST FEEDBACK SESSION

The case team had been scheduled to meet with top management for two hours for the first feedback session. The consultant in charge was interested in finding ways to engage organizational defensive routines that inhibited effective decision making as well as formulation and implementation of planning.

Although he had received acknowledgment from the clients that learning to learn was important, the consultant doubted that they knew the import of their agreement. He believed that he would have to wait to find the opportunities to move into the less traditional forms of consulting. The strategy may sound like easing in, but it is not like the easing-in processes discussed in Chapters 2 and 3. Easing in has as its intention to remain within the defensive routines including the defensive routines that cover up the defensive routines. In this case the consultant will wait for the opportunity to engage the defensive routines. When he finds one, he will make explicit what he is doing. Finally, he will encourage the clients to confront him on his actions, thereby encouraging them to choose the type of intervention they would prefer. The consultant does not place himself or the client in the position where an either/or choice has to be made. He also does not attempt to coerce the clients into the learning-to-learn mode if they do not prefer such consulting advice.

The consultant was, at that time, a relative beginner in producing interventions that engage defensive routines. Hence he not only moved slowly but also strove to provide choice to the client to make himself confrontable so he could reduce the possibility that he would make irretrievable errors.

The session began with a presentation that told a straightforward story. It included the following:

1. Description of some of the key economic facts of the clients' business (six slides).
2. Acknowledgment that the clients have improved features of the business and that they (clients) saw a need for improvement in the base business as well as adding new business.
3. Description of the consultant's view of the base business as inferred from client data, followed by identification of inconsistencies and weaknesses that existed in the business plans. The inconsistencies and weaknesses selected were those that the consultants believed were nontrivial, that did not require the clients to make complicated inferences from the data, and that therefore were easily recognizable and confirmable (or disconfirmable) by the clients.
4. Recapitulation of the improvements the clients expected to make in their new business, improvements that the consultants acknowledged were not going to be easy to make.
5. Identification of the next steps to be taken by the case team.

The theory of help involved in such a sequence is as follows:

1. Begin with data that the client can easily confirm as valid. This will communicate that the consultants understand their business and how to communicate such understanding.
2. The very act of organizing six slides to capture important features of the essence of the business will communicate to the clients that the consultant not only understands the business

but also can select the key features of it and present them in only a few slides.

3. The six slides also should give the clients insight into the consultant's premises and conclusions.
4. Communicate the message in increments the clients can manage but that challenge their actions and reasoning processes.
5. After telling the story in a way the clients recognize, begin to show implications that are not so obvious precisely because of the way the clients reason about their problems.

The discussion began with the clients asking for insights into the problems illustrated by the first two slides. A few inquiries were related to understanding the slides. The majority of questions explored the meanings of the slides or were what-if exercises based on the slides.

The consultants were not able to answer all the questions asked of them during the meeting. When they admitted they could not answer a particular question, they also asked if others had any ideas on how to answer the question. Often the clients were unable to suggest an answer. The consultants' "ignorance" was legitimized (in the clients' eyes) whenever the clients had no response. There was perhaps another, subtler consequence. The consultants and the clients probably know that an "I don't know" answer cannot be used frequently without loss of credibility. Hence, using one of these few time-outs means that the consultants have confidence that they will not be placed in such a situation frequently and that they can add value for the client.

The clients soon began to educate each other as they commented on features of the slides. This, as we shall see, creates a process where the consultants not only can make their distinctive contributions but also can minimize the we/they distinction that frequently occurs under these conditions.

Client 2: The decision to collaborate to make Product X was our response to a compet-

The clients are providing important information about decisions they appear to have

itive tactic taken by our competitors.

Client 3: Oh, okay, a shotgun wedding.

Client 4: Yuh, that was the worst goddamn decision that . . . made.

questioned. This may be new information to some or it may not, but it is now being discussed publicly and jointly.

The consultant could have moved the clients toward engaging potential defensive routines by asking if Client 4 felt that way at the time of the decision. If so, what prevented him from saying something? If he did, what was the reaction? The consultant decided against this action because he felt it was too early in the session. This is a judgment call. Such a decision could be made differently by another consultant or by the same consultant under different conditions. The point to be made is that the consultant also can choose when to intervene to engage.

Client 2: I can't understand why the market has fallen away on one of our most highly leveraged products.

Client 1: In other words, the consultant's slide shows that if we took Product A out of the whole equation, we wouldn't have that tremendous profitability falloff. . . . we weren't all that profitable to begin with back in the old days.

Client 5: They [competitors] took part of our market that we had. . . . they moved right in on that.

The clients continue to have dialogue with each other and with the consultants about their problems.

Client 2: Are we saying the line would have been up if it hadn't been for the Product A? The same as the rest?

Client 4: No, but it wouldn't have shown that kind of deterioration. . . .

Client 2: I don't think that's quite correct. [Explains.]

Client 3: I have a different view. [Explains.]

Client 1: That's not *our* definition of our business. . . .

The discussion moves from educating each other to questioning each other. Such questioning can be encouraged to build a climate of inquiry that could lead to engagement of the defensive routines that are related to these issues.

Client 3 educates Client 1 and others about the meaning the consultants intended. Acting as an interpreter implies understanding of and agreement with the slides, as well as a commitment to make them helpful to the group.

The discussion continued, with different clients explaining and justifying their own or their organization's policies and performance. This occurred even though the consultants had neither openly questioned or attacked the clients nor presented slides to evaluate the clients' performance.

Another consequence of the clients' educating each other about the meaning of the consultants' slides is that it helps to create internal commitment to the slide information. For example, when one client said to another, "I think that what they are *really* saying is . . ." he is saying at a minimum that he finds the ideas worth interpreting to others to make sure they are understood. Later on, as we shall see, clients use the consultants' slides to discuss openly some of the errors their company has produced to date.

Thus, we have a multilevel discussion going on: the consultants are communicating their ideas, and the clients are describing and justifying their actions, thereby confirming the validity of the consultants' ideas and communicating their concern and sense of responsibility to each other.

These consequences are also important for developing a strong steering committee to deal with the more difficult challenges to come as well as to help to integrate the consultants into the group. The clients can educate and disagree with each other without reinforcing the we/they relationship with the consultants that often exists at the outset.

About a third of the way through the presentation, the clients were shown slides that contained embarrassing issues about their performance. By now the climate had been created in the meeting so that the clients could make these issues explicit, and they did so. For example, the clients questioned their pricing and distribution policies.

Client 5: Let me open up Pandora's box. If we start looking back and go all the way forward in a reasonable amount of detail, its important, I think [to realize the mistake that we may have made in distribution].

Client 5 is apparently raising the ante of risky subjects that can be discussed.

Consultant 2: [Chuckles] Good point!

Consultant 1: All right. But what we really saw on this chart is [explains].

Consultant 2: Consultant 1, there's one point I guess I'd like to add, . . . if I can just step back a minute from what we've been talking about as to one of the reasons why we go about things this way.

Consultant reminds the clients that they have been hired to think differently from the clients but that they will do so with the goal of being helpful to the clients.

Our understanding is that the one thing you didn't hire us for is to come in and think the way you folks do. On the other hand, the one thing you did hire us for is to come in and be effective for you and with you in terms of doing things at the end, in terms of creative solutions. . . .

Consultant 1: And we weren't making any argument on what you should do. What we were observing is [the following relationship between the products in two different market segments]. Therefore, margin is the major determinant of profitability of either segment. And that, as we go through these, leads us more and more to say we really need to look at that margin issue because there may not be that much — although there are some things — that we can do with below-the-line costs which are in fact a much smaller nut than all the costs.

Does that make sense from your point of view?

Client 3: Essentially what is underlying your presentation this morning seems to me, to simplify it, product line management.

The consultant follows up the statement of difference in thinking with the promise that all ideas will be thoroughly discussed and understood. Progress will be a function of joint understanding and choice rather than by razzle-dazzle presentations.

Consultant describes what he believes to be some important factors, suggests where more analysis and discussion may be necessary, and encourages questioning of his views.

Consultant 2: To a great extent.

Client 3: All of this discussion is [slows down speech] product line management.

Consultant 2: It also demonstrates the way we begin to reason through a problem:
Take the basic data and unfold it.
See what the economics tell us about the questions we really ought to study.
Reason step by step.

Consultant again identifies that their reasoning processes may be different, that they are discussable, and that they are being used in the clients' interest.

Client 3: Very good.

Client 4: Makes sense.

Client 6: Somewhere along the line, you will get at the issue of what are the practicalities of product line management.

Consultant 2: Absolutely. I'd like to amplify a bit. These are major issues. We are coming more and more to understand the business. We also understand better why you asked the question you did originally but about which we had expressed some doubts.

Expresses view that consultants now better understand the client's early framing of the problem and see its validity from their view. Consultants commit themselves to exploring these issues.

One of the things that we'll be doing is getting information on those questions but focusing on key strategy sessions. As we get deeper into this [we'd like to bring in other members of the team].

Second, this is the first meeting where we have been behaving in our usual way, which is to do some [empirical] work, try to organize our logic and go over it with you, let you hear us, ask any questions you wish. [We'll send follow-up copies.]

A question I wish to raise is, is this process a comfortable process for you folks? Are there changes that you would like us to make that would make it more effective or more comfortable in the future, from your point of view?

Client 1: I think it is comfortable. It would be a little helpful when you go through one of these things again if you give us at the outset what it is that you are trying to prove rather than us trying to guess it.

Consultant 1: Yes.

Client 1: It will stop a lot of nitty-gritty questions.

The consultant changes subjects for a moment to focus on the way the discussion has been going so far as well as the intended design for such sessions.

FIGURE 8.1 *The Ladder of Inference in this Case*

4	The clients' plan imposed on the base and new business,
3	Inferences regarding improvements needed in base and new business,
2	Inferences as to the economic meaning of the data,
1	Data that clients define as basic to the business.

Summary and Conclusions

The first feedback session presented substantive information and initiated the executives to a more participative implementation process. The design of the presentation as well as part of the discussion followed the reasoning found in the ladder of inference (see Figure 8.1). The consultants began with six slides of data that were basic to the business (1). Next they made explicit the economic meaning of the data (2). Then they identified the improvements that the clients defined for the base and the new business (3). The final slides described key features of the clients' plans and policies (4).

Simultaneously, and this point is crucial, the consultants identified important inconsistencies and gaps at any of the four levels. The consultants' contribution was not only to feed back information that the clients knew but also to present it in a different form. They also raised important questions about the effectiveness of the clients' reasoning processes at each of the four levels in the ladder.

Using the clients' reasoning processes to design the presentation and to guide the discussion helped make it possible for the clients to ask meaningful questions, to educate each other, to admit to errors, to begin to question each other, and to perform mini thought experiments. These conditions also encouraged the clients to become more proactive in their responses and to begin to experience some degree of success in dealing with the problem. The consultants were able to make their contributions and at the same time to minimize the probability of a we/they relationship and the mystery-mastery tone that occurs when consultants, acting as experts, tell the clients what to do.

THE SECOND FEEDBACK SESSION

About six weeks later, the second feedback session began with the consultants bringing the client steering committee up to date on their activities. The consultants also stated what they hoped to accomplish during the session. Briefly, the opening presentation included the following messages:

1. This is a progress report.
2. We want to communicate what we are learning and get your reactions. We do not intend to state final conclusions.
3. We are exploring which products can be made more profitable. We are digging deeply into factors such as the determinants of margin, production costs, marketing expenditures, price realizations, and profitability by segment and by customer. We have some thoughts on these matters that we would like to explore with you.
4. We want to tell you what we have learned from the interviews about questions such as what our customers value us for. What is the basic drawing card for customers?
5. We want to go over the number, sample of customers, and so forth of the in-depth interviews.

Then the consultant asked the clients about the so-called salesman issue, which he believed was controversial:

Consultant 1: I guess I would think the types of things — let's just move on to another issue. These are things we've heard. . . . do they surprise you in any way? [Silence]
  This is about the sales force. [Someone says he can't see the quote so Consultant 1 reads it aloud — about the sales force "wearing three-piece suits and never leaving their paneled offices."]

Client 1: Do they not leave their paneled offices? First of all, I'm not sure their offices are paneled but I would *hope* they leave their offices! I don't know what in the hell they're going to do in their offices.

Client 3: I think what he's saying is . . . we're not out in the field that much, we're not in touch with all the responsibilities we have. . . . what I think they're saying is that "You guys are not as specialized in the marketplace as some of your competitors." Is that what they're saying?

Consultant 1: They're saying the others [competitors] are in here, they can help me directly, they know their product lines, they see me frequently and provide me great assistance, they know more about their product line than I do.

Consultant 2: I think your comment is a fair one also in that, yes, Consultant 1's summary of what might lead to that comment is a fair description of the situation. On the other hand, one of the things we also have to deal with is, that's the way a guy chose to put it. He said, in effect, "My summary of the way it is is 'the three-piece-suit guys don't leave their offices.' " And that says that even though that individual may or may not understand many of the things Consultant 1 said, his visceral reaction is to [state it in a way] which is a little more than you'd like to hear.

[The animated discussion continued.]

Client 3: The key other issue is that we don't have a career market guy. The rest of the market have career-oriented people. That's their job, that's where they're going to go, and that's where their growth is. All the young people we've got out there in three-button breasted suits want to be president [of our company]. A whole different category of people.

Client 2: As a result, we generally conclude that they're doing a lousy job.

Client 5: I don't think that.

Client 3: No, I wouldn't say they were doing a lousy job. I think that. . . .

Consultant 1: Can I intervene for just a second? When Client 2 said, "As a result, in this respect, they're doing a lousy job," what did you think he meant by that?

Client 5: Not doing their work. Not working hard, not doing their job.

Client 3: No, he didn't mean that. [Further discussion on what Client 2 meant. The differences in view begin to surface more forcefully.]

Consultant 1's intervention helped Client 3 and others check out their attributions about Client 2. In so doing, he illustrated the importance of testing attributions and at the same time signaled the group that he will intervene whenever he believes he can help them produce a more effective problem-solving process. It probably would have been counterproductive for the consultant to have interrupted, at this point, the substantive discussion to consider in more detail the group's problem-solving processes. The consultant can keep track of these interventions and develop a map of the defensive routines he identifies. At the end of the session (if there is time), or at another session (where time is made available), he can open up this new dimension. If the clients want to discuss it, that is value added. If they do not, it places the consultant in a position where he can predict some of the problems the group will have in implementing suggestions that contain difficult or threatening material.

The clients dig deeper into their views of their customers and compare them with what the consultants report. For example, after a lively discussion about dealers, Client 2 said, "Well, it has been our view that . . . , yet our dealers say [this]." Several people say, "No, no, that is not what the dealers are saying."

Client 2: Huh? Well, I say that is our perception here. It is different from what [they've reported].

Client 4: There is a way to explain the difference. [He does so.]

Then several people disagree with the explanation, and the discussion continues. The consultants let it go on until they have heard several points that should be highlighted. Consultant 1 then intervened. He began by summarizing several of the points already made so he could coordinate and build a more cohesive group.

Consultant 1: Isn't it fair to say that there are two separate questions operating here? One is, among those dealers that are [such a kind], what is it they say their business mix is?

The second question, which I think is one that we've talked about a number of times in this room is, are the dealers in the aggregate going to be an effective channel for reaching the X market? To which the answer I think is — and I don't think we've turned up anything to contradict this — that for most dealers, decidedly no. [He continues and repeats his interest in their views. Agreement is expressed by the clients.]

Next came a lively discussion among the executives about the quality of the customers they serve. The data presented by the consultants suggested that many of the customers held a second-rate status in the company. The second-rate status of many of their customers appeared to be an issue that was, up until this time, an undiscussable issue with the total group. The consultants made it discussable. In effect, the dynamics were:

- We have made the second-rate status of our customers a topic that is not discussable in this group.
- You (consultants) have violated the norm (because you had to do so in order to meet your responsibility).
- We can hold you responsible for violating the norm without condemning you. To condemn you would be tantamount to punishing you for performing the tasks we are paying you to accomplish.
- This frees us to behave responsibly and to discuss the undiscussable.

The discussion reached a peak when Client 2 said, "This whole exercise, this whole discussion, raises questions about whether we even ought to be in this Z business at all." The discussion continued, with the consultants rewarding the difficult, confronting questions (including those related to their presentation) by saying "Good" or "That is an important question." At other times, the consultants acted as group helpers, making sure the group members understood each other. Also, they strove to surface what may be important messages made tacitly by the clients, messages it may be difficult for them to state explicitly. For example:

Consultant 1: Is there an implication that you were drawing from that [addresses question to client]?

The consultants continued to present data that indicated that it was unlikely the clients would ever be profitable in the Z market. The more data they presented, the more the clients questioned the meaning of the data. Since the consultants were able to answer their questions, it became more and more apparent that being in the Z market was an error. The consultant then made an intervention that could get at some important defensive routines that existed within this top management group.

Consultant 2: A while back, when we first put up some of this stuff on Z, you said at one point, "Something's happening here," and everybody laughed and so forth. And you said, "Yuh, that sort of occurred," and so forth. I wasn't sure what all that meant. Let me tell you a question that went through my mind . . . that apparently the people in the room were aware of the fact that, given the kinds of discounts that you have to give to get business, the business was going to look pretty bad. Would I be correct in that? Was it a surprise that it was going to look bad?

The clients responded first by explaining their laughter. In doing so, they made public the difficulties they were having with each other in discussing the issue.

Client 3: That surprised us all right.

Client 1: I think we would have known there would be a loss.

Client 2: The reason I think the laugh came, and the discussion, was that we had just gone through an exercise to reduce, or do away with, the price allowance. We in sales were less willing to give that up. And the thing that hasn't been said here is, when you give that up, how much other business goes with it?

Client 3: Yeah, we just went through that exercise.

Client 5: We kind of postponed the decision, and Client 2 has asked for it now, so that's why I kind of laughed.

Client 4: Well, we didn't postpone the decision totally.

Client 1: We didn't go all the way.

Consultant 2: Okay, I guess what I was wondering was . . . given the magnitudes of the kinds of numbers we're talking about here, it looks like it may be very difficult to make the business a profitable business. And I guess what I was wondering therefore was, what is it that would prevent you from in fact closing in on the business and saying, "Let's build a case internally among ourselves as to whether or not we should get out of the business." Is there anything that would prevent that?

A very lively discussion followed about the way decisions were made in the firm and the impact of the culture upon the decision-making process. The consultant continued the explanation:

Consultant 2: Yes, and to some extent the culture that permits a management group to simultaneously have two things going on . . . : one is an urgent desire to improve profitability and yet that not getting readily translated into programs to identify the largest offending items, of this sort anyway, and then be able to close on them more rapidly. I find some inconsistency in that. What are your reactions?

Client 4: We already know where we've got trouble with product lines. What we need to sort out is the fear we have of losing business because we get out of these areas where we have. . . . where you can help us is to find a way to equate that possible loss. We have not found a good way yet. It's a cloudy area. It's a subjective area.

Consultant 2: So the question being, therefore, to what extent am I pulling out a crucial element and things can come tumbling down?

Client 4: Exactly. That's our worry. And we don't have a good way of quantifying that.

Consultant 2: Okay, let me make the distinction then. If I pulled something, and things collapsed, we'd be very concerned about that. But if I removed something, and if as a result I still have what we need.

Client 1: If we could see that, we could make those decisions a lot easier.

Consultant 2: That's what I'm hoping for, yes.

Upping the ante as to what the client will discuss publicly also increases the consultants' vulnerability. First, the clients may feel freer to criticize the consultants' ideas. Second, they may hold the consultants responsible if the discussion becomes heated and counterproductive. The consultants should encourage their criticism because constructive confrontation of their ideas can lead to a more effective diagnosis and resolution. The consultants can defuse the criticism by stating at the outset that, as the level of candor increases incrementally, it will be the responsibility of the group (including the consultants) to identify workable limits.

Client 2: I think our fear all along has been that we'll take out this little sore spot here, and everything collapses. And to what extent does that hurt us?

Consultant 2: Okay. Now that's helpful, and I think as we go forward now and talk about some other things, we may want to come back to that, either today or at some other meeting . . . these kinds of questions.

Summary and Conclusions

The basic processes of problem solving that were begun during the first session were continued (and at times, slightly modified) during the second session while the following new ones were added:

1. Seeking and testing for inconsistencies in the clients' reasoning, for gaps in their arguments, and for any anomalies in the clients' positions that they took for granted.
2. Seeking "how" explanations for identified inconsistencies and gaps. By "how" explanations, I mean the consultants sought to identify the mechanisms and actions by which events occurred. What led to the inconsistency or gap? What were the factors that kept the inconsistencies and gaps going once they were known to the clients? "How" explanations focus the clients on describing events and actions, whereas "why" explanations usually focus on espoused theories.
3. Conducting thought experiments of the what-is variety.
4. Clueing in on any subjects that the clients considered important but that they appeared to find undiscussable.

These processes were utilized for economic and behavioral issues, with a larger emphasis on the behavioral (organizational).

Making such interventions may make the clients feel vulnerable because they are talking about issues that have existed for years but probably have not been discussed with any openness. This vulnerability is important if the clients are to be motivated to correct major factors that prevent effective decision making, lead to organizational rigidity, and produce a culture that sanctions such features.

Acting in ways that may make a client vulnerable also runs the risk of making the client defensive and making the consultant (and the case) vulnerable. This does not mean that the consultants should not act forthrightly, however; to fail to do so would be to subsidize the defenses of the client. And those are the very defenses that may have to be overcome if genuine implementation is to occur. Conversely, neither does it mean pressing vulnerability to the point of rejection. Consultant 1 pressed carefully. He moved incrementally, and with every attempt, he obtained the clients' reactions.

In another case, some of the clients became anxious about such actions, and the consultant's response was, in effect:

- I do not intend to upset people.
- I am trying to identify the factors that have created difficulties so that they can be genuinely reduced and corrected.
- I am trying to create the proper culture for implementing the new program. I am trying not to be constrained by your reasoning because, if I am, you would in effect be paying me to think like you.
- I will not knowingly act to harm or to upset anyone or to behave insensitively. If and when you believe that I am going a bit too far or too fast, please let me know. Needless to say, I too, will be aware of those limits.

If handled carefully, this approach adds another dimension of choice for the consultant and for the client. Is it risky? Probably no more than any other approach, but it may be required if strategy professionals are to become leaders in implementation.

UPPING THE ANTE EVEN MORE

Several weeks later a third session was held with the top group. During that session the consultants discussed a problem that they had been told was touchy, especially with the CEO. The consultant attempted to design with the subordinates a way to make the subject discussable. They resisted doing so, saying that if it were to be brought up, the consultant would have to take responsibility for doing so.

The consultant decided to create the conditions where the subject could be surfaced. When it seemed appropriate, the consultant raised the issue as follows:

Consultant: It was very important for us to have this discussion with this group because a lot of people raised with us the possibility that it couldn't be discussed.

CEO: Why can't it be discussed?

Consultant: I do not know the answer to that question. I can tell you what I have heard. Some individuals reported that a decision had been made and that you were particularly committed to go in that direction.

CEO: Now wait a minute, the decision to do X didn't come from me. It came from marketing. It was supported by everybody in this room.

Consultant: Well, I would differ with that. My understanding. . . .

Here is a difficult task. The consultant is trying to make discussable an issue that was undiscussable, and he knew many in the client group would not support him. He began the intervention by reporting that the CEO was viewed as committed to do X. This placed the consultant in the role of communicating for others what they had not communicated to the CEO. Another strategy would be to ask the CEO's views to create an opportunity for others to comment. If they chose to do so, then the CEO would hear directly from his immediate reports. If they chose not to do so, the consultant would have evidence of how difficult or touchy the situation may be for the subordinates. The following might produce some results:

Consultant: I do not understand the situation fully. All I have is secondhand data. May I ask what was your position about decision X? How would you react to a re-examination of the way it was made or to our suggesting some new approach to the problem?

If the CEO answered that he was quite willing to examine new approaches, the consultant could have then presented his views. In addition, he could have taken the opportunity to use decision X as an example of how individuals hold different views about the members' interest to change their minds. The problem is framed as exploring more than one individual's views and the intention is to help the group examine its decision-making processes. Returning to what actually happened:

CEO: [Turning to the group] Speak. They're all here. Who did not support it?

Client 1: Well it was a split house, but I agree it was part of the plan.

Client 2: I supported the position once it was taken, but from my view it never made sense to me.

The consultant could have taken this opportunity to examine the group processes (not simply the attributions made about the CEO) by asking:

Consultant: [To Client 1] When it is a split house, how is the decision handled? How are differences explored and resolved? [To Client 2] Do you recall what was said that led you to believe that it was difficult for you to express your views, or if you did, what led to the fact that they were rejected?

Returning to what actually happened:

CEO: We do everything here by consensus. [It was discussed fully.]

Consultant: Let me spend one more minute on why I say there may be a question about discussability. Not speaking about the people in this room but for those below this group. They experience the decision process as follows: [He describes their views]. Therefore, they told me to be careful about examining this decision.

CEO: Somebody has to make a decision. I am ready to make it. It is very rare when I will overrule the majority. I do not think I overruled the majority.

Consultant: That's fine. [I would like to explore how this group] can communicate to the people below that even though a decision was made, if new information becomes available, it should be brought up. No decision is unexaminable. . . .

Client 3: The decision was made as the consultant says. It appears that some people at the lower levels felt a dictum was reached and there was no sense in discussing it.

CEO: But didn't your organization support the decision?

Client 3: Yes, but that isn't the issue.

Client 4: They [people below] are saying this after the decision was made.

CEO: In my opinion, there are no issues that are ever closed.

Consultant: That is an important statement. How do we communicate it to others?

CEO: You know if these issues were closed, you would never be hired.

Consultant: I realize that but there are people [below] who wonder why we were hired.

CEO: It's not costing us a small amount of money to hire you. We did this because we are interested in progress.

Consultant: And it is because we believe that is so that I raised it at this meeting. [He could have added "I raised the issue not because I doubted your or the group members' commitment to learning. It is because the people at the lower levels hold a different view in spite of the commitment here to reopen the issue that indicated to me something that should be explored."]

Client 2: Before we leave this, I would like to say that I believe the consultant has exaggerated the differences. I think you have interpreted a higher degree of conflict in the consensus of opinion than really is the case.

Consultant: How did others hear me?

Client 5: [No, the consultant is not exaggerating. For example, after describing it to . . . group] everybody's reaction was that the decision was a bad one.

CEO: [What do you mean by] everybody?

Client 2: I mean everyone [enumerates]. . . .

Consultant: [I would like you to consider that a game is played, one that is common in many large organizations.] The chain of command says be very careful about the way in which you disagree with your boss. If you were supporting a decision that was made, do not be seen as fighting it [once it is made].

The CEO continued to re-examine the decision-making process. The more he questioned the participants, the clearer it became that the consultant had diagnosed accurately some gaps in the process of consensus (as it was called in that organization).

Consultant: Let me repeat. Among all the people who said that the decision was wrong, they could cite the logic behind it. They were not unfamiliar with the bases of the decision. What they were saying was that given their gut understanding of the market, the decision would probably not work. . . .
    It is not our intention to identify individuals. But if you believe that we are representing fairly the groups below, then it says that the expectations that you as senior managers have for the way your organization operates are different from the expectations the junior people have. [If this is correct, it is worthwhile to examine it because] you may end up getting less good analysis, less good decision, and less good implementation.

CEO: I appreciate your concern. That is why I am also concerned. [I can understand it if you tell me people far away from here do not agree.] What bothers me is that senior people here may have these difficulties. . . .
    I think you are indicting our top managers.

Consultant: I think it would be unfair to indict any one group. I'm indicting the culture.

CEO: Okay. And that bothers me. . . . I can understand some people are opposed to it. What I cannot understand is that the people who recommended it, in the first place, are opposed to it.
    I think this is the most critical thing that you've

come up with so far . . . this bothers me. And if you are correct, I would rather turn our attention to that area because it will hurt us more than anything we are doing.

Consultant: I agree.

CEO: This comes as a shock to me. I frankly think that you may be overstressing. . . . I hope you are. It is hard for me to accept that it is true.

Consultant: I do not think that we are overstressing it. Nor do I think that we have to stop the analytical work to focus on this issue. It will be possible to work on both.

CEO: Fine. But I think that we need to address this issue very carefully. . . .

What we need is for you to prove this to us.

Consultant: What I would like is to design a way that you can prove it to yourselves.

CEO: Fine, you can certainly see that we are concerned. . . .

[Turning to his group]: I'm asking, is there any issue that anybody feels he cannot discuss with me?

The consultant intervened to say that he felt the way the question was asked might make it difficult for the individuals to answer it. We now have an illustration of a triple bypass. The consultant has helped the group to examine some of the organizational and some of the group's defensive routines. But he has not had an opportunity to help the clients examine their theories in use. Hence, when the CEO attempted to learn more from his group, he asked the question in a way that might inhibit the discussion. The consultant then focused on this possible impact.

The meeting turned to the remaining part of the technical agenda. After the meeting, the CEO invited the consultant to lunch. He repeated that the issue the consultant had raised was an important one and that he wanted the consultant to explore it further with the group.

nine

COMPETENCIES AND SKILLS REQUIRED FOR PREVENTING AND REDUCING DEFENSIVE ROUTINES

In the previous chapters we described consultants who attempted to engage defensive routines in order to provide better substantive solutions to formulate and implement strategy and to help organizations become more effective at learning. We described the rules that should be used if consultants were to act as we recommended. These rules represent the reasoning behind skillful action. When we produce the rules, then we will be acting skillfully.

Examples of the rules were:

Advocate your position as forthrightly as you can, but do so in a way that encourages others to question it.

Whenever someone states an evaluation or attribution about you that you do not agree with, ask for the data that he or she used to develop the evaluation or attribution.

Whenever you make an evaluation or attribution about others, illustrate it with the data you used to build your case and test its validity with the other.

If you act in ways that appear to upset others, apologize for upsetting them, assure them that this was not your intention (if that is the case), and state what you intended to do and the reasoning behind it.

If others' actions upset you, ask for the reasoning behind the actions so you understand their intentions.

There is a problem with stating these rules as I have just done. They are stated at a high level of inference. Therefore, as in the case of the advice in strategy implementation (Chapter 4), the rules may make sense or not seem particularly new, but implementing them may not be as easy as we think when the context contains threat and defensive routines. One way for readers to check this out is to complete the Bill and John case. If the answers are similar to any that was given in Chapter 2, then it is unlikely that they will be able to produce actions consistent with the rules (again, if the context contains defensive routines and threat). The readers who do not agree with the rules would probably not try to produce them in the first place. They might also complete the Bill and John case and see if their responses are different from those of Model I. If they are, then they are probably disagreeing with a set of rules that is based on the theory in use that I believe will help individuals engage rather than bypass defensive routines.

The theory in use found in these rules is called Model II (Figure 9.1). This model can be used to engage defensive routines to help individuals and organizations detect and correct difficult and threatening errors.

Model II, like its predecessor, is abstract. Being abstract, it is comprehensive. Unlike Model I, few people use it in everyday life to design and implement actions even though many people like and espouse it. There is nothing particularly new about Model II as an espoused theory of action. The challenge is to transform it into a theory in use.

Acquiring Model II as a theory in use does not mean that we should discard Model I. The latter is more effective for routine, nonthreatening issues. The former is more effective for nonroutine, innovative issues as well as those that are threatening and

FIGURE 9.1 *Model II Theory in Use*

Governing values $\longrightarrow$	Action strategies $\longrightarrow$	Consequences
Valid (confirmable) information, Free and informed choice, Internal commitment to the choice.	Advocate your position and combine with inquiry and public testing. Minimize unilateral face saving.	Reduction of self-fulfilling, self-sealing, error-escalating processes; Effective problem solving.

involve defensive routines. Thus, I am not recommending that we get rid of Model I. I am saying that we have two choices. Like any other situation of choice, we can define the rules under which they will use either theory in use, rules like those I just described.

The action strategies under the new theory in use include advocating ideas and making evaluations or attributions in such a way that you encourage inquiry into them (see Figure 5.1). This can be accomplished by actions such as illustrating your evaluations or attributions, asking for inquiry into them, and testing them publicly.

It is critical to note that all these actions will be counterproductive if they are used in the service of Model I values such as unilateral control, maximizing winning, and minimizing losing. They will be counterproductive because they are gimmicks. A gimmick is any action in the service of inconsistent values. It is inconsistent to encourage others to inquire, to become vulnerable, when your governing values are to be in unilateral control and to win and not lose. The recipients will soon sense that they are being manipulated and act accordingly.

The values that govern Model II actions are valid information, free and informed choice, and internal commitment to the choice. These values, like any others that govern our actions, are ideals and can only be approximated. We can never have all the valid information or a completely free and informed choice or be fully committed.

As we learn to produce actions that are consistent with these new values, we will find that we will naturally be making our reasoning more public. If we strive to illustrate evaluations and attributions, to test them publicly, and to encourage inquiry into our actions, we will soon find ourselves describing the reasoning that led to the actions. We will also be seeking to understand the reasoning of others. The more we make our reasoning public and subject to inquiry, the more we are predisposed to communicate it as clearly as possible, and the more we make it subject to public testing, the more we will strive to make our reasoning processes as compelling as possible.

The more all of these consequences happen, the more likely we can focus on using hard data from which to make inferences. By hard data, I mean data that are easily acceptable as valid descriptions of reality by those of us with contradictory views. Hard data do not necessarily mean quantitative data. Indeed, accountants and financial experts can provide many examples where numbers are highly soft and subjective. Tape recordings are often accepted as hard data when we are trying to understand what had been said during a difficult episode in a meeting.

The end result is that we will tend to move away from the defensive reasoning that was described in Chapter 2 toward productive reasoning. Productive reasoning makes it less likely that defensive routines will be created, but where defensive routines exist, productive reasoning makes it more likely that they will be engaged.

The characteristics of productive reasoning are:

- The use of hard data (that is, easily acceptable as valid descriptions of reality by individuals with contradictory views).
- Explicit premises,
- Explicit inferences,
- Publicly testable conclusions.

Behind productive reasoning lie the following:

- An explicit or tacit theory of strategy formulation.
- A set of interrelated concepts.
- A set of explicit rules of how to use these concepts to make permissible inferences, reach testable conclusions, and criteria to judge the validity of the test.

There is another result of holding Model II theory in use and using productive reasoning. Some of our most basic operating assumptions begin to change. Operating assumptions are rules about creating particular climates or contexts such as help and support, respect for others, strength, honesty, and integrity. We all recognize these states of affairs. They are are not rules for action strategies because different actions can lead to creating them in real life. They are consistent with the theory in use we hold. They are more like consequences that we wish to produce in everyday life.

For example, let us take the contexts just described and give the meanings the world presently assumes to be valid (left-hand column) and the meaning the same context would have if we engaged defensive routines and used Model II and productive reasoning (right-hand column).

Help and Support

Give approval and praise to others. Tell others what you believe will make them feel good about themselves. Reduce their feelings of hurt by telling them how much you care, and if possible, agree with them that the others acted improperly.

Through the use of publicly compelling and testable reasoning, increase the other's activity to reflect and evaluate his or her theory in use and operating assumptions.

Respect for Others

Defer to others and do not confront others' reasoning or action.

Attribute to others a high capacity for self-examination without loss of their sense of effectiveness or their exercise of self-responsibility and choice.

Strength

Acquire a capacity for winning, for advocacy, for holding your own position in the face of others' advocacy.

Acquire a capacity for high advocacy and high commitment that is combined with encouraging inquiry and self-reflection.

Honesty

Tell others no lies or tell others all you think and feel.

Create conditions that make it more likely that one can reveal to others (and hear from others) without distorting what would otherwise be subject to distortion.

Integrity

Stick to your principles, values, and beliefs.

Advocate your principles, values, and beliefs in a way that invites inquiry into them and encourages others to do the same.

Many of the cases used so far do illustrate the differences in meanings. For example, recall the consultant who identified inconsistencies in pricing policies that were confirmed by the top executives. He said that normally he would have stopped his intervention with the accolades he received from the client on his economic analysis. He chose, however, to ask a question that he said he would not have asked before learning to deal with defensive routines. He asked the clients, in effect, what is it about the way they manage that permitted pricing inconsistencies to exist when they were known, in varying degrees, by various members of the group.

In the present world view, such an intervention would be evaluated as ranging from inappropriate to foolish to dangerous. The reason for these beliefs can be seen by examining the meaning that respect, strength, honesty, and integrity have under these conditions. Respect means to defer and not to confront defensive routines. This is what the consultant would have done previously. Strength means advocating the position and winning. The consultant did that when he surfaced the pricing inconsistencies, was found to be correct, and the clients liked it. He was honest because he did not tell lies. He also would not previously have confronted the actions that permitted the pricing inconsistencies to continue. Finally, integrity meant sticking to his principles, which he did by focusing on the importance of reducing the inconsistencies in the pricing logic.

It is easy to see why the clients liked the consultant's first intervention. He surfaced three inconsistencies and made them subject to discussion. This led eventually to discussions among the top to correct the inconsistencies. In their eyes, he showed respect, strength, honesty, and integrity.

The consultant had now learned to engage defensive routines in order to solve problems in a way that they remained solved and to aspire to help organizations learn how to learn, which was another matter. Engagement of defensive routines could lead to dangerous consequences in the eyes of some of the executives. However, the executives in this case, and many others that we interviewed in other cases, valued highly these learning aspirations. Why would they become anxious? And why do not consultants take this route more often? One answer is that the executives who valued learning how to learn were also concerned about the dangers of engaging defensive routines, and many doubted that the consultants had the competence to help them succeed. The second answer is that both the clients and consultants usually have the same theories in use and therefore are predisposed to have the same doubts about the feasibility and value added by engaging the defensive routines.

In this case, the consultant now had a new set of meanings for respect, strength, honesty, and integrity. He indicated respect by asking his question. He attributed to the clients a high capacity for self-examination without losing their sense of effectiveness. He also attributed to them the capacity to choose if they wanted to continue the second line of inquiry. He indicated strength showing that he could advocate a difficult inquiry and self-reflection. He focused on honesty by creating the conditions that made it more likely that the clients could reveal to each other without distortion a discussion of defensive routines that would otherwise be subject to distortion. Finally, he showed integrity by advocating his beliefs, even though he knew doing so was risky, and he did so in ways that encouraged the clients to confront him and later each other.

If the clients raised objections or concerns the consultant would deal with them openly. For example, in this case, when the CEO said, "I don't think we hired you for this kind of help," the consultant responded:

Consultant: We value very highly the relationship with you and do not wish to act in ways that jeopardize it. The reason I raised the question that I did is my belief that unless we get at these factors, they could operate after we have gone to undermine whatever new strategy is put into place.

If you as a group prefer not to go in this direction, fine, we will work closely with you.

The consultant, in effect, advocated his position and provided a choice to the clients. In this case, the executives initially resisted, but the more they discussed the issue, the more they realized that the consultant was correct. In another example (Chapter 8) you may recall, the CEO and several top members became upset when the consultant confronted their view that they operated as an open, consensus-making group. Again, the consultant provided a choice. Again, the CEO chose to examine this issue. Indeed, he told the consultant that if what he said turned out to be correct, then the value added would be greater than developing a new strategy.

DEALING WITH DEFENSIVE ROUTINES

To be competent means to have the abilities required and the requisite qualifications to reduce reliably or prevent defensive routines from arising. Competencies are more comprehensive than skills. In order to be implemented, they may require several different kinds of skills. Seven competencies that we have found to be important are the following:

1. To identify the reasoning and actions that create defensive routines. Reasoning that helps to reduce defensive routines begins with hard data (See Figure 9.1). Hard data are relatively easily directly observable, and parties involved can easily agree

about the meaning of the data. The inferences made are explicit and the conclusions are subject to public testing.

These reasoning processes necessarily require actions such as advocating ideas and encouraging inquiry into them, illustrating evaluations or attributions, and subjecting these to public testing. These types of actions are especially useful to identify and deal with defensive routines such as mixed messages, undiscussability, self-fulfilling prophecies, and self-sealing processes.

2. To reflect on one's reasoning or actions to check for and minimize producing inner contradictions (such as saying that someone is wrong to prejudge individuals and to do so by prejudging the individual), inconsistencies between intentions and consequences (not intending to produce defensiveness in others yet doing so), injustice (identifying rules for reasoning and actions that are counterproductive yet using them as if they are not), and distancing and disconnectedness from self-responsibility (using explanations that place responsibility for defensive routines on others and on the system without exploring your impact).

3. To reflect on the reflections in number 2 in order to change reasoning and actions. The objective is to become an on-line experimenter where new reasoning and actions that produce fewer defensive routines can be tried out. This stance is one of continual on-line inquiry into reasoning and action for the purpose of detecting and correcting mismatches.

4. To construct maps that show how patterns of reasoning and actions create defensive routines at the individual, group, intergroup or organizational levels. The maps will also show how each defensive routine draws upon the others to nurture itself and how it provides reinforcement to the others. For example, in Chapter 6, we mapped how a pattern of interpersonal actions combined with another to produce a greater likelihood for an ineffective problem-solving process; how this, in turn, made it less likely that the organization will make effective decisions and more likely that they will create a culture of management by crisis and coalition politics and rivalries. Another example was the map of not only how management information systems were used to protect divisional planners but also how the ultimate consequence was to lead to corporate mistrust of those systems and their planning.

These maps of action not only describe what factors cause what consequences but also, as long as the terrain is not changed, indicate that they will do so over time. Moreover, their validity is not reduced if the users do not agree with the map. For example, the individuals agreed that the management information system map was valid and that they did not like what it said, but that did not make it possible for them to change it. They had neither the personal competence to change their theories in use nor the power to change the organizational defensive routines.

5. To select the point and time for interrupting defensive routines where and when it is more likely to produce learning and change. The dilemma of intervening with defensive routines is that the activation is necessary to understand them, but it also makes understanding and change more difficult. So far, it appears that the dilemma just described is more likely to be resolved successfully if the individuals involved:

- Connect the task of reducing defensive routines with the tasks of designing a more effective set of technical activities such as better planning processes. The more the exploration of defensive routines is connectable to a business or organizational problem, the more likely the intervention will succeed.
- Intervene as early as is possible in the thought-action process. For example, it is easier to interrupt a diagnosis, somewhat less easy to interrupt a solution that has just been invented, and even more difficult if the interruption comes after the action is produced. The more involved individuals are, the more they may resist having their actions interrupted if their values are to remain in unilateral control, to win, not to lose, and so on.
- Intervene when key individuals are willing to support the inquiry and/or when the group or organizational norms for reflection and inquiry are strong.
- Intervene in such a way that if others become defensive, you will not get caught up by their defensiveness. If you use publicly compelling and testable reasoning and actions, if you are willing to be vulnerable and confrontable, then it is unlikely that you can be the cause of the others' defensiveness. Or if your actions do cause defensiveness, you will be willing to explore your re-

sponsibility; otherwise, it is the recipients who should examine their stance.

If you act competently when others become defensive, then you are not likely to be infected by the defensiveness. This does not mean that you distance yourself from your possible responsibility for creating defensiveness. On the contrary, you seek to be open and confrontable. This is what we have described as combining vulnerability with strength.

6. To deal effectively with your own and others' feelings that may range from surprise to bewilderment to embarrassment to frustration to fear and to anger. By dealing with, I mean first to help individuals express their feelings, to empathize with the feelings without necessarily accepting them. You can say "I can understand how you would feel anger or fear" without feeling similarly or agreeing that such feelings are correct or just. Individuals can have feelings that are wrong in the sense that they lead to mismatches, injustice, and distancing.

The second feature of dealing with feelings is to help individuals to reflect on their feelings by using publicly compelling and testable reasoning more than privately compelling and testable reasoning. This means to help individuals face the facts about their feelings, which in turn means help them to explore how their feelings may be used to protect these individuals from understanding the basis of their premises, the nature of their inferences, and the validity of their conclusions.

Sometimes individuals will call this focus too rational or too intellectual. They want to express their feelings without analyzing them. Individuals are free to make this choice. However, if they make this choice, then they cannot learn about any inner contradictions, inconsistencies, injustices, and undue distancing they may be producing; and of course, it is not possible to learn about feelings or ideas without examining them.

7. To create conditions in which others can learn or can use the competencies described here. To design settings or contexts within which individuals can acquire and use these competencies under conditions of zero to moderate stress. The skills needed for such competence are to use publicly compelling and

testable reasoning as well as to advocate, evaluate or attribute, and combine these with illustration, inquiry, and public test (See Figure 5.1). But teaching others these skills goes beyond modeling them. As we shall see in the next chapter, it is possible to teach these skills — especially in the context of getting the technical job done — but it is not easy. Learning seminars are being developed, however, where these competencies can be taught to others (Argyris, 1982; Argyris, Putnam, and Smith, forthcoming).

Although modeling the competencies is not enough, it is key if the others are to test their credibility. One of the best ways to test the validity and usability of these competencies is to observe the consultants using them, especially under some degree of stress.

UNFREEZING THE COMPARTMENTALIZATION OF PRODUCTIVE REASONING TO TECHNICAL ISSUES

Productive reasoning, as we have said, underlies the thinking and action that often engage defensive routines. In studying executives and consultants, we have found those who use productive reasoning to solve technical problems tend to use defensive reasoning to deal with threat. It is ironic that these individuals have the competencies for the requisite reasoning to engage defensive routines but they do not do so. It is as if they have compartmentalized their productive reasoning and their defensive reasoning so they do not see how the former would be relevant in dealing with defensive routines.

For example, effective strategy formulation usually includes understanding the economic features of the business and its environment and knowing how to produce conceptually elegant and empirically rigorous analysis that stands up against tough inquiry. Strategists usually accomplish these requirements well and end up formulating an innovative strategy.

When they begin to try to implement the strategy, if individuals or groups begin to resist and defensive routines are activated, the executives or the consultants often think defensively and bypass the issues, a strategy they do not use in dealing with tough technical issues. They are often bewildered by resistance and anxieties to proposals that they believe are rigorous and sound. They may even become more upset when individuals appear to nit pick their strategy or generally make life difficult.

Under these conditions we have observed that these individuals try to defend their strategy by raising the level of proof, by showing concern and trying to be flexible with client demands, and by trying to educate clients if they are making the wrong requests. Unfortunately, there are times when the clients react in ways that lead the creators of the strategy to feel that their critics are judging them to be opportunistic or arrogant. They tend to feel bewildered and angry. They suppress these feelings during the meeting and explode after the meeting in the privacy of their own group. "What stupid people. Can you believe what they said?" "What the hell do you do when people are that dense?"

Two senior consultants, one internal, one external, described some of the strategies they used under these difficult conditions:

Consultant 1: In effect, what we do in a lot of cases where we do all the analysis . . . we come in with what I call a "drop dead" analysis. We avoid questioning the [client's] reasoning. Instead, we question facts.

The client often says, "We're going to do the following." We ask, "Why?" The client says, "Because the margins are better in that segment." So we do a month of analysis to prove that the margins are not better. We say, "We've shown you that the margins are poorer."

The client responds in one of two ways: (1) "I question your data," or (2) "Then using our reasoning, we shouldn't go where we were going because we had a factual error."

In effect, we often use the client's reasoning to change the facts in order to get them to do what we believe is in their best interest.

Sometimes it is necessary to do the analysis because [for example,] the client's reasoning is correct. "Let us go where the margins are better." Sometimes his logic is bad but his facts are good. That is often when he isn't seeing the second or third order effects. . . .

Consultant 2: In our organization, our way of handling this is to overwhelm them with data until the client says, "I yield."

The unintended consequences of these actions may be to lower the level of trust between the consultants and the clients and to lower the probability of effective implementation. The challenge is for the consultants or the executives to help the client engage and thus reduce the defensive routines to accomplish genuine frame breaking and help the clients learn how to learn.

I believe that consultants and executives do not have the choice to gloss over frame breaking, to bypass defensive routines in the name of the art of the possible. There is increasing awareness that organizations are becoming more difficult and costly to manage precisely when the most sophisticated management concepts and information systems are being made available. Action to reduce defensive routines cannot be postponed without peril.

This does not mean that people should take precipitous action. We can learn from our experiences in reducing air pollution. It is a model of being steadfast in purpose and moving sequentially. It is a model where all players become responsible for changing their actions as well as of organizations redesigning their policies and practices.

One of the first actions that can be taken to begin to bridge the gap is to focus on compelling reasoning and testing it publicly. This strategy is consistent with the emphasis on logic and justice in our society. The key is to expand the use of this strategy by dealing with the human dimensions of technical problems.

ten

LEARNING IS EASY AND DIFFICULT

Learning the competencies described in the previous chapter is both easy and difficult. They are easy to learn in the sense that they depend upon communicating as accurately as possible what you mean when you speak and selecting the words that make it most likely that the hearer will understand. They are easy in the sense that they are rule oriented because people understand the meaning and value of rules. They are easy because they do not require us to deal with features like the unconscious, which would mean having a rather select and highly specialized set of clinical skills and language that would be difficult to integrate with everyday discourse. They are easy in the sense that they are based on justice and competence, attributes most people value highly. They are easy in the sense that it is possible for us to recognize what is advocacy combined with inquiry or illustrating and testing attributions and evaluations.

What makes it difficult are the programs and rules that we presently use to deal with threats. Our competencies are based on bypassing, not engaging, defensive routines, on a set of operating assumptions that is more likely to reinforce the weaknesses and defenses of others as well as our own, and on our being in unilateral control and whenever possible — that is, winning rather than losing.

If our competencies are based on these factors, so is our sense of competence, confidence. Our sense of worth, as related to dealing with defensive routines is, in effect, built upon skills, operating assumptions, and a theory in use that are counter to the ones that are required if we are to engage and reduce defensive routines.

If this is so then learning the new competencies requires unlearning the old. However, unlearning the old is not a simple intellectual process. It means temporarily experiencing feelings of decreasing self-confidence, of not being in control, of vulnerability. These are precisely the feelings that trigger our bypass routines, which are the factors that have to be overcome. We will feel a sense of Catch 22 because the actions we take to defend ourselves are the very ones we are being asked to unlearn.

This does not mean that re-education is impossible, that it has to be painful, or that it must be dramatic. On the contrary, it is possible to learn the new competencies at a pace that any individual can control. Taking it slowly and taking a long time is not a problem because most of us rarely forget what we have learned and can build upon an insight obtained months before.

The key opportunity required is to practice, and practice requires an opportunity to experiment, and the best experiments are the ones that are carried out in real life. Thus, we can wait for several months until the appropriate context arises for us to practice our new competencies.

In our experience, once individuals get going they find that learning the new competencies adds new challenge and new interests in their lives. Many of the strategy consultants that I worked with said that learning the new competencies reversed their sense of burnout from the kind of consulting they had been doing.

In order to get going, we have to understand the new competencies, operating assumptions, and theory in use. By and large this is the easiest step. Next is to unfreeze our automatic predisposition to use defensive reasoning when dealing with threat and instead to experiment with productive reasoning. Finally we need the ability to design opportunities for practice that are rich with learning.

In this chapter, I illustrate a somewhat extreme reaction on the part of several strategy consultants who would be considered in the category of the "best and the brightest." The young consultants reacted strongly to the new requirements that would be placed upon them if they were to use the new competencies in a client setting. However, even with all the complaining and emotionality, they learned and the client received some valuable consulting on a very difficult economic problem.

In all fairness, I hold myself responsible for part of the strong reactions in this case. I agreed with the officer who was ready to conduct the experiment because I was impressed by his capacity to learn and his willingness to experiment. I also believed that the younger consultants were very bright and committed to learning. Reflecting on that belief, I now realize that I did not get enough data. I watched the younger consultants use productive reasoning for technical problems with creativity and ease. They were so good at it that I assumed it would not be difficult to transfer the productive reasoning skills to dealing with threat. I was mistaken.

First, they had very strong bypass routines built up to dealing with threat. As soon as they realized the challenge they had accepted, they became quite threatened. Second, the experiment was not only one of learning new competencies. To the credit of the officer consultant, he realized that learning the new competencies required also designing new intracase team relationships as well as new relationships with the clients.

Two prominent features of these new intrateam relationships were a high degree of interdependence and teamwork coupled with a minimal sense of win and don't lose. The younger professionals found these requirements difficult. They had made their reputation of being first-rate strategy professionals by making individual contributions. They had not worked cooperatively in a way that their contribution was so integrated with those of the others that it would be difficult to distinguish. Finally, the consulting firm, as a firm, had not given any clues that it would reward people if they used these new competencies or created these new cooperative teams. The firm was waiting to evaluate the outcome of experiments like these so it could decide what position it might take.

We would not have these difficulties if we were to start

anew. The officer has continued to experiment and to learn. The new, younger consultants who work with him now do so with a more informed view of what they are getting into, and the officer has a history of dealing with difficult clients effectively by using these competencies.

There is another value of the experiment described in this chapter. It provided excellent re-educational opportunities for the young consultants to learn some of the more difficult competencies without jeopardizing the client relationship. Also, the young consultants learned to cooperate, to be less loners, and to reduce their brittleness. It also appears that those who learn are willing to become more reflective on their practice. This means that they examine their errors in order to correct them. But they cannot do this by themselves; they need the feedback and help from others. The result is that conditions are being created where the consultants (be they officers or nonofficers) learn to evaluate their performance openly. They become resources for each others' growth. They help to create one of the most sought-after conditions among professionals — namely, the ability to monitor the quality of their performance. Now to the case.

A case team of two junior and two senior consultants was formed. The vice-president interviewed each member so he could tell them that he wanted to experiment with a different way of organizing and managing the case team and to ask for their cooperation. He asked any individuals who did not wish to participate in such an experiment not to join the team.

The officer described two critical differences. It was normal practice in such a case to assign each member to a different functional group: one to marketing, one to production, and one to finance. Each consultant then became an expert in that functional area.

There were several reasons for such a practice. First, efficiencies could be created by specializing each member. Moreover, it tended to be easier to establish a good working relationship in each area if the same consultant was contacting the same given department. In a client system that has cross-functional rivalries and mistrust, it was also best to have separate consultants. The result was that the team structure mirrored the structure of the client organization. The unintended consequence of this structure was that case team members developed some of the cross-functional difficulties mirrored in the organization.

The officer wished to experiment with organizing the team members according to the intellectual problems they would eventually solve. He also wanted to have the consultants respond with a greater sense of the problem as a whole, especially when they were talking with clients who might prefer to think within narrow specialties. He realized that this move ran the risk of the clients' mistrusting the consultant. Instead of seeing this as a danger to be avoided, however, he saw it as an important opportunity to help the client. If each case team member could act in ways to overcome the mistrust due to cross-functional rivalries, they could help show the clients how to accomplish the same in their organization.

It was also common practice in case team management to decompose the problem into parts in which each consultant could work relatively autonomously from the others. This made it easier for consultants to work on two cases. But the more important reason had to do with the case team dynamics. The officers found that the young consultants were better at working on problems alone than cooperatively. The vice-president wanted to create case teams where the cohesiveness was not due simply to the skill of the officer but also to the effective relationships among the case team members.

For such team effectiveness to work, the team members would not only have to help each other but also be able to evaluate each other's work and actions. This was contrary to normal practice. Usually the officer or the manager evaluated performance, and this was usually done in private. However, the young consultants were often in a position of evaluating clients, and clients often felt that they were not very good at it. The officer believed, therefore, that if the experiment worked, the case team members could create a team that mirrored the features they would ask the client organization to develop. Again, it made good sense to model a small organization that had few defensive routines.

Finally, the vice-president believed in the importance of consultants' capacities to reflect on their experience and practice. This was the basis by which they could learn how to learn. It was ongoing practice development. The vice-president described these ideas to two junior and two senior consultants, as well as a manager. They all agreed with a good deal of enthusiasm.

ESTABLISHING A CASE TEAM WITH CROSS-FUNCTIONAL ORGANIZATION

Almost at the outset, the young consultants balked at being organized in the cross-functional model they had accepted.

Vice-president: I presume that in taking the marketing area, it is marketing and sales that you are getting involved with, right? Not just marketing.

Consultant 2: No, I think there's a distinction, because I'm not doing the economics of the channel. Say I find out [the following]; that's feedback I should give, I think, to Consultant 3 because he's doing the cost of distribution.

Vice-president: Okay. We are now surfacing one of my great concerns about this case, which is: that's the way the client is structured; if we specialize that way, we may reflect the problems that exist in the client organization.

One of the senior consultants also objected to the cross-functional organization.

Consultant 2: I'd like to make a pitch for mirroring the organization. I believe in empathizing with the guy I'm dealing with and understanding his problems from his point of view. I like to get him to believe he can trust me, and he may be very guarded if he knows I'm talking to people in other functions.

Consultant 1: I agree with Consultant 2. If you have a cross-functional problem, you need the respect of both departments if you're to be effective in getting them to work together.

Vice-president: You're arguing your case now. Let's talk for a minute about why this case team has so many strong guys on it. It's because we think that in order to get them to operate better in a cross-functional way, there is a need to have people out there on line with the client, frequently, who are knowledgeable, who can defend and argue positions, and who can also work on the process aspects of the case. If that's true, and that's why we staffed it, I expect that you're going to be doing a lot of arguing of positions, where you're going to be the only one out there who is arguing these issues.

The young consultant defended the established way of working with clients by making the following arguments:

1. They were for empathizing with clients and understanding their problem from their point of view.
2. The way to be trusted in one department is not to talk to clients in other departments.
3. Working with one client makes it possible to get into the depth of the organization.

The reasoning behind the argument is important. The consultants begin by being for empathy and understanding, something with which the vice-president would agree. Then they jump to the conclusion that these conditions plus trust occur if consultants do not talk with clients in other departments. This may be true under the usual conditions, but the point of this experiment was to try to build trust, empathy, and understanding without reproducing or depending upon the tunnel vision created by functional myopia. Again, working with one client could make it easier to go into depth; it could also make it more difficult. Moreover, having a cross-functional view could make it easier to go into depth within a function because the consultants may have more complete knowledge about the organization's problems.

BUTTON PUSHING

The vice-president and Consultant 1 continued to have differences about styles of operating. Consultant 1 did not appear to me to be interested in any reaction except to protect himself. This is not to say that the vice-president's actions were always consistent with inquiry. However, he did try to reflect on his errors and to examine the way the team was operating, as well as on his own style.

It was not surprising to learn that a blowup occurred during one meeting. Consultant 1 accused the vice-president of "zinging him," of being hostile, of judging him as incompetent, and so on. The vice-president tried to explore these attributions but did not succeed.

PUBLIC EVALUATION OF MEMBERS' PERFORMANCE

The third meeting began with Consultant 2's presentation of some slides to describe his thinking on the marketing issues. The other members of the team had many questions and suggestions. Consultant 2 replied to several of these comments by saying, "Sure, I'm coming to that," or "I plan to do that." It began to look as if Consultant 2 was not as prepared for his presentation as he wanted to be. The vice-president asked him about his preparation.

Consultant 2: The problem I'm having — I'm being bombarded by a lot of things. I haven't had the time to sit back and think about all this.

I don't approach a problem the way everyone else does. You're pushing me out into the field. I can't think that way. I have spent four days in the field. That is a big problem I'm having with this case: the time limitations you are putting on me.

Vice-president: I don't think you've ever said to me to let you sit back for a day, but maybe you've said it to the manager.

Do you [manager] object to his sitting back for a day? If it will help?

Manager: No. I don't know where the four days in the field are. We only did a half-day in the field. . . .

> Vice-president: Then maybe we should not spend two hours on stuff that you believe is not ready.

> Consultant 2: Fine.

MAPPING WHAT HAPPENED*

The case team experimenting with a new approach experienced several differences among team members as to how the team should proceed. They were how best to solve the technical problem, illustrated in this case by the debate over how to design the first presentation, and the argument whether it was legitimate for the vice-president to question openly how team members interacted. The difficulty is not the differences per se but the way in which case team members deal with their differences. Rather than resolving differences, team members acted in ways that led them to become entrenched. The patterns of behavior that created problems can be summarized in the phrase *Model I theories in use*.

Unillustrated Attributions

Case team members typically made assertions at a high level of inference and did not illustrate these assertions with relatively directly observable data. For example, when arguing that their approach to designing the presentation would not have a negative impact on the relationship with the client, one consultant said:

Consultant's Statement	**Unillustrated Attributions**
My feeling is, you can say things well and yet be em-	One can use our provocative approach and still be empathic.

*Robert Putnam contributed in writing this section.

Consultant's Statement	**Unillustrated Attributions**
pathic. You can be encouraging and yet still be provocative.	
I don't think they're mutually exclusive.	You are claiming these features are mutually exclusive.

Advocacy, No Inquiry

When advocating their position, often by making unillustrated attributions, case team members rarely encouraged others to inquire into the validity of that position. The preceding example was illustrative. Case team members often go further and actively discourage inquiry. For example, when the vice-president asked how others saw what Consultant 1 had been saying, Consultant 2 said:

Consultant's Statement	**Unillustrated Attributions**
I don't think Consultant 1 is wedded to the position as strongly as I think the vice-president has the impression he is.	Consultant 1 is not firm in his position.
I know that Consultant 1 likes to argue a position very strongly. If that's not the issue right now, which it isn't, let's move along.	Discouraging inquiry: The way Consultant 1 argues is not the issue. Let's move on.

The impact of not encouraging inquiry or of actively discouraging inquiry is that there is little public testing of the validity of positions that case team members advocate. This means that case team members are unlikely to learn of errors that may exist in their position.

Discounted Data

In the preceding example, Consultant 2 was discounting the persistent arguments that Consultant 1 had been making for basing the structure of the presentation on his view that the client could not become competitive in the market at large. Another example of discounting occurred when Consultant 2 argued that people in this organization would not lock in on theories. When the vice-president offered to cite examples of people who had locked in, Consultant 2 said, "I would attribute to that person, that he really has got to have a lot of problems." Thus, Consultant 2 makes attributions that disqualify in advance any data that might disconfirm his view.

The cumulative impact of making unillustrated attributions, advocating without inquiry, and discounting data is to make arguments self-sealing. The reasoning used by case team members becomes circular because arguments are built on premises that are not illustrated, are not the subject of inquiry, and are exempted from potentially disconfirming data.

Inconsistencies

There are inconsistencies in many of the positions argued by case team members. In the preceding example, it is difficult to see what might induce Consultant 2 to change his view once he has discounted potentially disconfirming data. Hence, he appears to be locked into the theory that people in this organization will not lock in on theories. We heard Consultant 1 saying it was wrong to do psychoanalysis in the case team at the same time he is psychoanalyzing the vice-president's motives.

Unawareness

In each of these examples, and in many others, case team members appeared unaware of the circularity and inconsistencies in their reasoning. They were also unaware of their unawareness.

Undiscussable

The circularity, inconsistencies, and unawareness are reinforced when case team members treat the behavioral dimension as undiscussable. For example, when the vice-president asked how others saw what Consultant 1 had been saying, Consultant 2 said that he thought the question was pejorative and refused to answer. Consultant 1 objected to the vice-president's discussing how people worked, saying "I will be very uncomfortable every time this case team cycles off to psychoanalysis." And when the team was discussing the vice-president's evaluation of Consultant 2's work, Consultant 1 said, "I don't think the case team time is well served by this discussion." Notice that when case team members argued that such matters should not be discussable, they made unillustrated attributions, advocated without inquiring, and employed the other features that made their views self-sealing.

Hold Another Responsible

Case team members typically focused on the responsibility of the other person for difficulties in the team and did not focus on their own responsibility. For example, in a conflict over speculating, the consultants focused on how the vice-president's way of participating squelched them. They defended their way of arguing as standard practice and appeared not to consider that it may also have counterproductive features. Similarly, on the several occasions when Consultant 1 angrily withdrew, he communicated "the vice-president is so controlling, there's no point in arguing with him." Thus, he held the vice-president responsible for his withdrawal. Also, he did not test his attribution that the vice-president wanted to make him submissive and held the vice-president responsible for creating conditions in which it was not possible to test (for example, he tells the interventionist, "He's saying, 'if you question the truth of my comment, you are incompetent.' And you're asking me to go back and question it again").

Focus on the Negative

While the features identified here characterized much of the interaction in the case team, there were exceptions. In particular, the vice-president often encouraged inquiry into team process. However, his process comments often had both positive and negative features, and team members selectively responded to the negative features. For example, the vice-president asked the team how he should handle a dilemma that he experienced: when team members made sweeping statements, he feared they might say such things to the client if he did not point out exceptions, but he feared that if he did this, team members might feel squelched. Consultant 1's reaction was, "I think you're being unnecessarily nervous about his team doing things that would hurt us with the client." This reaction focused on a negative feature of the vice-president's intervention: his unillustrated attribution that team members might make an error with the client. It ignored the positive features of the intervention: the invitation to design jointly a way to deal with a team process issue.

Three other types of consequences that occurred can be described as first-order, second-order, and third-order consequences.

First-Order Consequences

Perseverance Based on Personal Privilege and Impatience

Since case team members continued to believe that they were right and the other was wrong, they persevered in the approach they believed was right. For example, the consultants persisted in speculating, and the vice-president persisted in citing data to show how the speculations were in error.

When case team members saw others persevering in an approach that they were increasingly convinced was wrong, they became impatient. For example, the vice-president was impatient with the consultants' speculating, and the consultants were impatient with the vice-president's nit-picking their speculations. Perseverance and impatience fed back to reinforce differences in approach, and they reinforced the negative ways that case team members dealt with their differences.

Increasing Data that the Other Is Wrong

When case team members saw others persisting in an approach after they had explained what they thought was wrong with the approach, they took this as further evidence that the other not only had the wrong approach but also was unable to see errors. When case team members became impatient and their behavior increasingly took on the negative features associated with impatience, then others took this as further evidence of error. Increasing data that the other was wrong fed back to reinforce differences.

Second-Order Consequences

Double Binds

These processes created double binds for case team members. For example, when the vice-president participated actively in the way he thought was most competent, then case team members felt he was squelching them. When he kept quiet, he felt irresponsible for allowing what he thought was unproductive activity to continue. From the case members' point of view, if they participated actively in the way they thought most competent, then the vice-president got impatient and they felt negatively evaluated. If they were more passive, then the vice-president designed the case, and they felt dissatisfied that they were no more than data hounds.

Third-Order Consequences

Button Pushing

When case team members felt impatient, found themselves in double binds, and began to attribute that others intended these consequences, then their ways of dealing with each other escalated. The form this escalation took in this case was button pushing: each person said things that pushed the other guy's button. For example, Consultant 1 said that the vice-president was "unnecessarily nervous." The vice-president said to Consultant 1, "Why must I listen to your speculation before you know half the facts of the case?" Consultant 1 communicated that the vice-president was so controlling that he wouldn't let the consultants think for themselves. The vice-president suggested that he had doubts about the consultants' competence.

Each of these statements might be a genuine issue and worthy of inquiry, but they were used in the case team as needles in the course of arguments about something else. Each participant seemed unaware of his own zingers but highly aware of the zingers sent by others. Button pushing thus fed back to reinforce the impatience felt by team members and provided further data that the other was wrong, and it reinforced the meta-attributions that were made about the nasty motives of others.

Hopelessness

These features can reasonably lead case team members to doubt that things can get better. Differences become entrenched, and more discussion just seems to make things worse. Other case team members seemed unable to learn of the errors in their position that seemed so obvious to those on the other side. Others were seen as increasingly unreasonable and intentionally so. In this case, Consultant 1 came to believe that there was little point in continuing. He thought that little improvement would occur, and he assumed that the vice-president did not want to change. Both Consultant 1 and the vice-president thought that the other could not be influenced to see another direction.

IMPLICATIONS

Professionals enter firms with Model I theories in use. As long as the work of the firm does not require professionals to question their accustomed ways of working, Model I theories in use can be reasonably effective. But when professionals must engage in frame breaking, the counterproductive features of their existing theories in use about frame breaking come to the fore.

When case teams experiment with a new approach to the firm's practice, team members' accustomed ways of working will be called into question. We predict that team members will act in ways that reenact the error-escalating, self-sealing map described on previous pages.

To the extent that the officer on the case uses these same behavioral strategies, then the team processes described in the map will require the officer to choose between two options: he may take unilateral control, or he may back off on the proposed change (or some combination of these two). In either case, there will be little progress toward developing a new approach if team members are not able to design the case jointly.

In the case studied here, the vice-president wanted to create a third option. He sought to learn and to use Model II skills to encourage inquiry into the team process and joint design of the case. As we have illustrated, he and the team experienced many difficulties. Several lessons can be drawn from this experience.

As is to be expected when someone is learning a new theory in use, the vice-president's interventions had both positive and negative features. Case team members often focused on the negative features and responded with the behavioral strategies associated with Model I. They were both unaware of the negative features of their responses and genuinely believed they were right. The vice-president had difficulty responding effectively.

In addition to his newly developing Model II skills, the vice-president sometimes acted in ways consistent with his older Model I skills. Behavioral skills that we use automatically are difficult to change. The first step is interrupting the unawareness of these skills. Several times it appeared that the vice-president was acting in a Model I way, becoming aware he was doing so, and correcting himself. This points to the necessity for iterative learning. However, iterations of escalating error will not be helpful. It will be necessary to create conditions in which the escalation of error can be interrupted so that case team members can reflect on their actions. In this case, such interruption was made possible by the presence of an interventionist.

Case team members can learn to act in ways that help interrupt the cycle of escalating error. For example, when two consultants inquired why the vice-president did not argue his substantive points, he explained his dilemma, and the consultants confirmed the vice-pres's fear that he would be seen as squelching them if he participated freely. In so doing, they helped create conditions in which the team could reflect on the dilemma and begin to design alternatives. Such action acknowledges that they share responsibility and treat the dilemma as discussable. It would seem that this had been made possible by the team's experiences in earlier meetings and that these consultants had come to believe that the vice-president was confrontable.

We are unaware of the conditions that require iterative learning. When automatic responses are repeated, case team members may assume that the actor cannot change or does not genuinely want to change. For example, when the case team experimented with a substantive discussion to see if they could work effectively, the vice-president again became impatient with the consultants. Consultant 1 inferred that there had been no change in the vice-president's behavior and that problems would continue. Our interpretation is that the vice-president's impatience is a repetition of an automatic response, and upon reflection, he saw that he might have been wrong to become impatient and encouraged the team to continue. This illustrates one iteration in a learning cycle that could produce genuine change. By that point, however, Consultant 1 had given up. He had seen the repetition of impatience and had taken it as proof that the vice-president did not genuinely want to change.

The famous Hawthorne effect — that is, stimulating accomplishment in workers by putting them under observation in an experimental situation — did not occur in this experiment. Although the consultants were excited about being part of an experiment, they did not suppress their needs in order to help the experiment work. Why was this the case? Although this was the first time such a team had been created in the organization, the espoused commitment of the players, their superlative record of being among the best and the brightest, and their professed interest in integrating the technical side with the people side of planning seemed to be a good base with which to begin. There was inadequate pretraining, a condition that can be remedied. I accept responsibility for not realizing the necessity for more pretraining and team building than was done. By the time it was clear that this was needed, the young consultants were reluctant to participate.

Another factor was that the officer who dealt with the team members' defensiveness was also relatively new at engaging defensive routines and in designing the client-consultant as well as the case team relationship. He worked very hard developing further skills in engaging others' defensiveness without allowing these defenses to infect him. This learning helped him not only in dealing more effectively with other case teams but also in becoming a more skillful consultant with difficult clients as well as a more effective officer in dealing with fellow officers. He also became a leader in the education of young consultants and managers who wanted to learn to deal with individual-organizational defensive routines.

As difficult as these conditions may appear, they can be overcome with mostly on-the-job and a little off-the-job education. The problem is not time or money. The biggest and most difficult challenge is the brittleness of the young consultants.

The Brittleness Syndrome

The consultants hired by the organization were the intellectual elite of their undergraduate and graduate programs. Almost all graduated with honors or better. In addition to their intellectual superiority, the consultants had a very high level of aspiration to succeed and were willing to work very hard. As they described themselves (Argyris, Putnam, and Smith, 1985):

> Pressure on the job is self-imposed . . . almost completely [laughs]. . . . I must not only do a good job but I must be the best, or damn close to it, in whatever I do.
>
> People around here are very bright, hard working, and highly motivated [to do an outstanding job]. They will work beyond the purple heart stage.
>
> Most of us not only wish to succeed but succeed at maximum speed, *which is really what is at issue* [emphasis in original].

These comments also suggest that the consultants were continuously comparing themselves with the best around them and continuously trying to better their performance. At the same time, the consultants did not appreciate being asked or required to compete openly with each other. They considered such actions crass and inhumane. The role they preferred at work was to be an individual contributor where they added value for the client and the connection to their individual performance was clear. They may be described as productive loners.

Coupled with their high aspiration for success was an equally high fear of failure:

> You must avoid mistakes. I *hate* making mistakes. I feel terrible and embarrassed.
>
> Many of us fear failure whether we say so or not.

When the organization hires young men and women like these, they also hire individuals with a high degree of susceptibility to shame and guilt whenever they experience failure. This may be coupled with an equally high avoidance of, and fears about, such feelings. These feelings combine to create brittleness (Figure 10.1). Brittleness is an inappropriately high sense of despair or sense of despondency when the high levels of aspiration are not achieved as intended.

The consultants used several metaphors to illustrate inappropriate response: "doom loop" or "doom zoom." I often ob-

292

FIGURE 10.1 *The Psychological Success-Brittleness Syndrome*

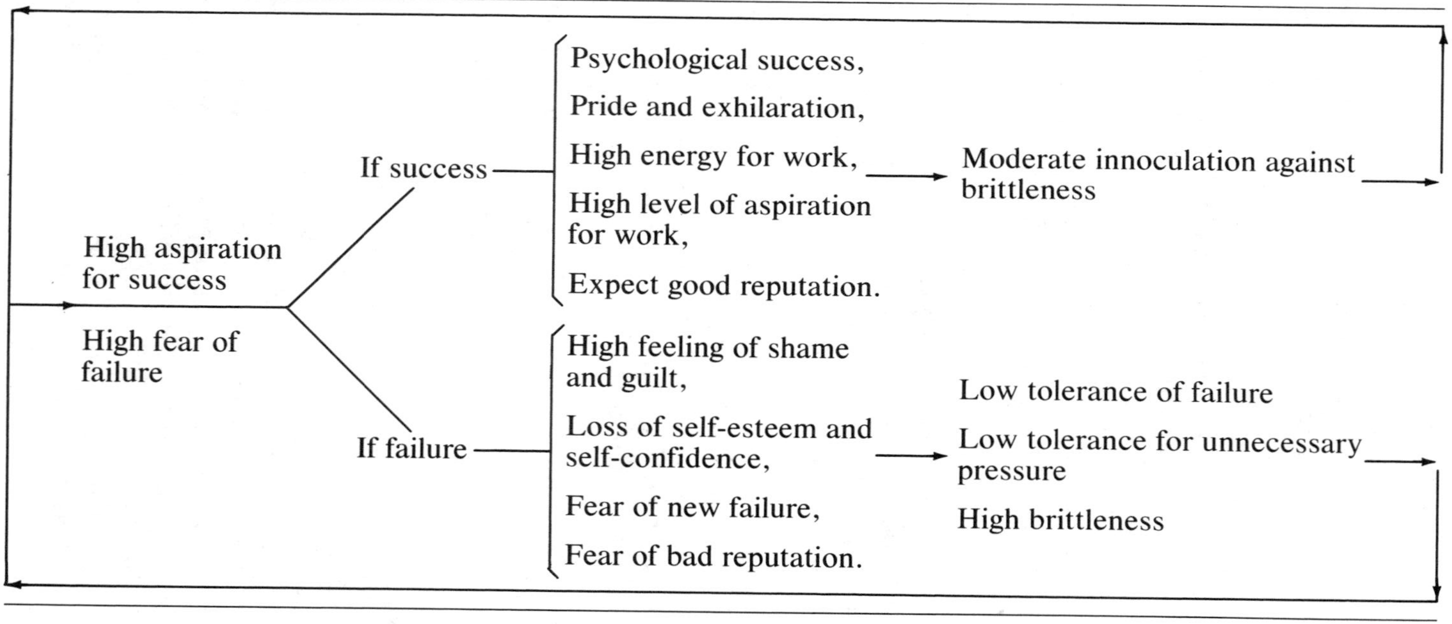

served consultants perform well in the case team, but because they did not do it perfectly and/or receive accolades from the manager, they went into a doom loop of despair, and they zoomed into it, did not ease into it.

To the extent that the consultants experienced success, they did not have to be concerned about failure and the attending feelings of shame and guilt. But to the extent they succeeded, they also did not develop the tolerance for, or the skills to deal with, feelings of failure. This, in turn, led them to fear the feeling of fear of failure as well as failure itself because they knew that they would not cope with them superlatively (their usual level of aspiration). This, in turn, would increase the probability of quick and inappropriate reaction to failure and, hence, reinforce the brittleness.

The most important feature of effective case leadership, in the eyes of the consultants, was the ability to decompose the technical problem so that each consultant was assigned a manageable part that he or she could accomplish without a high degree of interdependence with the other team members. Another feature of effective case leadership was that any negative feedback about performance should be done carefully and privately. Carefully was equivalent to easing in, as described in Chapter 2. It is interesting to note that many of the consultants would deny that they preferred easing in to forthrightness. As we saw, when officers learned how to be more forthright in their evaluations and simultaneously to invite confrontation of their views, the consultants often described them as honest but tough or even brutal. However, an analysis of the tape recording by an independent party could not confirm the brutality.

Another feature of effective case leadership was to involve the consultants, early in the case history, in creative freewheeling discussions about the technical problem. An officer or manager who decomposed the problem and managed the case team strictly was seen as overcontrolling and authoritarian. Thus, the effective leader had to find the balance between autonomy and control of the professionals. This was not an easy task especially because of the success-brittleness syndrome. Early in the case the officers and managers usually bent backward to let the freewheeling discussions continue to provide a sense of participation in the creative process as well as to educate the young consultants on how difficult it is to conceptualize a complex strategy problem. They also found themselves feeling frustrated with some discussions and were in conflict about how to bring them to a halt without appearing overpunishing and producing doom zooms. Often, precisely because they were walking on eggs, they failed.

The young consultants therefore came into the organization with at least two personal and powerful bypass loops: first, their Model I theory in use and, second, the success-brittleness syndrome.

There are several reasons why this combination of factors did not harm strategy formulation and development or the clients. First, the quality of the technical work was outstanding and could be done mostly by consultants acting as loners. Second, the dedication to the work by all consultants was very high. Third, the officers were willing to absorb costs so that clients would not be unfairly charged.

The difficulties arose whenever implementation required the engagement of client defensive routines. It is not easy to deal with client threat and defensiveness under the best of conditions. It is even more difficult to do so with case teams composed of individuals who are predisposed to be brittle when feeling failure, managed by processes that bypass the brittleness, and cover up the bypass (Argyris, 1982).

This was the challenge the vice-president took on when he decided to experiment with developing a case team that would minimize bypassing its own defensive routines, hence increasing the probability that it would deal more effectively with the clients' defensive routines. As we saw, this was not an easy task. In spite of the difficulties, however, the clients evaluated the products of the case team highly. Thus, it is possible to have these problems, to learn to overcome them, and simultaneously to get the job done. This should be encouraging to consulting firms and clients who wish to develop these new competencies and get on with the job.

eleven

ORGANIZATIONAL CHANGE

It is not farfetched to think of defensive routines as living systems that can figure out how to protect themselves and grow. The core of their integrity depends upon privately compelling, privately tested reasoning coupled with action strategies that are self-sealing and antilearning. Defensive routines take kindly neither to being changed nor to being discovered. Thus, changing defensive routines is a challenge precisely because their survival depends upon not being changed.

We easily agree that in order to reduce defensive routines we have to identify them. But unlike other kinds of things to change, identifying the routines may actually call them into action to defend themselves. Once these defenses are activated, they will camouflage themselves by influencing the way we reason, what we perceive, and how anxious we feel. They do this by activating the bypass routines we use to deal with potential threat.

How are we going to get at the defensive routines if they pull a disappearing act by activating the bypass routines in the very people who may be seeking the change? The first step is to help us realize what are the personal bypass routines that we activate when we have to deal with organizational defensive routines. A second step is to help us become aware of the program in our heads that keeps us unaware of when we are using our personal bypass routines.

A third step is to identify the change program not as one to reduce defensive routines but as one to design a better planning process, a more effective information system, and so on. Start with those features of the executive stewardship that are easily recognized. As we have seen, most executives easily recognize the importance of realistic job descriptions, correct reward and penalty systems, valid and useful information systems, planning processes, and so forth.

While any of these is being designed or redesigned and while careful thought is being given to implementing them, then defensive routines will pop up automatically without our realizing it. They will surface naturally as we deal with technical or organizational problems. We will be therefore more likely to identify them accurately and to do so without overly activating them.

Once the defensive routines are out in the open and connected to the design and effective implementation of the new planning process (or whatever), then we can be asked to deal with them for two reasons. One is to assure the development and effective implementation of a new planning process, and the other is to reduce defensive routines and ultimately to prevent them. Again, these features are at the heart of the stewardship of management.

KEY FEATURES OF EFFECTIVE ACTIVITIES TO REDUCE AND PREVENT DEFENSIVE ROUTINES

A program is a design that specifies the end results plus the steps of how to get from here to there. Designing a new planning process is a program because competent professionals can formulate a new planning process and stipulate what steps would be needed to implement it. It makes sense, therefore, to think in terms of specific and complete plans to get the job done.

This is not true for reducing and preventing defensive routines. Specific plans require a complete and accurate map of the defensive routines, their impact on the organization, and their capacity to be changed and the ability of the players to effect the change. It is difficult to obtain this information because, as stated, the very act of getting it can activate and energize the defensive routines. Even if this were not the case, it would take an army of specialists with lots of financial resources and time and with carte blanche to study everything. The latter would also trigger off defensive routines. Under these conditions, the strategy most likely to succeed is one that will change defensive routines.

Start Small

Begin with one or two relatively clearly defined technical or organizational problems that will require reducing the defensive routines if they are to be solved effectively.

Think and plan carefully the objectives and the actions to be taken during the first step. Define clear public tests of the progress and its effectiveness on the organization. Commit the organization so that the program will be allowed to be implemented and so that no one who works genuinely to reduce and prevent defensive routines will be harmed.

Start at the Top

None of these steps can be accomplished without the commitment of the top. The top has the greatest power to encourage change, to nurture it, to monitor it, and to take responsibility for the direction and pace of development.

Change activities to reduce defensive routines require continual validation by the top. The organization will always be asking, do they really mean this? The best and most powerful validation that the top can give is through its behavior and actions. Only as they embody the new competencies and actions will the organization come to believe that the activities are not a fad or a manipulative device.

Start with Important Problems

A program that works with trivial problems will produce trivial results. Conversely, a program designed to change too much all at once is also doomed to failure. The goal is to identify moderately tough problems where there is a serious challenge and a serious probability of success.

Defining an important problem is not a static affair. The very act of individuals agreeing on what is an important problem is a big step. These discussions often produce defensive reactions. As they are dealt with effectively, the players may re-examine what they have just defined as an important problem.

Start with Clearly Defined Change Processes

Although the direction, pace, and target for change may have to be kept open ended, the nature of the change activities as well as the criteria for defining high quality progress should be stated un-ambiguously at the outset. One reason is that if everything is open ended, then there is a danger of the program going out of control. What should be defined is a process of monitoring the changes that are occurring to inform the players of the progress. It will also help them to make informed decisions concerning the next steps, including whether or not to stop.

Another reason why the change processes should be defined clearly at the outset is that the processes used to reduce or prevent defensive routines are going to be inculcated in the organization. These processes represent the most enduring learning that will take place. They will define the new competencies, values, and norms. All involved should know clearly what they are wishing for themselves and for the organization during the very early stages.

The third reason for defining the process unambiguously is to provide the client a way to evaluate continuously the progress (or lack thereof) as well as the competence of the consultants. It also provides the consultants with guidelines to assess their effectiveness.

CASE ILLUSTRATION OF A CHANGE PROGRAM

This section shows how the ideas just described were illustrated in a leading consulting firm. I select this case because it illustrates what might be done in any firm that utilizes a lot of very bright professionals. The case also closes the loop in the sense that it shows how an organization that helps clients to reduce and prevent defensive routines soon finds itself examining its own. In this case the partners, managers, and consultants involved developed some interesting learning experiences and policies.

The relationship began small. We started in the largest office. We began at the top. We selected a problem that concerned the company: the career development of its professionals at all levels. We utilized a change process to deal with defensive routines that began by helping the players examine the reasoning and the theory of action they used when dealing with threat. This process also generated data to diagnose the organizational defensive routines related to the career development of the professionals at all levels. We collected data on the value of every session held by interviewing the players and by reviewing tape recordings of almost all the key sessions.

The first step was a three-pronged program. First, we observed the partners and others in action during meetings while they were managing the firm. Second, the top completed a case that described how they dealt, or might deal, with a difficult human problem that they face as administrators or consultants. They used the same format as in the John and Bill case.

Third, we interviewed at least 65 percent of the junior consultants to diagnose what they believed were problems, if any, in the human resources area. We knew that if the program succeeded and the change activities were enlarged, then the junior consultants would also have to be observed in action and asked to complete cases.

The second step was a two-day feedback session. During the first day, an analysis was presented of the interview data. A map was also presented depicting some of the major organizational defensive routines related to the problem. The participation was lively. Many ended the day recommending that they commit the firm to spend more time and resources to take corrective action.

I cautioned at making any decisions about next steps before the next day's presentation. I knew, given their reasoning processes and theories in use, that if they were to double the financial resources and time spent interacting with the younger consultants, they might make things worse. To compound the problem, they would be unaware that this was the case (a statement that holds for all the other organizations that we have studied). Moreover, the subordinates had similar defensive routines. This led to a lively closing discussion around the question Are you telling us that we will make things worse even after we have become aware of what we do that is counterproductive? The answer was:

> I am saying that so far you have learned about the organizational factors that cause some of the human problems that you wish to correct. The next step is to examine what contribution, if any, you make in causing these problems by the way that you reason and act in dealing with threat and defensiveness.
>
> For example, you appear to agree that you should spend more time with the younger consultants in discussing their performance and the future in this organization. Many of you are willing to double your efforts. Tomorrow I should like to show that doubling your exposure with the consultants may actually make things worse because the way you would reason and act during these sessions could create further problems.

The next day, we began the session with one of the cases that a partner had written. I selected his case because he was highly oriented toward learning about people skills, and if he became defensive, he would probably deal with it in ways that encouraged his own and others' learning. The prediction turned out to be correct. The dialogue that followed produced the kinds of insights and puzzles described in Chapter 2, but it was directly connected to the problems of their organization. Next, a second case was discussed, written by another partner who was open to learning and encouraged others to do the same.

As a result of the discussions, the participants became aware of their own and others' defensive routines as well as how unaware they were of their own. Although the specific nature of each defensive routine varied, they all produced data publicly that showed they had defensive routines and that they attempted to deal with them by bypassing them. Just discussing these issues publicly began to make it easier to consider using publicly compelling and testable reasoning and action when dealing with defensive routines. This is the first experience the players had had in using nondefensive reasoning to deal with defensive routines.

Not all reacted positively, however. The fears described in Chapter 10 began to surface here. Should we have such discussions publicly? Are people accustomed to having their reasoning examined publicly? Would such discussions make some people feel defenseless? I encouraged the participants to raise these questions with each other and to assess the degree to which the fears are justified. As is true in most cases so far, the very raising and discussing of these issues provides concrete evidence that the end results can be positive. This does not mean that there are not some individuals who still have doubts and concerns. Again, my task was to support their discussing these doubts and concerns and to seek further ways to test them. After all, they had in the room all of the top executives of the firm.

Next, the executives began to transfer the lessons they were learning in the here and now to the problems that had been identified the day before in the organizational analysis. They could now begin to see how the younger consultants felt that the performance feedback had not been very effective. They could also see that the ineffectiveness existed at the officer and manager levels and did not vary by age or years as a consultant. This meant that they were all in the same boat, and this fact meant that the executives could discuss defensive routines more publicly than they thought previously was a good idea. Moreover, they could also begin to see that although the subordinates may be correct, the executives also may have the same defensive routines. If so, some of their frustration, impatience, and hostility toward the top was unfair.

Toward the end of the second day, the participants turned to the question, "What's next?" The partner who administered the office began by saying:

> If all that has happened yesterday and today is valid, then we have much to learn. I can predict, for example, that when I try to feed back the yearly evaluations of the non-partners [in this room] by the partners [in this room], I am likely [and perhaps they, too] to make mistakes and be unaware when I am doing so. I know what I should like to suggest as a next step. I should like to have our consultant join us in these evaluations if the respective manager agrees, so that we can continue to learn from our actions.

The request was greeted with a great deal of favor. I added a request to tape record these sessions for two reasons. One, the participants could reflect more effectively on what happened by listening to the tapes. The conditions were that the tapes would be kept by the consultant and would be considered to be the property of the individuals present at the meeting and that participants could use the tapes any time they wished but could not permit anyone, including spouses, to listen to them without the permission of all players. I warned against granting such permission, but of course the choice was theirs. The second reason for the use of the tape recorder was that I could listen to the tapes with the goal of producing a document to be used within the firm on how to conduct effective performance evaluative sessions throughout the firm. Again, any participant could veto the use of the tape recorder with impunity. The tape recordings were used frequently by the officers and managers.

Another officer suggested that I continue to sit in on the officer meetings and officer-manager meetings to help them develop more effective ways to deal with defensive routines. This suggestion was also accepted without any dissent.

SPREADING THE UNFREEZING AND THE CHANGE ACTIVITIES

Note what has happened. Once the officers and managers approved the organizational diagnosis, once they examined their personal responsibilities for these problems, and once they realized they had to learn to deal with defensive routines differently, they took the next step easily. They began to select contexts in which they could continue to learn and, at the same time, deal with tasks. The partner in charge of feeding back performance evaluations asked that he be permitted to continue the learning in those sessions. Once accepted, the directors and the other partners involved automatically committed themselves to further learning.

If, on the one hand, no one volunteered such next steps, then I would have asked what would lead them to agree with what they have learned but not wish to continue the learning? As the barriers or fears were identified, we would assess how widely and deeply they were held. Next, we would focus on designing actions to overcome them. This would automatically continue the unfreezing and the spreading activities. If, on the other hand, the worst case occurred where the group resisted continuing the process, then I would help them to consider the impact that such an action would have on the organization. It might be possible to design some transition experiences such as exposing the rest of the organization to these seminars. If nothing could be done then I would ask them if they thought it would be wise for them to continue.

The feedback sessions with the managers were successful. Many errors and misunderstandings were corrected on the spot. The officers illustrated their commitment by meeting with the consultant before the feedback session to plan the session as well as meeting afterward to reflect on how well it went. This increased the learning for those who participated significantly.

The culture also began to be changed. The facts that the sessions were tape recorded and listened to, that the officers were willing to interrupt the session to examine their errors, that the consultant seemed to do the same toward officers and managers, and that the managers left the meeting reporting a significant increase in the sense of justice began to change the corridor gossip about the firm and the cultural norms around what was and was not discussable.

Innovations were developed as learning occurred. For example, managers were permitted to select, if they wished, an officer to join them with whom they felt most secure. Another change was in the predisposition of officers to collude in corridor gossip for the sake of the company. Under the old conditions, a consultant or manager would go to an officer that he trusted and, after asking for secrecy, tell the officer something negative about the actions of another officer or manager. Under the new conditions, the officer administrator announced that he would not agree to such sessions unless the information could be given forthrightly to the individual under question. He was also willing to have the informant join in the design of the feedback session to help assure the confidences that he felt were needed. The policy, during the administration of this officer and the next one, led not only to more forthright discussions but also to the reduction of requests for such collusions. What happened was that the officer, managers, and consultants dealt with these problems more directly. At the outset, the consultant was invited to facilitate. Again, as the success of these meetings, which began to include young consultants, got around the hall, there was a greater willingness to make undiscussables discussable.

Finally, the partner developed innovations in the process of firing someone. For example, if a consultant was not doing well, the partners usually built up their evidence until they felt that they had a sure case. Then the partner took the candidate to a fine restaurant and fed back the negative decision. At the same time, the partner would offer very generous separation arrangements, including help in finding another job. Finding the consultant another job was not difficult because the firm was known to hire consultants of the highest quality and to maintain very high technical standards. Other firms were more than willing to hire alumni of this firm.

Under the new arrangement, the officer told the prospective candidate of his or her status early. "At the moment, it is our belief that you will have difficulty in making it. We are telling you early because we want to check our attributions with you. Maybe

our data are wrong or incomplete, and maybe they are not. We also want to design with you a series of actions that you agree would disconfirm our conclusions."

The results were encouraging. For example, one young consultant felt that the data used were valid but incomplete. He felt that one officer and a manager in another office where he had been located for several years would provide different evaluations. The partner encouraged the consultant to arrange a meeting where this could be accomplished. The meeting was held with the officer and manager present. Neither supported the consultant. Both said that they were not as positive about his performance as he recalled. Under questioning of the partner, they admitted that they probably had not been as forthright in the past with the consultant because they did not want to upset him. They were in the dilemma of giving him the bad news in a way that they thought he would hear it. They now realized that they had to be much more explicit and less easing in. The partner then asked the consultant if he wanted to design some other actions because he had not received valid feedback in the previous office. A frank discussion, managed by the consultant, ensued. He concluded that he did not wish to continue but wanted help finding a new job. This request was granted immediately. Again the corridors were somewhat aghast when the consultant told his friends that the session had been fair and that he had decided to leave on his own volition.

As the number of successful experiences increased, officers and managers began to enlarge the activites to other settings. For example, several officers decided to do some case team evaluation. One example was described in Chapter (5) where the team reflected on what caused it not to perform as well as it could. Another example was that several officers invited the consultant to observe and facilitate the case team discussions as they were going on (Argyris, 1982).

As the success of these experiments increased, one officer invited the consultant to help him redesign a different client relationship and a different case team activity. This was described in Chapter 10. The point is that success seemed to feed upon itself, and slowly a larger number of partners began to use the consultant to learn more of the new skills under conditions where they were dealing with client or internal problems. The exact number of these opportunities and where they would arise could not be predicted ahead of time. As they arose, they were staffed. Rather than repeat examples of changes described in the previous chapters, I present two new examples of how consultants began to examine their personal defensive routines in dealing with difficult client situations.

CASE A: HELPING CONSULTANTS CHANGE THE PERSONAL DEFENSIVE ROUTINES THEY USE TO DEAL WITH CLIENT DEFENSIVE ROUTINES

Robert and Dick are senior consultants in a firm that was hired by a major corporation to help them explore the marketing and financial futures the firm will be facing in the next decade. They were asked to become consultants to an internal case team created by the CEO to study the issues. The case team was composed of officers of the company (including the planning vice-president) and chaired by a senior line officer.

Robert and Dick were becoming increasingly frustrated with the progress of the case team. As they viewed the problem, they were in a predicament that they could not solve without endangering the client relationship.

First, the case team members were not technically competent to conduct the kind of sophisticated analysis that was required. They also did not see their responsibility as immersing themselves into the raw data to try to understand the complexity involved. They were willing to do what Robert and Dick told them. But Robert and Dick had difficulty in assigning the team important tasks because the client members did not know how to do them and to teach them would require much more time than was available.

Second, none of the client members in the case team took initiatives to throw out ideas and discuss them. Some worked hard and some did not. The case team did not have a set of norms about excellent analytical work. The team leader often blustered and inhibited people from participating.

Finally, Robert and Dick did not believe they could take corrective action because, "We have no control over the group so we cannot give orders. "We are not sure that we understand the technical features well enough to tell them what to do."

If Robert's and Dick's diagnosis is correct, they are encountering several layers of defensive routines:

1. Client organizational defensive routines that had led the CEO to appoint a team that was not technically capable of conducting a study;
2. Case team defensive routines that tied up its deliberations so they did not take the initiatives required;
3. The consultants' defensive routines about engaging the first two sets of defensive routines.

The consultants bypassed the issues by asking for more technical help from their consulting firm in order to get the work done, bypassing discussing their diagnosis with the team, and acting as if the team or the consultants was not a problem.

As the consultant to Robert and Dick, I saw it as my responsibility to help them examine their defensive routines and to alter them so that they could engage the clients' defensive routines more effectively. Robert and Dick began by telling me that the problem existed in the client group. I did not doubt that their clients were partially the cause of the difficulties. I wanted, however, to begin by focusing on the ways they may be responsible for reinforcing the problems they wished to overcome.

The strategy I used was to help Robert and Dick reflect on their own thinking and reasoning about their relationship with the clients. If this worked, it should not only help Robert and Dick solve their problem but also provide them with a model of how they could teach their clients to reflect on their actions. For example:

Interventionist: To what extent is it possible for you to say something of what you've been saying to me to them? What prevents you from saying this to them? . . .

As the session progressed, I tried to illustrate how they were responsible for their difficulties by pointing out inconsistencies in their reasoning while trying to be clear about my own.

Interventionist: So, [your] frustration is as much due to the ambiguity and complexity of the technical problem. . . .

Robert: Yes.

Interventionist: And I don't understand how you can then get [frustrated] at theirs . . . when they are less competent technically speaking and, second, are much more prone to saluting because they have grown up in that culture.

Robert: I'm frustrated by the situation. . . . It's just something about those days spent there that is frustrating.

Interventionist: And I'm agreeing with you. . . . I'm suggesting that it is just as much your doing as theirs . . . from the description you are giving me.

I further emphasized their responsibility by illustrating the possible negative consequences of their actions. For example, Robert reveals that he has commiserated with the vice-presidents about their frustration with the project, attributing it to their once having had authority over thousands of people while now they must do the work themselves as equals. I noted:

> The unintended consequence of that is it could reinforce [their] pattern [of not accepting responsibility] because they could use that as the explanation and say, "Okay, Robert, now you see my point. I used to be in charge of 2,000 people, now I'm [not]. You empathize with it, now please, get on with it [Robert laughs] and feel even less responsible."

The interventionist thus challenges not only their diagnosis but also their perception of the cure. This is important in getting Dick and Robert to take responsibility for changing the nature of their interaction with the task force and not perceiving themselves as paralyzed.

A theme that runs throughout the session is the nature of the consultant's role: Must the consultant be an expert in the given business in order to be effective? Dick and Robert repeatedly state that the only way they can get themselves out of their current impasse is to become experts in corporation P's specialty. The interventionist agreed with them that they should learn more about the technical aspects of the problem, but he cautioned about the way they might use the knowledge under conditions of feeling frustrated. He recollected that they said if they knew the business problem better they might feel free to give orders and confront the ineffectiveness of the team. That strategy may run afoul of the executing leader. He recalled Robert's statement, "It's hard to kick people and tell them to follow my directions when I'm not clear what the directions should be."

Robert responded that he understood that I wanted to help them help the case team become more reflective, but the trouble was that he was finding the whole experience "terribly boring."

Interventionist: And how do you account for the boringness? . . .
Is it that you're not good at it and you deal with it by saying that it is boring, or is it that these are boring people?
Robert responded that he actually felt challenged when he was not good at something.

Interventionist: Yes, and if that is so, how come this is boring?
Robert attributed his boredom to the slow pace of the meetings. I placed the responsibility for his boredom back on him.

Interventionist: Well, let me push you a little. If you were good at dealing with these issues, maybe you could . . . speed up the pace.

As the discussion continued, Robert and Dick began to see that the interventionist's view was that they were not taking enough responsibility to engage the clients' or their own defensive routines. This bewildered Robert and Dick. Both felt that the real problem was the clients' actions and not theirs.

Robert took the initiative to express his concerns and frustrations with the interventionist. Robert asked in effect, "Do you *really* believe we should describe our frustrations to the client? Couldn't that make things worse?"

This made it possible for Robert to ask the interventionist some specific questions about his strategy:

Robert: How would we express our frustrations?

Dick: How would you describe my views to the client?

The discussion now shifted to how they can engage the defensive routines without risking seriously the client relationship. This was a more productive shift because one reason people bypass is that they do not believe that there is a way to engage without rupturing the relationship. I turned to role playing my answers for Robert and Dick to test the validity of my views by producing them. For example:

Interventionist [role playing what Robert may say to the team]: "Dick and I are experiencing a dilemma. On the one hand, we believe that you feel somewhat frustrated by the pace and ambiguity, . . . and we do too. And we'd like to then begin asking ourselves the question, how do we begin closing the ambiguity?" That would be a beginning. What is your [reaction]?

Robert: I certainly think it is worth talking about. . . .

Dick and Robert now began to show more receptivity to the interventionist's suggestions. Gone are the earlier rationalizations that characterized their responses to his role plays. However, they continued to raise concerns about the case, presenting the interventionist with what appeared to be major obstacles in implementing his ideas.

Dick: There are a couple of people that quite clearly don't do anything at all. . . . They have not produced a single slide, graph, document of any kind. . . .

[A] high degree of organizational ambiguity is necessary within that group in order to allow for that to function without a loss of face on the part of the individuals involved.

Interventionist: Well, what you are saying to me is that if we are going to remain within their system of defenses we can't do what we think might be a good idea. That's why I say I don't know how much risk you want to take. But I wouldn't remain within their defenses. I wouldn't do that kind of face saving. I wouldn't reward that because someday it might come back at you. . . . Somebody might say, . . . "Why didn't you do something about it? Why didn't you come to me?" . . .

Robert: They look to us to deal with that ambiguity and we can only deal with it partially. . . .

Interventionist: Now that helps me. . . . Let me suggest an additional. . . . I'm now being Robert again: "I believe that one of the problems here has to do with ambiguity at all sorts of levels. It is not possible for me to predict all the ambiguities you may be experiencing, so if you are experiencing them, let me know.

In these examples, I do not discount the clients' concerns. I show how they can manage the problems by openly discussing them with the group. I do not deny that ambiguity and lack of data are important concerns, but I see the larger problem as the clients' inability to cope with these concerns.

Once the inconsistencies and negative consequences of their reasoning and actions had been made clear to them and alternative strategies had been illustrated for each of their major concerns, Robert and Dick understood and accepted their share of the responsibility for the difficulties they have had.

Robert: I guess what you are suggesting goes back to the theme of what our responsibility is in this process. . . . I think [the interventionist] has a good point there. Maybe we haven't been as proactive as we should about saying [to the group what they need to do].

The next phase is one where Robert and Dick tested their understanding through simulating the interventions they would try with the client. In his practice, Robert demonstrates that he has begun to achieve a balanced sense of responsibility for the case. He is open about his own uncertainty and his negative evaluation of the group. He sees his role as helping the group to think reflectively, and he invites them to help him do this by telling him what they would like from him — a significant change for someone who advocated earlier for a leader who would "step up and say, 'I'm in charge.' " For example:

Robert (role playing what he might say to the client teams): "You'd think everyone is having a hard time, you and me, with the complexity . . . of this project, and it is very important . . . that we keep trying to understand what is your responsibility in this and what is ours. . . .

"One of our responsibilities is bringing to you the strategy expertise that we were hired for. And sometimes I am having a hard time knowing the best way to communicate that to you. Part of that is moving the process forward substantively. Part of it is teaching you to think reflectively. And it is hard to teach someone to be reflective. I will need some help from you in that process, and [need for you to tell me] what you'd like more of. Conversely, I feel a little frustrated because . . . you are the ones who are supposed to do the analysis, and data often come back in forms that take too much of our time to use."
Does that make sense?

I supported what Robert said because I believed that it would enable him to clarify any misunderstandings with the task force about their respective roles. By having this discussion he may obtain information about the corporation's expectations of him and Dick, information they can then use to plan their consulting strategy. I reminded him that he should be prepared to be very specific in his evaluation of the task force. Robert ended the meeting by saying that he found it helpful. He wanted to experiment in dealing more with the issues that engage defensive routines than those that bypass them.

In conclusion, neither Robert, Dick, nor I believes that this experience would mean that the problems of overcoming their predisposition to bypass their own and client defensive routines were solved. The episode was the beginning. Reflecting on the process of engaging Robert's and Dick's defensive routines, I sensed it went as follows:

Activities during the Episode	Interventionist's Intentions
Robert and Dick were encouraged to fill in apparent gaps in their diagnosis.	I want to indicate a genuine concern in helping Robert and Dick express their diagnosis in as powerful terms as possible. I try to help them to fill in gaps in the logic as well as to illustrate their points by giving examples of actual conversation.
Inconsistencies were identified in the diagnosis and were tested with the clients.	I would be tough on their description. I would state any evaluations and attributions that I was making in order to test them publicly with them. In doing so, I am making myself vulnerable because I could be wrong. I do not mind vulnerability that leads to my learning and my client's learning.
	I will not use vulnerability, however, as a cover-up for my sloppiness. I make evaluations and attributions, fully believing that they are correct. I test them because I could be wrong. If indeed I am more wrong than right, then my rea-

Activities during the Episode

Interventionist's Intentions

soning can be called into question.

Robert and Dick were encouraged to seek alternative ways to reason and to act. The presentations included inventions and actual conversations of how they would produce the inventions with the clients.

I present the conversations because they present a more complete basis for the clients to understand my inventions as well as a stronger base for them to question or accept them.

I keep asking clients for illustrative conversations because they represent the most valid window into the way they reason when they act. I must therefore include conversations so they can get a window into my mind.

The clients experimented with ways to confront defensive routines. The experimentation included their making explicit the problem they were trying to solve, the inventions to solve the problem, the actual conversations that would have to be produced, and an evaluation of their probable effectiveness, which could lead to a reformulation of the problem or the invention.

I want to help the clients reflect on their thinking by using the model of discovery-invention-production-evaluation and by learning how to do the above and test publicly the outcomes.

I want to help them to make their thinking about dealing with defensive routines more explicit, more precise (including when they are not precise), and more testable by those who have relevant information.

Several months later during a conversation with Robert, he reflected on what he had learned during the session. First, he had become clearer about what were his responsibilities and what were the responsibilities of the clients. By clearer, he did not mean simply that he understood them better. He meant that he could invent solutions and produce conversations to implement the solutions.

> My immediate response was to see the clients as being responsible for the problem. And often my diagnosis of what they were doing was correct. The problem was that I never acted on that diagnosis because I could not see a way to do it that was constructive.

Second, he realized that structurally, the strategy that they had been using was not going to work. The strategy tended to escalate the problems rather than reduce them: "I now can see more ways to solving these problems than hiding them, which made them worse." Robert also said that he also found that he could apply the ideas to other clients as well as to interactions within case teams:

> I just had a difficult meeting this morning. A young consultant was blaming the manager for his [consultant's] poor performance. It was very useful to me to think through together with him whose responsibility it was and how he arrived at his conclusions.

He left realizing that he was responsbile for not communicating effectively with his manager about the problems he was attributing to the manager.

CASE B: HOW PERSONAL DEFENSIVE ROUTINES CAN HELP TO LOSE A POTENTIAL CLIENT

Phillip, a principal who was an expert on formulating and developing strategy, was competing with another consulting firm for a contract. Phillip believed that the competing consulting firm was not as good as his was in rigorous empirical analysis but that they were probably better at, what he described as, "hand holding clients to make them feel better especially in the behavioral area." What worried Phillip was that the potential clients implied that they were looking for a consultant who was strong not only on the technical features of strategy formulation but also on overcoming behavioral blockages to implementation.

The clients eventually chose the other consultant. Phillip decided to reflect on the experience to learn from it. Phillip's explanation to himself of the loss of the client included the following:

1. The client had just achieved unexpectedly fast success on a new product and, hence, became less interested in strategic analysis.
2. The competitors had an inside track with the president of the client firm.
3. The president was a lawyer and, hence, probably not interested in rigorous systematic analysis.

I have observed consultants use several of these explanations when they experience a loss of a potential client. First, the explanations are true but incomplete. The company did produce a new product, the other consultant did have an inside track, and the president was not a strong supporter of quantitative analysis. Second, the explanations placed the responsibility for the loss with the client. However, as the consultant learned later, the client wanted him but felt he was not concerned enough with the human problems of implementation and that he distanced himself from those problems during the early meetings. Third, the explanation acted as a bypass mechanism for the consultant not to focus on his responsibilities.

As a result of several long conversations, Phillips identified three actions he took that could have contributed to losing the client. First, he dealt with the client's possible desire to focus heavily on implementation by "feeling them out" during the meeting. After examining the reconstructed conversation, Phillip concluded that his strategy to be flexible could have caused him to be seen by the client as wishy-washy, as trying to agree with whatever position the clients preferred in order to get the contract. For example:

Phillip: I think we can help you. But it's not clear to me whether it would be more effective for us to work closely with you, have your people do a lot of the work, and us direct and interact with you or whether we should come in, gather the right data, go away and do the work, and then present the solutions. How would you feel about either approach?

Client: We don't know what would be more effective. Our guys don't have that much time to be doing a lot of work. On the other hand, we're not sure that giving us the right answer at the end of three or four months is going to transfer enough of the workings and the dynamics of how you get that answer, in order to make us effective at doing it from now on.

Phillip: I think that means we have to work more closely with you and have you be more integrated in the process.

Client: Yeah, but we don't have enough time.

Phillip: In that case, we can do the other alternative.

A second action that Phillip recalled he took was to emphasize the importance of not staying on too long. He did so because the competing consultant had the reputation of staying longer than necessary. During the meeting, he said, "Look, we are here to help you as long as you need help. But when we see the job is done, we will go away. You want to be careful because some consulting firms prefer to stick around forever."

Later Phillip thought that this comment could have contributed to the difficulties because he had the reputation of being good at strategy formulation and less effective on organizational implementation issues. Hence, when he said that he would leave when he was done, the client could have interpreted that as evidence that they leave before implementation is carried out.

Finally, Phillip had made a fifty-slide presentation on economics and competitive issues that he learned later had impressed the clients immensely. They concluded, as he believed was the case, that he produces better analysis. Phillip also reflected that he had only one slide on implementation. If the clients compared the thoroughness of the analysis with the superficiality of the organizational issues, they could have concluded that he was not as effective in implementation.

Dealing with Difficult Personal Relationships

A third area into which the consultant was invited was the domain of difficult personal relationships — between partners, between a partner and a principal, or between a consultant and a partner. As many subordinates as superiors initiated meetings to discuss this problem. It was becoming safe for subordinates to initiate actions, something that had been most difficult to do in the past.

In one case, a principal initiated a discussion with a partner. He felt the partner was unfair, unilateral, and at times brutal. The partner asked for and received illustrations of each of these attributions. The illustrations helped him to see where he could agree with the principal. He told him that he could see how the principal would interpret his actions as he had done.

However, the partner gave examples of the principal's actions that led the partner to conclude that the principal was not very good in managing a case team or a client relationship but was very brittle around these issues. What the partner had done in the past was try to bypass the issue so he did not hurt the principal. He would, for example, suppress his feelings and frustrations, only to find out later on that they would erupt with an intensity that surprised and embarrassed him. He dealt with these feelings by promising to control himself more and not to work with the manager again. He also distanced himself from the principal and worked whenever possible directly with the case team. Sometimes the case team members would find themselves receiving contradictory advice. Some would deal with the conflict by going either to the principal or the partner. In either case they extracted the usual secrecy commitment. The partner would then act in ways that appeared unilateral and brutal to the principal. The principal would act in ways that seemed devious to the partner. Since none of these attributions was discussed and tested, the situation became worse.

The session helped the partner and the principal become more candid and reduce the cover-up of defensive routines. It also made it easier for each to identify valid weaknesses and strengths in each other and work cooperatively to deal with them.

In another case, a young consultant admired officer A very much and was excited when A selected him to be a member of the case team. As they worked together, the consultant found the officer to behave in a mixture of genuine participation and genuine unilateral control while appearing unaware of the latter.

As a result of the discussion, the young consultant was helped to see how his actions had left A worried about his competence. Often A preferred to be participative, but he reverted to unilateral control whenever he felt that the consultant was not taking enough initiative. The consultant, in contrast, had reduced his initiative because he thought that was upsetting the officer.

Once these issues were cleared, a highly productive relationship developed. The consultant also encouraged other consultants to do the same when they had problems with other officers or managers. Thus, such encouragement had an impact on the culture.

Helping Officers Deal with Problems Where There Were Strong Differences in Views

The consultant sat in on an officer and officer-manager meetings when they were discussing difficult issues. His objective was to identify defensive routines that made problem solving less effective and that inhibited building a cohesive officer group. As pointed out previously, one of the important concerns was the issue of career development for consultants and managers.

Some officers believed that career development programs were needed to attract outstanding young professionals. Another group had serious doubts about career development programs, believing that if the firm hired the right type of professional — that is, one with high analytical and conceptual skills — such professionals would be so engrossed in their work that it would be easy to attract and keep them. This second group was not necessarily against career programs; rather, its greatest fear was that the programs might be used to retain dull professionals. This group also feared that, in the long run, these less competent professionals would depend on these programs for their commitment rather than on the actual job tasks. Hence, career development activities might attract and retain professionals who really should leave the firm. The former group of officers was known as the liberals, and the latter group was known as the conservatives.

The debate about the career program had been going on for several years. Every time a young professional quit (not often), the liberals used his or her departure as evidence for the validity of their position. The conservatives expressed doubt of this. They maintained that if professionals with the right attitude and proper skills were hired, they would not leave.

Both sides saw the problem as a central one that required some action. A committee made up of liberals and conservatives was formed and asked to recommend future policy. I focus now on some of the problem-solving dynamics of the meeting in which the committee made its presentation to the executive group. The data presented here were collected from tape-recorded interviews and from observation of several preliminary group meetings.

How the Liberals and Conservatives Framed the Problem

We learned in interviews held before the final meeting that the liberals framed the problem as follows:

1. The firm is being unfair, foolish, and irrational about education, evaluation of professionals, and career development programs.

2. The conservatives are, mostly, well-meaning people who are blind to the unfairness and irrationality of the present policies.
3. The conservatives see the liberals as overprotective alarmists: "If the liberals were let loose, they would produce policies that require much more attention and money to implement, and this might spoil the younger professionals."

The conservatives believed the following:

1. There is a morale problem among the young professionals. The problem can be solved through proper recruiting.
2. The liberals are overreacting to the cues of dissatisfaction. If the conservatives are not careful, the liberals may undermine the firm's emphasis on high standards, analytical excellence, and autonomous professionalism.
3. The liberals see the conservatives as well intentioned but out of date with the current social changes about careers.

These lists illustrate that there is a basic agreement that the firm should hire and keep first-rate personnel. There is also honest disagreement on what action to take. These agreements and disagreements are discussable. The liberals can talk about career programs in general, and the conservatives can talk about proper recruitment procedures in general.

The difficulty arises when the whole group tries to design the specific actions the firm should take. Before an agreement can be reached, each side must explore the doubts it has about the other. The difficulty is that each side questions the other's reasoning processes. To compound the problem, each side privately explains the ineffective reasoning of the other side by making attributions that the other side is unfair, irrational, foolish, blind, overprotective, and overreacting or that it is responding to political pressures from its coalition group.

Although doubting each other's reasoning processes, each side explains the other's ineffective reasoning by using motivational or political concepts — as if the explanation lay in the motivations and defenses or in the political action of individuals. It is as if each person assumed that when others act, they intend the consequences that follow. However, this belief assumes that they are aware of the consequences of their action and that if they are acting ineffectively, their ineffectiveness is related to motivational or political factors. The possibility that their reasoning processes are wrong and that they may not be aware of this is not considered. We have already glimpsed that people may be unaware of the consequences of their own actions at the same time they are aware of the consequences of other people's actions. Moreover, their reasoning processes may be automatic but flawed, and accompanying each automatic response is yet another that keeps people unaware of their ineffective reasoning and the consequences of their actions. The motivations and political factors may be the cues that trigger off the automatic responses. Hence, they are necessary but not a sufficient focus for detecting and correcting errors.

It follows that both groups will have to suppress most of their diagnostic frame about the other side when they meet to discuss the issues. It is not surprising, therefore, that both the liberals and conservatives affirmed prior to the meeting that their meeting strategies should be guided by good common sense. The definition of good common sense varied somewhat. For example, the liberals framed their action as follows:

1. Do not do or say anything that makes the conservatives publicly defensive. Such action would be viewed by all as unfair and uncivilized and could lose us support for our position. Therefore, do not mention the conservatives' blindness and irrationality.
2. Focus on the negative consequences of the present policy by citing data that clearly support our views.
3. Do not polarize or overstate the case because the conservatives will interpret such statements as confirming our alarmist tendencies and will confront us on those issues. That would lead to personal attacks, which would get us away from the issues.

The conservatives framed their action as follows:

1. Do not say or do anything that makes the liberals publicly defensive. Such action would be viewed as unfair and uncivilized. This could lose us support for our position. Do not discuss the view that the liberals are blind, are alarmists, and tend to overprotect the young professionals.
2. Let the liberals talk so they cannot accuse us of being obstructionists. Respond with data that clearly illustrate our views.
3. Do not polarize because that will only confirm the liberals' fear of our rigidity and stodginess.

The two groups appeared to hold the same views about factors that would inhibit effective problem solving. Both ruled out discussing their view of the other side's poor reasoning. In doing so, they ignored the opportunity to test the validity of their views but continued to act as if these views are valid.

After the meeting, representatives of the liberal and conservative positions were interviewed and asked whether it would have been helpful if they had tested the validity of their attributions. The automatic responses included the following reasoning:

- "Of course; that's obvious."
- "That is not possible, though, because it would only upset others."
- "If people are upset, you get neither a valid test nor a civilized discussion."
- "After all, all of us are striving to be rational."

Is a paradox evident in this reasoning? At the heart of rationality is the rule that inferences should be subject to testing. It is fundamentally irrational to assert that a premise is true when it has never been tested. The paradox, therefore, is that, in the name of rationality, the participants are acting irrationally.

However, at another level this irrationality is rational. It is rational in the sense that if people act on the basis of attributions they know others will not confirm, then to state these openly will indeed upset others, and this may block that particular action.

When the participants said they were acting rationally, they meant that they wanted to minimize the expression of negative feelings and defensiveness, and this is rational. But it makes little sense to expect that such expression will be minimized if each side believes that the other is reasoning incorrectly and if each is making unjust attributions about why that is so. Because both sides planned not to discuss these matters, a powerful norm was generated that all would hesitate to violate. The norm assured that negative feelings and defenses would not be expressed, but it did not influence the way people secretly felt.

What Happened during the Meeting

The meeting was opened by the liberals. They recommended establishing a high-level career development committee to define and monitor policies. They frequently repeated the following points, making suggestions for new career development initiatives:

• Career development is not a panacea.
• It will do better what we are already doing. We are building modestly on existing practice.
• It will not alter the firm's norms on first-rate technical competence.
• It will be experimental.
• It will be informal. It is not designed to threaten anyone.
• Such a program should be managed by officers with a wide range of perspectives.

The liberals also noted that a study of the young professionals suggested that one of the most important complaints had to do with the executives' behavior when evaluating subordinates. They recommended that this topic undergo further study — a recommendation that might be described as an easing in, cautious approach.

The conservatives interpreted the approach in precisely these terms. They began their counterreaction with statements like "I'm glad to hear that we are moving carefully and experimentally, that we are trying to make better what we are presently committed to." Interviews after the meeting confirmed the inference that those who spoke this way saw it as a means of publicly holding the liberals down.

At the same time, the conservatives agreed that there was room to improve the quality of the feedback to young professionals, emphasized the importance of recruiting fine professionals. with "the attitudes of the builders of the firm," and agreed that they may not have fulfilled their share of career development responsibilities but mentioned that they were an already overloaded professional group.

Not all liberals and conservatives followed the guidelines. At times, a liberal's impassioned plea cited dangers like impairment of the firm's growth and excellence if the firm could not get the best professionals. The response was that there was little evidence that the firm was not getting its share of the best professionals. One liberal said that young professionals were overcommitting themselves to insure promotion, to which a conservative responded that this might be a plus for the firm if kept within appropriate limits.

The meeting concluded with a vote to create a career development committee and program. The career committee was explicitly told not to generate initiatives costly in terms of attention and money without reporting these to the total partnership. The conservatives asked that the committee's representation include an appropriate range of views. The managing partner assured them that this would be done and asked for volunteers. The meeting ended with public comments about the spirit of cooperation, the common sense used, and the progress made.

One of the consequences of feeding back this analysis was that many officers wanted to reduce the defensive routines, especially the mixed messages and intergroup games. Some succeeded in doing so, others less so. The overall impact on the group processes was, according to all the officers, a positive one. However, the very success led to their upping the ante and finding new issues upon which to work.

DEFENSIVE REACTIONS TO CHANGE ACTIVITIES

These successes should not be interpreted to mean that some officers, managers, and consultants did not have doubts. As far as the consultants were concerned, the few who had concerns were highly competent in rigorous empirical analysis and in conceptualizing client problems elegantly and successfully. They could not see the sense of dealing with defensive routines, their own or anyone else's. Often they would add that their clients never exhibited such defenses. In many of those cases the clients had told the officers that the consultants had excellent technical skills but that their people skills left much to be desired.

Managers and especially officers did not have to be convinced of the importance of people skills. They not only had more experience but also were responsible for the success of the relationship. Their big concern was whether it made sense to use these new skills. Six defenses were often used by officers and managers (as well as by clients) when exploring the idea of engaging defensive routines.

Couldn't Becoming Candid Lead to People Being Destructive?

"What are you recommending — that I call someone an SOB or that I tell him that he is a narrow-minded lousy performer?" Individuals who express such concerns appear to have heard the idea to make the undiscussable discussable but have not heard the advice not to do it in a way that will discourage learning. To call someone an SOB or a lousy performer is to make hostile evaluations and attributions without illustrating them and without subjecting them to test. These are precisely the actions that we wish to avoid (as indicated in Chapters 2, 3, and 5).

There is also the question of why individuals have to frame the problem in these terms in the first place. Why is it that their automatic way to frame the problem and to act is counterproductive? Why do they frame their evaluations and feelings this way? Perhaps their hostility should not be focused on the way they reason and act about others, which appears to be destined to be hostile.

If We Said the Truth, People Would Leave or Clients Would Fire Us as Consultants

A second defensive routine is to invoke the worst possible case. It is as if the only alternative is to continue the defenses or lose. The basic assumption of this approach is a mistrust of the others' willingness to engage their defensive routines. There are cases in which the mistrust is probably valid. So far, however, the actual number is significantly less than such fears would suggest.

Whenever the danger is high, the cues given by others are so obvious and powerful that it would not make sense to act in ways that would upset others. Defensive routines are useful under such conditions, but most individuals do not give such cues. In most cases, we have seen that people are much more open and willing to discuss the undiscussable than is attributed to them. Could the worst case strategy tell us less about the world out there and more about the fears the individuals have of their capacity to deal with candidness effectively?

It Is Dangerous to Become Candid Because It Could Hurt People or They Could Take Advantage of You

If being candid means doing it so incompetently, then it is dangerous. But, as we have shown that is not what is being recommended. The subtler issue is the fear that if individuals discussed the undiscussable, someone may take advantage of them. This may be valid in a competitive, mistrustful world. If we stop here, however, then we have a self-fulfilling prophecy and a self-sealing process. It is an example of a defensive routine that causes individuals to protect themselves by reinforcing the defensive routines.

The task is to begin to engage the defensive routines step by step while, at the same time, creating structures and policies that reward and protect individuals who are trying to reduce the defensive routines. Again, we have found few cases where the danger is as great as this defense implies. As long as the steps are taken one at a time, it is possible to learn from each experiment. If, at any point, individuals conclude that there is danger, then they can call a halt to activities.

The other side of the coin is that whenever there is danger, not dealing with it does not reduce it. All we do is create conditions where the dangerous actions go underground. This, then, rewards playing it safe and getting as much power as possible that can be used if it becomes necessary.

Isn't It Important to Permit Individuals, Especially Subordinates, to Protect Themselves Through Privacy and Secrecy?

Nothing in our approach suggests that individuals do not have a right to privacy or secrecy. The problem arises when individuals use their private reasoning or keep some of these actions secret in ways that harm other individuals or the health of the organization. If unilateral self-protection through privacy or secrecy (by superior or subordinate) leads to harming individuals, then those actions are not self-protective. If they are, they are simultaneously destructive of others, and if the latter is the case, they eventually become self-destructive.

Recall the case of Gerry (Chapter 2). He felt that he had to keep his ideas and feelings private and not to test them because (in his view) his superior was authoritarian and manipulative. Our analysis showed that his actions could have helped to produce such behavior on the part of the superior. By keeping his reasoning private, he was not able to test it publicly. Since "not testing publicly" is an appropriate rule when reasoning defensively, Gerry eventually became distanced and disconnected from his own reasoning.

There are no doubt times in which it makes sense for people to protect themselves privately and secretly. One example would be dealing with an unbearable boss who is closed to learning and who may use his or her power to harm you or an unbearable subordinate who may act to undermine you.

Our position is that individuals should strive to test if they should withhold their views and that organizations should develop conditions in which this public testing can be carried out with impunity.

If I Behave This Way, They Will Think I Am Crazy

Much depends upon how the new behavior is introduced. For example, whenever I introduced the new behavior in the early sessions in each firm, no one thought I was crazy. They evaluated my actions quite positively and voted overwhelmingly to learn the new skills. Some began to feel that others would think they are crazy as they went from watching me perform to designing how they might implement such behavior.

The introduction of the new behavior should be done incrementally. Recall that in the first sessions, I selected cases written by officers who I judged were more open to learning. My strategy was incremental. I was hoping that the early sessions would produce enough success to induce individuals to continue.

It is true that discussing the undiscussable is often seen as a deviant act. It is also true, if it is done well, that it is often accompanied with a sigh of relief and a desire on the part of people to learn how to do it. If, in contrast, it is done well and rejected strongly, then the client and the consultant have better data as to what it would take to overcome defensive routines and whether they wish to do so or not.

I Do This All the Time. Aren't I Just Being Thoughtful and Honest?

This is a difficult defense to deal with because, unlike the others, expressing it does not require the individuals to go public with their doubts and fears or how they would behave. If someone believes that being candid means to call someone an SOB, it is possible to show how this is counterproductive. It is possible to discuss the fears individuals have that others will take advantage of them if they become more candid.

When individuals say that they engage defensive routines correctly and leave it at that, it is difficult to deal constructively with the defense. If they are asked to illustrate and their response is highly abstract (which is often the case), then discussing that may be threatening. One reason why it may be threatening is that this defense is often used by conflict avoiders. To ask for illustration is to produce some conflict. The irony is that individuals create the conflict because they have the option to illustrate their views concretely. Thus, there is the additional threat that they could feel mistrusted.

There are two conditions under which these conflict avoiders get in trouble. One is a situation in which they have, for whatever reason, disappointed a client. Strange as it may sound to some consultants, clients do have their defenses about upsetting "nice guys." In one case, the consultant was considered to be a nice guy by a CEO. He often told the COO (Chief Operating Officer) that he wished the consultant made it easier to say negative things to him. The CEO never did. One day when the CEO retired and the COO took charge, he fired the consultant for that reason and, of course, never told him the truth. The new CEO realized that his organization was going to have to go through some difficult cultural changes, and he doubted if the consultant was prepared for the job ahead.

The other area in which this strategy does not work is in an organization that is beginning to change successfully. For example, in both of the consulting organizations mentioned, there were three or four officers who expressed that they already behaved consistently with Model II. However, when asked to illustrate their assertion, they either seemed unable to do so or they did it at a very high level of abstraction. These same officers tended to resist participating in the innovative feedback sessions described earlier or in holding case team meetings to reflect on their practice. The difficulty arose when the young consultants and managers learned of the progress being made in other case teams — they, too, wanted to experience the same learning. In all cases they either hesitated to ask or did so with such hesitation that it was difficult either to see it as a request or to trust it. Soon these officers got to be known as nice guys who supported the status quo. The officers, in turn, began to have difficulties in getting managers and consultants for their case teams. The difficulties were not too great because you may recall that some consultants had the same doubts. Also, these consultants, for the most part, were technically excellent. Combining technical excellence with conflict avoiders can be powerful as long as the implementation issues are not great.

INSTITUTIONALIZING THE CHANGES

Another step was to develop educational experiences to teach the learning to others within the firm. Seminars were designed with officers and managers attending who were experimenting with the new approaches.

For example, a partner designed a seminar around a recurring problem. What do you do when a client nit picks your ideas? Briefly, the clients had begun a new venture that they believed could become a billion-dollar-plus business. The consulting team was asked to help the clients take advantage of the opportunity. The team worked cooperatively with the client organization. After several months of work and periodic lengthy discussions, the consulting case team presented to the client hard data to show that it was unlikely that the business would be more than a seventy-five-million-dollar one (at least in the immediate future). "As the presentation wore on," the officer stated, "we became aware that there was a lot of nit-picking of analytical points. For the first time we were asked questions such as, 'When did you get that number?' or 'How do you know your assumptions are correct?' "

The officer then asked his colleagues how they would diagnose what was going on. An analysis of the tape-recorded discussion indicated that all agreed that the clients' nit-picking behavior was caused by the clients' defensiveness. "What would make the clients defensive?" asked the officers. Three reasons were given:

1. The consultants had come to a different and much more pessimistic solution than had the clients using the same data. The nit-picking was caused by the feelings of embarrassment on the

part of the clients as well as the fact that they did not know how else to react.

2. The consultants have not only just told the client that their projections were wrong but also have created the possibility that at least some of the people brought in to build the new business may not have jobs.

3. The surprise itself could be the cause of the client defensiveness. If the consultants had spoken with some of the key individuals before the meeting, they could have prepared them for the surprise.

As one consultant said, "Their nit-picking is a survival process to be expected by anyone who is threatened." Many participants nodded their heads approvingly or said "Yes," "Correct," "Right on." He added "Would we not act in the same way if we had an outsider tell us that our practice was wrong?" Again, many nodded their heads in approval, and several said "Yes." Hence, we have an example where the consultants agreed that the clients were acting defensively. They agreed that the causes of the defensiveness were that the consultants had arrived at a different conclusion than what the clients expected and had done so using the very data the clients had used to develop the wrong conclusion.

The officer leading the discussion asked what actions they would recommend. The responses could be categorized as follows:

1. Ask the clients to "raise their sights . . . and help them to see the big picture."

2. Encourage the clients to examine "our numbers any way they wish and see what happens to the analysis. If we are correct they will eventually realize it."

3. Invite the clients to express all their views. "[W]e then promise to think about them and promise to respond. In the meantime, let us get on with the presentation."

4. Begin the presentation with more positive findings, and ease into the negative conclusions.

The first feature about this advice is that it made sense to most of the participants. By making sense I mean that they appeared to agree with the hypothesized positive effect of such actions on the client and they appeared to know how to implement the advice.

There is a second feature about the advice that is more complex and problematic than the easy agreement implies. All these strategies assume that clients who are feeling defensive have the capacity to reduce their defensiveness either by asking them to raise their sights, by promising a response, or by beginning with some positive examples. It is as if human beings can distance themselves from their feelings of threat and then continue to focus dispassionately on the data that are causing the threat in the first place. There is also a plea for suppressing the defensiveness to overcome it. The clients are expected to place their defensiveness on hold and discuss threatening subjects with dispassion. These strategies are being recommended even though earlier many of the consultants had agreed that they too would have reacted defensively if someone had told them something that was equally surprising about their practice and had used their data to make the point.

A third feature of the strategies is that all of them attempt to bypass the defensiveness. Moreover, there is no suggestion that they should state to the client that this is what they are doing. This is understandable because to discuss a covert bypass strategy is to violate its face-saving features. Hence, the defensiveness is undiscussable and the undiscussability of the defensiveness is also undiscussable.

During the discussion, consultant A said that he would have asked the client "to temporarily suspend disbelief, to focus less on the details, and more on the major pieces of anlayses." Consultant B responded, "But that would be adding insult to injury. Moreover, the clients could experience A as acting in a patronizing manner." There were a few moments of awkward silence since this was the first time one of the participants had evaluated negatively the contributions of another.

The officer asked A how he felt about B's response. A said that he felt B had not understood him. The officer then asked, "If the conversation continued as it did, would you have felt that B and others would be nit-picking?" A responded, "Yes." He then pointed out that A had concluded that his colleagues were wrong, acted as if that were not the case, and continued to hold his views more strongly while discounting the views of his critics. B smiled when he heard A's comments and said, "To be honest and I guess that's the idea of these sessions, I would have probably reacted the same way as you did."

The point is that the moment the threat occurred in the seminar, the participants also acted in ways to bypass the threat and to distance themselves from it. These strategies make it unlikely that individuals will ever test publicly their inferences and attributions to understand the defensiveness or will ever obtain the cooperation they seek to overcome it. Hence, the strategies that clients may use when they become defensive may also be used by the consultants when they become defensive.

In this connection it is interesting to note how the consultants tended to react if the clients questioned their conclusions, analyses, or models in a way that did not begin with defensiveness. The fundamental strategy, as one consultant stated it, was "to up the level of proof and overcome them with evidence." The clients were aware of the brilliance and rigor of the consultants' analyses but not necessarily of their sense of concern or compassion. At worst, the clients felt put down and ignored. Both consequences would tend to lead to defensiveness, but then the consultants could switch to the strategies described earlier.

Next, the officer helped the consultants to try to redesign the behavior within the room as well as the behavior toward the client. The consultants found it difficult to do this. The officer then described what they tried that was new, how the clients reacted, and asked for the consultants' reactions.

We are just beginning to collect examples of how strategy professionals may use Model II interventions to solve strategy problems and to help the clients learn how to learn. The officer said that he had decided to deal with the issue by commenting, in effect:

> You are asking a lot of detailed questions of the sort
> that you have not done before. This leads me to
> wonder if some of you may be feeling unhappy be-

cause you signed up for jobs [that may not continue to exist]. We may be a partial cause of the problem. Do any of you feel that way?

The question was greeted with a resounding silence. Finally one individual said, "Well, I do not know about others, but that is exactly how I feel. I came here to do a job. I left a good job. I feel hurt and unhappy."

This led others to discuss their views and feelings and was followed by a constructive problem-solving session as to what they could do to save jobs and design other ventures. Then one client said, "Let us go back to your presentation." To quote the consultants who were there, "The nit-picking stopped." "There was no more nit-picking." "There was never any further argument about our figure."

In another seminar, a transcript of an intervention with a client was given to a group of managers and consultants. They were asked to evaluate the effectiveness of the consultant. They did not know that the case represented an example of an officer who was learning to deal with client defensive routines.

The consultants were overwhelmingly negative in their written evaluations of the clients and the consultants. For example:

- Nothing was solved. Nothing was really ever investigated or examined. . . . Participants used generalizations and rhetoric and did not expose themselves to criticism/confrontation. [Rarely] tested their views.
- What does all this mean? It sounds like they're talking and not really saying anything.
- I perceive the clients and the consultants to be skirting around the issues (perhaps I do so because the transcript is short). The real problems are lightly touched on and dropped like hot potatoes before honest evaluations are arrived at.
- I am left uncertain about the following:
    1. Has the client been alienated by the way consultants have interacted with the organization previously?

2. Is the problem between functions, between a division and headquarters, or both? If both, they should be separated and discussed individually.

- It appears that the consulting team has not been able to help the clients understand their own problems. It is not clear that they have done a good job of developing a client relationship in which the clients feel as though they are working with the consultants to recognize and solve the organizational or other problems.
- Clients and consultants seem to be skirting the issue to protect their own positions. They use escape clauses to avoid facing up to the issues.
- Classic gobbledygook.
- Clients are not honest.

The consultants were then helped to examine the way they framed their diagnosis in the same way as the respondents were in the John and Bill case. They became aware of the same paradox — namely, if they communicated openly what they had written to the consultants and to the clients, they would have produced the defensive routines that they condemned in the case. This led to a spirited discussion that began with blaming others and changed to becoming more reflective of their own actions to accepting more responsibility for the probable counterproductive features of their own actions to asking to learn skills that would prevent these difficulties.

twelve

SUMMARY AND IMPLICATIONS

DEFENSIVE ROUTINES ARE POWERFUL

Defensive routines exist in most organizations. The routines most dangerous to organizational learning and effectiveness are those that are used in the name of support, concern, strength, humanism, and realism. These ideas are culturally taught and accepted to be true.

Threat is dealt with by defensive reasoning and a defensive-prone theory in use. This, in turn, produces learning systems in organizations that are actually against understanding how to deal with threatening issues so they can be eliminated.

The three resources upon which practitioners can understandably depend for guidance also reinforce these conditions. The researchers on strategy implementation and, indeed, management in general, acknowledge the importance of defensive routines yet provide advice that is fraught with defensive reasoning, defensive theories in use, and defensive organizational cultures. The second source — the consulting firms — are, for the most part, not much different. They appear to deal with threat primarily in ways that bypass these defensive routines. Finally, the same may be true for most university and executive programs. They may teach that defensive routines exist, but we know of no course that is dedicated to helping us become aware of our defensive reasoning or our theories in use and how to provide opportunity to change them.

Thus, a multitiered set of defensive loops exists, to my knowledge, throughout the world, that reinforces defensive routines. It is for this reason, I believe, that defensive routines can be acknowledged as one of the most powerful factors that inhibit organizational learning and learning how to learn. However, teachers do not discuss them, organizations have no formal rules to support them, and to my knowledge, most strategy or management consultants do not deal with them in the name of being realistic, the art of the possible, and holding on to their clients.

What makes it possible for organizations to be productive under these conditions? First, much that goes on in organizations does not contain threat, or where threat does exist, there are times when it cannot be hidden and ignored. By the way, the dream of many management information systems designers is to design a tamper-proof, guaranteed-to-catch-the-culprit information system. If they succeed, they will also succeed in superimposing on defensive routines a control system that will call the individuals to new heights of creativity on how to bypass the threatening features of the information system. The strategy most often used by systems designers is to translate nonroutine, difficult problems into routine ones. Once this is done, a good deal of threat is supposed to be taken out of the system. Again, this could work for the short run and create a long-term danger. The long-term danger is that the routine, easily programmable mentality takes over. This not only may drive out creativity but also may become so rigid and inflexible that the most threatening challenge is to change the routine.

A second reason why organizations can get on with their business is that there are useful bypass solutions. In strategy, for example, defining a sound planning process, defining the new roles and the new structure, creating new management information systems, and rewarding the individuals are strategies that can help keep the organization effective.

The problem is that an increasing number of organizations that do these things well still find themselves crippled by defensive routines. Moreover, these defensive routines eventually become immune to any corrective features that may be taken to eliminate them. This is related to the most important fear expressed by top management and first-rate consultants. They do not fear designing and putting in place all these corrective actions. Their biggest fear is once this has been done, the corrective actions will work for a while and eventually lose a good deal (but not all) of their effectiveness.

This fear is realistic for a very fundamental reason. Whenever new jobs are defined, new structures, new management information systems, they are designed with the explicit or tacit assumption that threat is ruled out. If you examine the written material that makes any of these solutions operative, you will probably find little about how to deal with distortions and cover-ups.

The implicit assumption in most organizations is that employees, especially managers and professional contributors, are intendedly rational, have a sense of their stewardship, and are loyal. These characteristics are expected to combine to create an ongoing monitoring system against distortion and cover-up. This assumption is partially valid. The difficulty is that when threat occurs, defensive routines are created by individuals because such actions appear to them to be rational, indicating their keen sense of stewardship (they are trying to keep the place afloat), which therefore means they are loyal.

In addition, the designs are often developed with individuals knowing they were partially a cover-up. Recall the university that created the job of provost to separate the president from the faculty, the firm that created a corporate planning office because they gave up on divisional planners, and the organizations that demanded of their strategy professionals new planning processes and simultaneously gave tacit or explicit clues that they did not wish to touch the defensive routines with a 10-foot pole. Again, the intentions are clean. Top management believes that to change defensive routines is the equivalent of changing the world, a belief that I share with them. They conclude that the most realistic solution is to bypass them — a conclusion I see as understandable, shortsighted, and leaving a polluted organization to the managers of future organizations.

A third reason why some organizations perform in spite of

defensive routines is that they may have dedicated hard-working management, especially at the top. Once they create new structures and policies, they keep driving home their point that they value risk takers, individuals who blow whistles, people who keep organizations flexible, and so on. This is consistent with the fundamental messages of the recent best seller on organizational excellence (Peters and Waterman, 1984) that organizations should tend to their knitting and keep strategies that depend on their proven skills, listen to their customers (who can give feedback of the kind that defensive routines dread), and have a CEO who will take on the defensive loops in a multilevel, continual, unabating offensive. The long-range cost of this advice may be to burn out those dedicated individuals and to allow the defensive routines to flourish.

DEFENSIVE ROUTINES ARE ALTERABLE

The second lesson we are learning about defensive routines is that they are changeable. It is surprising but true that given a commitment to change defensive routines, it can be done relatively easily compared to the staying and proliferating power they have. I believe the long-run barrier to progress will not be appropriate change technology but whether society will encourage and whether individuals will take the initiative to tackle the challenge.

There are many forces that make tackling defensive routines realistic. First, it is not necessary — indeed, it may be counterproductive — to think in terms of massive change programs. Recall our advice to start small and at the top.

Second, the change technology being developed places the control over the direction and pace in the hands of the players. There is little danger of things going out of control. The advice is to move slowly and iteratively. Let the organization learn from each experiment so it can make the next one even more successful and build up organizational intelligence on these change processes that can be disseminated throughout the organization. Each attempt should be focused on a real technical problem. For example, designing a planning process or pricing strategies are types of changes that require careful inquiry, experimentation, and iterative learning.

Third, it is not necessary to have executives or consultants completely educated and highly skilled in changing defensive routines. In several situations in which I was involved, the top executives or the consultants were learning as they were doing. Most of them had the kind of appreciation learning seminars described in the previous chapter. Most had experience in trying out the new ideas and skills in small and manageable activities.

Be they line or consultants, individuals should be able to use publicly compelling and testable reasoning when dealing with defensive routines, be able to minimize using their own defenses to protect themselves or to protect the client, be able to translate an error into an opportunity for new learning, and be smart enough to design programs within these competencies and not to overpromise (which would make them feel anxious and the client to be wary).

In most cases, the executives and consultants made up for their gaps in knowledge and skills by learning while they were doing (with the help of a professional more competent than they). For example, the consultants described in Chapters 6, 7, and 8 were able to learn and stay ahead of their clients by spending several hours working with an adviser after every session with the client and then designing what to do next.

I was particularly impressed how quickly the participants learned to identify and correct errors, how good they became at designing new encounters, how little they forgot so they could use their knowledge not only in their own work but also in helping others, and how, after six months or a year of such efforts, some of them began to design interventions and examine current practice in ways that contributed to new advances in practice and theory.

I am sure that not all executives or consultants can learn as easily and as fast as those with whom I have been involved. I am also quite confident that, because of my lack of knowledge and competence about teaching the new competencies, some of those who appeared to be slower learners were not. Also inhibiting their learning was the lack of sound theory about such interventions about which they could read and that would answer their burning questions.

As our knowledge increases, I believe that we will be able to help an increasingly larger number of individuals to become competent and to do so more quickly than is presently the case. The same knowledge should also help us to identify where it is unlikely that we can be of help either to individuals or to organizations. My belief is that if there are limits they will be related more to individuals than to organizations because it is more likely that the latter will have a wide variety of individuals and, hence, some who can learn the new ideas and competencies.

Another encouraging sign is that although changes usually start very slowly, they are often additive and spread throughout the organization. Moreover, they appear to deepen and be resilient to defensive routines that are threatened by changes. Even in very defensive organizations where the changes were suppressed by anxious senior executives, the competencies were not forgotten. A year or longer after the organization became more supportive, the individuals were able to take their skills and the conditions they had begun to develop out of mothballs and place them into action relatively easily and quickly.

NEW SKILLS CAN BE USED IN SITUATIONS WHERE CHANGE IS NOT BEING CONSIDERED

We often meet executives and consultants who, after learning the skills in our seminars, believe that their organizations or their clients are not ready for engaging defensive routines. These individuals tell us that the ideas and competencies they learn are still very useful, however.

For example, in a survey, clients who used strategy consultants identified five criteria that were important in selecting the consultants with whom they worked:

1. A tough, analytically rigorous mind accompanied with high standards,
2. A continual concern for implementation,

3. A capacity to train the organization in the skills they use for strategy formulation and implementation,
4. Experience in the business,
5. The ability to create conditions where the top management could feel comfortable to think out loud, make errors, feel stupid, and in general work with them as they were growing.

It is interesting to note that relative experience was overwhelmingly voted as the least important attribute and that working in a personal effective relationship was the most important one.

The knowledge and skills that individuals learn to cope with defensive routines are very helpful in establishing close, enduring relationships with the clients (peers or subordinates in the case of line executives) where there is little thought, at the outset, to engaging defensive routines. These skills can also help the individual become a more effective diagnostician of organizational routines and the routines the players used to bypass them. They lead to a much richer picture of what is reality as well as what can or cannot be done to begin to sensitize the organization toward the need to change.

Along with a more realistic picture of the scope and depth of defensive routines, the individual is also able to be more empathic and patient about change. Change agents can be less defensive about dealing with others' defensive routines. There is less anger toward clients who genuinely do not wish to change or are ambivalent about doing so.

Another payoff is that any recommendations for change that are developed will tend to be more valid as well as more realistic about what can and cannot be done. Finally, all these combine to make it more likely that the individual can help the clients who are not ready for change at least not to get into worse difficulties.

DEFENSIVE ROUTINES AND CHANGING THE STATUS QUO

It is possible to use the concept of defensive routines to explain one of the most persistent findings in trying to change the status quo in organizations. I refer to the fact that such change rarely lasts. Every time I dig into the histories of attempts to change organizations significantly, I find that during the early states, especially with the help of a driven charismatic leader (and financial resources), changes are made. The problems arise when the players begin to face dilemmas, paradoxes, and threats; that is when defensive routines come into play. The knowledge and competencies people have to deal with them are not only inadequate but also create regressions to the status quo.

Take schools as an example. A decade ago, many alternative schools cropped up that were the creative experiments to change the status quo. To my knowledge, most have not succeeded in doing so. I examined several where the schools had funding, the teachers and students volunteered, the curriculum was jointly controlled, and the players were left alone to create their brave new world. In all cases they failed. When I dug into why this was the case, the key factors were related to defensive routines. For example, as long as the teachers and students were designing the easy aspects of the curriculum or the easy features of the school culture, everything went well. But when the difficult issues such as evaluations of performance, the choice of standards, and the level of commitment to learning the academic disciplines had to be faced, then all sorts of conflicts arose. Moreover, the students became as authoritarian and manipulative as they had accused the teachers of being before they joined this school. The teachers, who had volunteered, were deeply shocked and hurt because they believed that they could eliminate unilateral control and manipulation. The teachers tended to withdraw and become depressed. The students were left with their manipulative tendencies, which they then turned on each other (Argyris, 1974). In another case, we observed a dedicated, bright group of faculty trying to create a democratic culture in an inner city school in order to raise the level of moral development (which, in turn, might help the educational performance). The students who "bought" the dream dealt with the dilemmas and paradoxes by acting not only Model I but also Model I cubed! The teachers eventually became discouraged and withdrew (Argyris and Argyris, 1979).

The same problems exist in the area of worker participation and ownership. Witte (1980) provides vivid data that experiments in worker democracy begin with an outburst of enthusiasm that soon begins to wane. He concludes that one of the causes of the regression is the lack of effective leadership and authority to insure stability. When one digs into his rich data, it is possible to see why such leadership is lacking. For example, the dynamics of the planning councils are full of competitive, win/lose activities or easing-in diplomatic activities. As we have seen throughout this book, the groups are faced with threat; some members react aggressively while others react passively. The groups never deal with the tension between the two reactions. The result is often misunderstanding coupled with compromises that cover up the misunderstanding and cover up the cover-up.

Witte (1980) wonders whether genuine equality will be possible. He notes that often management dominates the conversation not because they have a dominating style (although some do) but because they have the relevant information. Workers are quite willing to speak less and listen more if they believe they do not have the relevant technical information to get on with the job. It is interesting to note that management in Yugoslavia dominates more than does the management studied in the United States (p. 73).

Bradley and Hill (1982) report similar problems in their study of Japanese and Western management styles. They studied the introduction of quality circles in two relatively comparable chemical and pharmaceutical firms, one in the United Kingdom and the other in the United States. They found, for example, that despite the introduction of quality circles, managers could not be regarded as pursuing high-trust relations when it came to providing the information the employer needed. Managers, at times, acted to keep the quality circles off subjects they did not want discussed even if it meant reducing the quality of the discussions. Another approach was to frustrate either the initial formulation or the subsequent implementation of circle suggestions that were seen as threatening (p. 303).

Quality circles did improve communications and social relations, but they failed to allay suspicions of management or the awareness that the interests of management and labor were not the same. Another consequence was the emergence of an insider-outsider division between members and nonmembers as the result of quality circles that, as far as I could tell, were not engaged by the respective firms.

Bradley and Hill (1982) conclude that quality circles do produce efficiency gains with quantifiable financial returns. The biggest gains are made in the early period. There is little positive impact on the employee-employer mistrust partially, I suggest, because both sides attempt to manipulate each other when difficult issues arise. It is interesting that similar results were reported in attempts to gain worker participation in India (Pylee, 1975).

Finally, Raelin (1984) conducted research among professionals to show how they tend to deal with the problem of mismatch between what they are seeking from work and what is available to them on the job. He finds that professionals may use a wide variety of defensive routines to deal with the mismatch that, I believe, they are likely to cover up. For example, on the job, they may engage in projects that will benefit their personal career but not the organization, they believe they are too busy to get to the things that might prove more useful to the organization, or they do exactly what is required of them, never more and never less. They may combine these actions with feelings that they are burning out and becoming distanced from the organization. These consequences are accompanied by seeking greater autonomy, requesting professional privileges like attending professional meetings, and searching for new employment.

In all these examples, the theme is the same. Whether threat is generated, the defensive routines individuals use are counterproductive, they tend to be bypassed by the players, the bypass is covered up, which means that the players begin to feel that they are not in control. Disenchantment and disappointment follow, and these, in turn, are not discussed.

DEFENSIVE ROUTINES AND THE MEDIA

Defensive routines are especially powerful in the media. What makes it difficult to deal with them is that the media people often use a tails-you-lose, heads-I-win strategy to argue their point, and when they see that this is no longer working, they revert to a defense that is even more profound. They claim, in effect, that their defensive routines should be protected by the First Amendment and, hence, by the courts.

For example, in the study of the newspaper mentioned earlier, I found that reporters would describe their colleagues (and themselves) as "highly competitive," "partially paranoid," "out to show the emperor to be without clothes," "willing to commit substantial shady acts to get a story," "people who, when under stress, magnify reality," and people who are almost always under stress. Building upon their descriptions, I would then ask if such predispositions had any influence on the way these newspeople might perceive and report reality. The response was immediate: the press must be protected by the First Amendment and any exploration of these issues by citizens could lead to the loss of their freedom. The ultimate of the latter argument that I have heard was the Nieman Foundation adviser who remarked that even the irresponsibility of the media people should be protected by the courts.

In another example, I observed a long discussion among reporters, columnists, and editors. The editors were trying to find ways to deal fairly with the issue of subjective-objective reporting and to define the conditions under which each was appropriate. The essence of the reporters' and columnists' arguments was that all reporting is subjective because it is all selective and, when published, highly incomplete. They polarized the issue so they could argue that nothing could be done.

As I listened to the reporters and columnists, I attributed to them a sense of fear and anguish about having to face the daily responsibility of writing minimally distorted stories under the pressure of deadlines. I empathized with the problem because it is one that I face in my work as a diagnostician of individuals, groups, and organizations (and I am rarely under the time pressures they experience). But what impressed me was that they fought any attempt to define ways to increase the validity of their reporting. The social scientists in my field would never get away with such a response because it is basically against learning. Much evidence has been accumulated that indicates that social scientists who are against such learning also tend to distort reality without realizing what they do.

Let us dig a bit deeper. In previous interviews, all the reporters and columnists had identified two reporters who were models of what they called "old-fashioned objective reporting." They admired the abilities of these two reporters to write a "straight story." The only trouble was that their stories had little color. These data appear to illustrate that some objectivity is possible. The result admittedly was colorless stories. But if they did not value colorless stories, how could they speak of these two senior reporters with such admiration and warmth? Further discussion surfaced the fact that the reporters themselves were ambivalent on this issue. On the one hand, they could see that the two straight reporters were a valid model of objective reporting. On the other hand, they believed that such reporting ignored the responsibility of newspapers to discover injustice.

This led to the discovery of another pattern of motivations and attitudes. On the one hand, many of the reporters had a very strong desire to identify and correct society's ills — especially since these ills were created by powerful individuals in powerful private or public organizations. On the other hand, all but one admitted that they would "be fearful as hell" to take a position in which they would be responsible for curing some of these ills. They enjoyed discovering the ills, but they feared taking a position where they would be responsible for correcting them.

Could these fears and this ambivalence influence the intensity of color in the story? "Yes, I suppose so," was the most frequent response that I was given. However, none of the reporters wanted to explore ways of identifying and correcting the possible distortions that could come from these defenses.

People who are fearful of taking action may also attribute to themselves a degree of cowardice. It is difficult to live with such feelings. One way to overcome the injustice implied in having cowardly behavior protected by the job is to escalate investigative reporting and dig out injustice. When injustice is discovered, report it relatively accurately but with color enough so that you can justify your fear of taking on the job required to correct these errors.

Perhaps this explanation may be overdrawn. Consider the following experience. A Nieman fellow described how he (and his newspaper) had paid to obtain information that led to the jailing of a banker. A distinguished professor of constitutional law who heard the story asked the reporter why he did not turn over the data to a grand jury. The reporter replied that he did not trust the courts. Someone asked why not reproduce the material, give it to the courts, and give them some sort of deadline. Before the reporter could reply, another Nieman fellow said, in effect, "Let's be honest, he published the story because he was hoping for a Pulitzer Prize and the editor published it because he had paid for it." Neither the reporter nor any other Nieman present rejected that possibility.

Back to the newspaper. I can recall vividly the elation and euphoria in the newsroom when the difficulties of the Nixon White House were being discovered and published. Many statements were made in the stories, and even more in the newsroom, that a milieu had developed at the upper levels of the White House that had caused the president and his chief advisers to distort aspects of reality and to be blind to that fact.

I was able to show that the innards of the newspaper had many of the same dynamics of the White House. I found the same kinds of interpersonal dynamics and internal politics, the same mistrust and win/lose competitiveness. The same deception and miscommunication existed among the reporters, between the reporters and their immediate editors, and between the reporters and the top editors. These similarities were confirmed by the reporters and editors. But the moment I suggested that the distortion of reality created in the White House (which they believed was caused by mistrust, deception, and win/lose competitiveness) could also exist in their organization (due to the same factors), their reaction was an immediate closing off of inquiry (back to the high road).

ROLE OF CONSULTING FIRMS

The biggest nemesis to professional firms that consult with organizations in any field where implementation is the name of the game is the defensive routines in each system and the more encompassing defensive loops in which they are found. Immediately after competence in their respective domain of service is the capacity to engage defensive routines wherever they exist in order to reduce them. We have seen how defensive routines lead consultants to hedge on their diagnoses and advice in precisely the areas in which the clients are most blind and defensive. This may even lead to a first class piece of analysis and conceptualization being reduced in quality in order to bypass the client's defensive routines.

I am not suggesting that consultants should not modify their proposals in order to implement them. I am suggesting that they first test their attributions that they must bypass either with their client or with some outside professional who may act as reviewers of their practice. I have illustrated that the former can be done without serious danger to the client relationship. To my knowledge, the latter is rare. I am a consultant, for example, to several consulting firms where I periodically review several cases to evaluate how they are dealing with defensive routines. The results, I believe, have helped the firms to redesign certain aspects of their practice. They are also used to develop some ongoing reflection on why they did not see what the outsider saw that has led to changes in the ways these firms manage themselves and their case teams. Finally, the results produce case material used in the ongoing re-education of their professionals.

Another important reason why consulting firms should consider seriously engaging defensive routines is that clients must have professionals who can help them intervene in the organizational factors that lead to slow deterioration in a way that is reminiscent of entropy. Defensive routines pollute the system and undermine it the same way air pollution undermines our lives. Consulting firms are to organizations what medical doctors are to individual health. Part of their stewardship is to detect those features that harm organizations, especially features that the players may resist examining. I say especially because organizations require individuals who will protect them from self-destructive defensive routines.

Consulting firms also have a responsibility to the societies from which they derive their practice to examine how that society may be structured to create the very problems that organizations must overcome. The massive defensive loops must be interrupted and altered if societies are not to have their capacity for learning impaired.

Another reason why consulting firms should develop competencies to deal with defensive routines is that the practice is self-regenerative of the professionals. I have watched consultants who are economists, statisticians, applied mathematicians, and management experts who found that after a decade of active work, some of their practice was becoming routine and not as exciting as it used to be. However, this same practice was a financial necessity to them as individuals and to the firm.

Learning to deal with defensive routines and integrating this knowledge with consultants' practice have several positive consequences. First, they help to reduce client conservatism and make it possible to conduct even more challenging studies in their technical field. Second, they reduce the probability that defensive routines from the client, or even from their own case team, will blunt the implementation of the more exciting technical results. Third, it becomes easier for consultants to reduce the burnout factors in their lives that come from the dilemmas, conflicts, and double binds that defensive routines would create. An extension of this consequence is that the consultants (and their firm) find themselves increasingly more reflective and innovative. They report feeling more at the forefront of their practice.

To my knowledge, the consultants or academics who can genuinely integrate recommendations and implementation in their specific fields by engaging defensive routines are very few in number. Some such professionals exist in the firms within which I have worked. More may be in consulting firms whom I have missed because they do not publish much about their practice.

Two of the first consultants to develop a genuinely integrated developmental strategy are Gisele and Göran Asplund. They have published a thoughtful analytical account of how they have integrated fields such as strategy, marketing, and management consulting by engaging defensive routines at the upper levels of management. They are also candid about their own defensive routines and how they tried to overcome them. It is a model of how practice can contribute to theory (Asplund and Asplund; 1982 a and b).

The Asplunds describe, for example, the case of the Eagle Corporation that was not able to market effectively the many new products it produced. Salespeople blamed the prices, and manufacturing blamed poor marketing. The situation was self-reinforcing. Using an integrative format, the Asplunds were able to show that the divisional managers mistrusted the capability of the sales companies when it came to more sophisticated marketing of the products and that prices were set for all products by using a conventional cost-plus-pricing method.

These two revelations seemed trivial and everybody knew about them. The problem was they contradicted the espoused theories of the company on marketing and pricing. This means that everyone knew something was going on that was contradictory to policies and that either they were unable to stop the counterproductive behavior or they did not wish to do so. The Asplunds present data that it was more the former than the latter. A set of nested cover-up activities was created that had to be covered up. This cover-up led the players to avoid the real issues. Examples of the cover-ups were some individuals' covering up facts about the profitability of certain products and others' letting it happen without comment. When someone estimated a topic to be threatening, he or she played down these estimations in order not to hurt anyone.

The initial reaction of the top was to make jokes about the findings. As they dug into the defensive routines, however, they unearthed important ineffective business policies and organizational activities such as rigid control systems, incorrect segmentation criteria, and product innovation that was not market oriented. The Asplunds helped the clients to alter these counterproductive practices and to explore the behavioral and cultural features that made them possible. The result was a restructuring of the research and development and marketing departments, which has led to improved performance.

UPPING THE ANTE

The most fundamental professional and moral responsibility of managers is their stewardship to the organization. In order to fulfill the stewardship, managers at all levels must understand and act within and upon the world in which they operate. Underlying understanding and action is reasoning. The reasoning required for effective leadership is productive reasoning.

Organizations are blessed with people who act as their agents. Human beings make organizations come alive. Unfortunately, people also can lead organizations to wither and die. They carry the seeds of organizational illness through their tendency to use defensive reasoning, especially when threat is involved.

Defensive reasoning produces defensive routines. Defensive routines combine to produce the equivalent of an organizational pollutant that makes it increasingly difficult for organizations to manage themselves as well as to design and be in control of their destiny. As is true of most pollutants, defensive reasoning and defensive routines are by-products of everyday actions that are required to run organizations. It is therefore difficult to see how they can be reduced and eliminated without opening up Pandora's box.

Eliminating defensive routines represents one of the most basic challenges to consulting professionals. How can consultants help organizations to reduce their defensive reasoning and routines no matter what the business or organizational problem? Providing this help is not easy for at least two reasons. First, we are being taught, around the world, that defensive reasoning is humane because it helps us to bypass threat. What we are not being taught is that bypass activities have profound unintended consequences. They may reduce threat or pain temporarily, but they harness the organization with increasingly comprehensive and deepening defensive loops. The legacy of bypass activities is slow but sure strangulation of productive reasoning and effective action.

The second reason why providing this help will be difficult is that as defensive loops become more comprehensive, not able to be influenced, and difficult to manage, the less likely clients will wish to take the risks to overcome the defensive reasoning and routines. As this fear becomes more prominent, then a self-fulfilling prophecy is created because it is precisely this kind of fear that reinforces defensive loops.

To my mind, we cannot bypass this dilemma. Management is increasingly being influenced by the information science technology that makes it possible to process amounts of information that hitherto was deemed unlikely. This possibility usually translates, in the minds of senior executives, into a demand from those who monitor their stewardship to have the information required to manage the organization effectively. The assumption is that having access to valid information helps.

Observers have pointed out that the information science revolution can provide the organization with too much information. I do not believe, strictly speaking, that this is a valid explanation. It is not the information science capabilities that produce too much information but the defensive routines surrounding the production and use of the information. The underlying assumption of information science is that truth is a good idea. The underlying assumption of human beings is that truth is a good idea when it is not threatening.

It is the task of consulting firms to have as one of their underlying values the production of valid information. Without it, the basis for their help will be threatened. The concepts, analytical activities, models, and metaphors that inform their practice all assume the existence of valid information. The success of consulting firms will depend very much on their being able to reduce defensive reasoning when it infects the chances of productive actions.

The conclusion, I believe, is inescapable. Consultants will have to take the lead in overcoming defensive reasoning in their clients and in themselves if they are to use the knowledge that will be increasingly available. As progress is made in understanding organizations, defensive reasoning will no longer be accepted in the name of caring, being realistic, or playing it safe. It will be seen for what it is: a poor, if not dangerous, second choice. I realize this questions many of the ideas of good currency. That is why we are upping the ante.

NOTES

CHAPTER 1

1. I use *individual-organizational* to mean the whole range of defenses in an organization, beginning with individuals, going to groups and intergroups, and finally to organizations as a whole (which includes key features of their culture).

CHAPTER 2

1. For a more detailed discussion of the evidence, please see Chris Argyris, *Reasoning, Learning and Action* (San Francisco: Jossey-Bass, 1982).

2. Adapted from Argyris, *Reasoning, Learning, and Action*, pp. 109–120.

CHAPTER 4

1. I am not including the problem that recollected conversations might be subject to distortion. That is not a problem because individuals cannot distort actual quotations to the point that they are different from

Model I. It is not possible to produce the kind of conversation we recommend in the next chapters without a different theory in use (Argyris, 1982).

CHAPTER 5

1. For a more detailed discussion see Chris Argyris, *Inner Contradictions of Rigorous Research* (London: Academic Press, 1980).

2. What makes it possible to use this method with a respectable degree of validity is the empirical fact that Model I behavior is so prevalent and that Model II behavior is rare. That means there is little variance, which in turn means that errors between models will be rare (Argyris, 1982). If we were to find situations in which Model II behavior was not rare, then a more complex system would be needed. However, it is precisely under these conditions that the players would find little need for the quantitative figures.

3. Adapted from Chris Argyris, *Reasoning, Learning and Action* (San Francisco: Jossey-Bass, 1982), pp. 121–135.

BIBLIOGRAPHY

H.I. Ansoff, A. Bosman, and P.M. Storm. *Understanding and Managing Strategic Change*. Amsterdam: North-Holland, 1982.

Chris Argyris. "Human Problems with Budgets." *Harvard Business Review*. 31(1953):97–110.

Chris Argyris. *Interpersonal Competence and Organizational Effectiveness*. Homewood, Il.: Irwin-Dorsey, 1962.

Chris Argyris. *Integrating the Individual and the Organization*. New York: John Wiley & Sons, 1964.

Chris Argyris. *Behind the Front Page*. San Francisco: Jossey-Bass, 1974.

Chris Argyris. *Inner Contradictions of Rigorous Research*. London: Academic Press, 1980.

Chris Argyris. *Reasoning, Learning and Action*. San Francisco: Jossey-Bass, 1982.

Chris Argyris and Dianne Argyris. "Moral Reasoning and Moral Action: Some Preliminary Questions." Mimeographed, Harvard University, Cambridge, Mass., 1979.

Chris Argyris and Donald Schön. *Organizational Learning*. Reading, Mass.: Addison-Wesley, 1978.

Chris Argyris and Donald Schön. *Theory in Practice*. San Francisco: Jossey-Bass, 1982.

Chris Argyris, Robert Putnam, and Diana M. Smith. *Action Science*. San Francisco: Jossey-Bass, (forthcoming).

Gisele Asplund and Göran Asplund. "Increasing Innovativeness through an Integrated Development Strategy." Stockholm: Erhvervs Økonomisk Tidsskrift, FDC no. 1–2, 1982a, pp. 15–28.

Gisele Asplund and Göran Asplund. *An Integrated Development Strategy*. Chichester: John Wiley & Sons, 1982b.

Louis B. Barnes. "Managing the Paradox of Organizational Trust." *Harvard Business Review,* March/April 1981, pp. 107–116.

H. Boothroyd. *Articulate Intervention*. London: Taylor & Francis, 1978.

L.J. Bourgeoiss III, and David R. Brodwin. "Strategy Implementation: Five Approaches to an Elusive Phenomenon." Mimeographed, Stanford University, Palo Alto, Ca., May 1982.

L.J. Bourgeoiss III, and David B. Jemison. "Analyzing Corporate Culture in its Strategic Context." *Exchange,* 7(1982):37–41.

Edward H. Bowman. "Strategic Decision Making." Presented at Symposium on Strategic Decision Making in Complex Organizations, Harriman, Arden House, November 1983. Mimeographed, pp. 1–10.

Keith Bradley and Stephen Hill. " 'After Japan': The Quality Circle Transplant and Productive Efficiency." *British Journal of Industrial Relations* 21(1982):291–311.

Otto Brodtrick (Office of the Auditor General). Talk given at the conference of personnel heads, Ottowa Public Service of Canada, May 3, 1984.

C. Roland Christensen; Kenneth R. Andrews; Joseph L. Bower; Richard G. Hammermesh; and Michael Porter. *Business Policy — Tests and Cases,* 5th ed. Homewood, Ill.: Richard D. Irwin & Co., 1982.

George Day. "Gaining Insights through Strategy Analysis." *Journal of Business Strategy.* 4(1982):51–58.

Peter F. Drucker. "Drucker on Drucker." *New Management,* 3(1985):7–9.

Peter F. Drucker. *The Effective Executive*. New York: Harper & Row, 1966.

Peter F. Drucker. *Management*. New York: Harper & Row, 1973.

R.G. Dyson and M.J. Foster. "Making Planning More Effective." *Long-Range Planning* 16(1983):68–73.

Feigenbaum, Pittsfield, Mass., General Systems Co., Inc., Lecture, May 3, 1984.

Steven P. Feldman. "Culture and Conformity: The Case of a Telephone Company." Weatherhead School of Management, Case Western Reserve. Mimeographed, May 1984, pp. 1–24.

Samuel M. Fulton, Robert E. Kelley, and Ian H. Wilson. "Scenarios: A Means to Avoiding Strategic 'Groupthink'." *Strategic Planning Management,* July/August 1983, pp. 1–5.

George H. Gage. "On Acceptance of Strategic Planning Systems." In Peter Lorange, ed. *Implementation of Strategic Planning*. Englewood Cliffs, N.J.: Prentice-Hall, 1982, pp. 171–182.

Fred Gluck, Steve Kaufman, and Steve Wallick. "Strategic Management for Competitive Advantage." *Harvard Business Review* 58(1980):154–161.

Leston Havens. *Participant Observation*. New York: Jason Aronson, Inc., 1976.

Bruce Henderson. *Boston Globe*. May 1, 1984, pp. 25 and 31.

Richard J. Hermon-Taylor. "Strategic Decision Making at the Crossroad: A View from the World of Practice." Symposium in Strategic Decision Making in Complex Organizations, Columbia University, New York November 1983.

Charles W. Hofer and Dan Schendel. *Strategy Formulation: Analytical Concepts*. St. Paul, Minn.: West Publishing Co., 1978.

Jacques Horovitz. "New Perspectives on Strategic Management." *Journal of Business Strategy* 4(1984):19–33.

La Rue Tone Hosmer. "The Importance of Strategic Leadership." *Journal of Business Strategy* 3(1982):47–57.

Laurence G. Hrebiniak and William F. Joyce. *Implementing Strategy*. New York: Macmillan, 1984.

Irving Z. Janis. *Victims of Group Think*. Boston: Houghton Mifflin, 1972.

Ernest A. Kallman, Leon Reinharth, and H. Jack Shapiro. "Resistance to Planning." *Planning Review* 11(1983):34–36.

Michael M. Lombardo and Morgan W. McCall, Jr. "Coping with an Intolerable Boss." Greensboro, N.C.: Center for Creative Leadership, January 1984.

Peter Lorange and Declan Murphy. "Considerations in Implementing Strategic Control." *Journal of Business Strategy* 4(1984):27–35.

Laurence E. Lynn and David de F. Whiteman. *The President as a Policymaker: Jimmy Carter and Welfare Reform*. Philadelphia: Temple University Press, 1981.

Tom MacAvoy. "The Corning Glass Case." Cited in Richard F. Vancil. *Implementing Strategy. The Role of Top Management*. Videotape 179-074. Boston: Division of Research, Harvard Business School, 1982.

Ian C. MacMillan. *Strategy Formulation: Political Concepts*. St. Paul, Minn.: West Publishing Co., 1978.

Daniel McCarthy, Robert J. Minichiello, and Joseph R. Curran. *Business Policy and Strategy: Concepts and Readings*. Homewood, Ill.: Richard D. Irwin, 1979.

Tom McGuire. "The Vick Case." Videotape 179-068. Harvard Business School, 1981.

Henry Mintzberg. "Beyond Implementation: An Analysis of the Resistance to Policy Analysis." In K.B. Haley, ed. *OR '78*. North-Holland Publishing Co., 1979, pp. 106–162.

Thomas H. Naylor, ed. *The Politics of Corporate Planning and Modeling*. Athens, Ohio: Planning Executives Institute, 1978.

Wim Overmeer. "An Inquiry into the Managing of the Resource Allocation Process." Cambridge, Mass.: School of Architecture and Planning, MIT. Mimeographed, 1983, pp. 1–34.

Richard Neustadt and Harvey Fineberg. *The Swine Flu Affair*. Washington, D.C.: U.S. Department of Health, Education, and Welfare, 1978.

William H. Newman and Boris Yavitz. *Strategy in Action*. New York: Free Press, 1982.

Stanley Peterfreund. "Fighting the Trust Busters." Stanley Peter-
        freund Associates, Claster, N.J., June 1984, p. 1.
Thomas J. Peters and Robert H. Waterman, Jr. *In Search of Ex-
        cellence*. New York: Warner, 1984.
M.V. Pylee. *Worker Participation in Management*. New Delhi:
        N.V. Publications, 1975.
James B. Quinn. *Strategies for Change: Logical Incrementalism*.
        Homewood, Ill.: Dorsey Press, 1980.
Joseph A. Raelin. "Culture and Professionalism: Cultural Expla-
        nations for the Maladaptive Behavior of Salaried Employ-
        ees." 1984 (Mimeographed, to be published in Academy of
        Management).
Robert B. Reich. "Regulation by Confrontation or Negation."
        Harvard Business Review, May/June 1981a, pp. 82–93.
Robert B. Reich. "Strategic Management Planning Review." *The
        New Republic*, June 27, 1981b, pp. 27–32.
K.A. Ringbakk. "Why Planning Fails." In David Hussey, ed. *The
        Truth about Corporate Planning*. Oxford: Pergamon Press,
        1982, pp. 351–365.
Paul Rizzo. *The Bubble-Memory Incident*. Videotape 180-042.
        Boston Harvard Business School, 1981. Copyright Presi-
        dent and Fellows of Harvard College.
A Director's Viewpoint: An Interview with ·Peter G. Scotese."
        Planning Review 11(1983):3–13.
George A. Steiner. *Strategic Planning*. New York: Free Press,
        1979.
George A. Steiner. "Formal Strategic Planning in the United
        States Today." *Long-Range Planning* 16(1983):12–17.
George A. Steiner and H. Schöllhammer. "Pitfalls in multi-na-
        tional long-range planning." In David Hussey. ed. *The
        Truth about Corporate Planning*. Oxford: Pergamon Press,
        1982, pp. 387–409.
Noel Tichy. "The Essentials of Strategic Change Management."
        Journal of Business Strategy 3(1983):55–67.
David C. Wilson. "Electricity and Resistance: A Case Study of
        Innovation and Politics." *Organization Studies* (1982):119–
        140.
John F. Witte. *Democracy, Authority, and Alienation in Work*.
        Chicago: University of Chicago Press, 1980.

INDEX